One Shot One Kill
One Mission

GreatCommissionSociety
SEMPER FIDELIS, SEMPER PARATUS

One Shot One Kill One Mission

By Neil Obbard

Based on a true story

Great Commission Society

Published by Great Commission Society
Suite 1, 4 Queen Street
Edinburgh
EH2 1JE
Scotland

DISCLAIMER
This book tells the true story of Neil Obbard. Some scenes have been
dramatized with authentic though not necessarily actual dialogue, and –
to protect the author and his family, and the rights of those whose paths
he has crossed – some of the names, places, and details
of the events have been altered.

British Library Cataloguing in Publication Data
A catalogue record for this book is available from the
British Library

ISBN: 978-1-908154-32-3

Cover design by EKDESIGNS
Typeset by Avocet Typeset, Somerton, Somerset, TA11 6RT
Printed and bound by Nørhaven

Prologue

The early morning light alters almost imperceptibly. Wildlife stirs, unaware I lie in their midst, my limbs stiff through so many hours of waiting. I want to sleep but know I cannot break my concentration, so I revisit old scenes in my head to pass the time.

I run through a list of targets, the subtle differences between each approach, their only constant being the danger they pose to others, the need for them to be removed.

I am good at this. Granddad would have been proud. He told me they were targets, not people. If I took time to dwell on them as family men, as men with wives and children, with purpose…then I might not survive myself.

Moments pass.

Stillness concentrates the mind, makes you focus on this moment.

Makes you focus on who you are.

We are the sum of events. We are formed by what happens to us, like pebbles on a beach, knocked and pummeled and shaped into what we are.

Knocked by piles of headless bodies, by blue nylon rope, by petrol bombs and rioting men, by starvation and control and everyday weapons. Pummeled by street fights, a tractor ride, a failed suicide attempt, strangers in cars in warzones. Shaped by other people's greed, other people's love, other people.

It is not their actions that change you, it is how you perceive those actions.

I check the distance points again, check for movement, glad of the lack of wind.

One day I will hold a real pebble in my hand and it will change my life.

Movement.

The target comes into my sights at the 600m mark. I have two seconds. I control my breathing and take up the trigger slack.

The lightest of pressures and there is no going back. There is a fleeting whisper of time before the target drops. I catch the case, re-cock my rifle and leave.

Where was the evidence I had been there?

Part 1 – Childhood

Chapter 1

I hadn't known anything could hurt that much. I felt as if my head had been cracked in two, allowing my first sense of agony to run over every shard of bone and every nerve ending.

Above me the blue summer sky, behind me the verdant garden, both with their promises of freedom and fun, the desires of every child. Yet, underneath me, I could feel the sharpness of the small wall with its apex top. It had served as a weapon after I'd committed some crime against my sister.

I stayed still, my little frame, not yet three years old, draped over that wall. I waited for my sister to be sorry or my mum to comfort me and, whilst I waited, I watched the first drop of blood that had slipped from my broken face drop silently onto the grey slab below my head, on the other side of the wall.

The first drop having broken free, the rest followed.

One tiny drop at a time.

And whilst I waited for my sister to be sorry or my mum to comfort me, the pool of blood grew and grew until it almost covered the whole slab, replacing the grey and dank with a vibrant, fresh red.

This is my earliest memory.

My mum had been in the kitchen of our semi-detached house and must have seen everything from the window. Me, her little boy, and my four-year-old sister Judith playing, until a wrong decision on my part, or a wrong reaction on hers, led to disaster. Mum marched out of the house and down the garden, hauled me off the wall to check me out. I was in a bad way but it was not so bad that caring for me and cleaning me up couldn't wait until she had belted Judith and told her off. I don't remember Judith's reaction, but at least my mum had defended me and put things right somehow.

Around a year after this came a happier memory. I was squeezed into tight shorts, a crisp white shirt and a waistcoat and bustled off to my Godmother Ethel's wedding. My parents, Judith and I made our way down the hill and gathered outside the Methodist Church, its tall facade defined by false columns and arched windows.

People gathered to chat with us or did the slow, semi-solemn walk into church that accompanies such occasions. Being two of the youngest there, Judith and I enjoyed some attention, especially from women and older relatives, who specialized in pointing out how adorable we both looked.

'Ah, Little Neil! Doesn't he look cute in his little waistcoat!'

'That's a pretty dress, Judith!' Judith was a bridesmaid and was thrilled.

No one mentioned the shorts, which were not the most comfortable. However, because I thought it was normal to have that amount of chafing, I didn't complain about it. Looking back, they must have been for a one- or two-year-old, because I was always much skinnier than average for my age.

As the start of the ceremony approached, we left Judith to do her thing and crept inside and found a pew on the bride's side, jostling down until the three of us were lined up to face the plastered walls and the wooden cross, which I didn't understand. There was the faint scent of flowers and the low buzz of conversation, women looking excitable and men pulling at tight collars and glancing at watches.

When Ethel came in, people craned their necks for a look, but I could barely see, so I tugged at my mum's sleeve until she looked down and, with a sigh, swept me up for a quick look before returning me to my place amongst everyone's knees.

I soon realised this was going to be a trial and looked around for entertainment.

'Mummy! Mummy!' My stage whisper to my mum did not go down well. She shushed me with a hint of impatience and continued to watch the bride move down the aisle, her proud father by her side.

I noticed my mum's bag on the pew and, more excitingly, the brightly coloured edge of a packet of sweets peeking out of the open zip.

My eyes widened and my entire being focused on that packet.

This was a good sign!

'Mummy! Mummy!'

This time the slight impatience had morphed into something far more threatening. Luckily for me, the solemnity of the event and the overwhelming need to keep me quiet worked in my favour, and – joy of joys! – my mum opened the packet!

This was beyond exciting!

It was a packet of Jelly Tots!

Mum gave me a couple and turned back to the action. Ethel had been handed over to the groom, David, and someone was saying words I could barely hear and would not have understood.

However, I soon learnt that Jelly Tots don't last long and dared to ask for some more.

'Shush, Neil.'

'Mummy! Please?!'

'Later, if you're good! Shush!'

This went on until my mum must have spotted someone looking over, distracted momentarily by the noise. To my delight, I was allowed a couple more Jelly Tots every few minutes and, in return, I chewed them without talking at all. By the time the ceremony ended, my mum had forgotten I had been annoying and we moved on to the reception, and its promise of more food, on the wave of a sugar rush.

My memories of those early years are naturally rare and there was never a time Judith and I didn't know we had been adopted, from two different mums. There was no big announcement, no discovery by accident: we just knew.

I had been plucked from the arms of some distant stranger and given to this couple, with its extended family of aunts and uncles, most of them awarded this title for living nearby or because of some unimportant and long-forgotten kindness.

My Aunty Karen used to tell me how happy my parents were when they heard I was to be given to them and my mum would tell me how very wanted I had been. This made me feel special, and the wondering about my biological parents came much later.

My dad did many different jobs, but at this point he was a sales rep, and a good one! He travelled a lot with his work but always came home at the end of the day. My mum stayed at home and ruled her domain with determination. She was the decision-maker, and apparently this meant little contact with my dad's family, but regular involvement with and from her own parents. My father's unquestioning acceptance of this confused me as I grew up, but I didn't challenge it, because the nan I *was* allowed to see was the heart of my world.

I visited Nan and Granddad Hayes in their council home several times a week. They had moved into their house in the 30s, on the very same day as their neighbour, who was now, as you might expect, called 'Aunty Millie'.

My mum always made it clear that it was she who was in charge of me, and the only one to make decisions over me. She also made it clear that Nan's ideas on my upbringing were not welcome and would not be respected.

She may have retained the last word on practicalities but she could not stop me feeling close to Nan, could not stop the love that was between us; nor could she stem the compassion my nan had for me and which I sensed even in the way she told me off for saying naughty words. It was as if she had to play to a moral script that conflicted with the role she held as my loving, funny, indulgent grandma. Another treat, overseen by my nan, was my Thursday night tea at Aunty Millie's, where I was awarded jam rolls and a comic, and sometimes even the opportunity to decide on a change: another type of sandwich? A new comic? I loved the fuss, the food, the being full, which was a rare feeling.

Aunty Hilda lived with Nan and Granddad Hayes. She was Nan's older sister, a sparse, grey little thing with white hair, a permanently attached handbag and a hat and coat, whatever the weather. She had worked in the munitions factory during the war and had a bank of fascinating memories she shared with me from time to time. Despite hearing some stories over and over again, I still regret not asking for more. Nan cared for Hilda and sometimes Hilda cared for me.

'Let's walk along here, Neil! We can see if we can find some good conkers! Hold my hand?'

I looked up at Aunty Hilda solemnly. This wouldn't do. I was three now.

'I'm a big boy now, so I don't need to hold anyone's hand.'

'Oh, I see, Neil. How about you just hold my little finger, then?'

'Oh, alright then…'

So Aunty Hilda and I looked for conkers on the way to putting Aunty Hilda's bet on the 'gee gees', my childish hand clasping her little finger as a symbol of my slow maturity.

We arrived at a sandstone house with a huge wooden door. Aunty Hilda knocked and we waited until a massive man opened to us, accompanied by swathes of cigarette smoke and whisky fumes. We entered, my eyes stinging, and made our way into the front room, where Aunty Hilda was rewarded with a welcome whisky before setting a bet.

Back at their home we went into the garden, a relic of the 'make do and mend' mentality of the war years. My memories of that garden now hold ghosts of my earlier self, skipping in and out of the rows of vegetables, helping Aunty Hilda to collect beans or carrots or peas for tea, chopping wood for pocket money, and later, digging over the soil when Nan, Granddad and Aunty Hilda had grown too old to cope. All of these memories were created free of my mum, even if her pervasive influence hung in the air, not quite ignored by us.

Aunty Hilda would often babysit us on Saturday nights with her boyfriend, Walter. He had served in both wars and would have been the source of so many interesting stories, had I had the wherewithal to ask about them.

'You can have your piece, then we'll bring you a drink.'

So I would eat my 'piece' – usually a cheese sandwich – and

wait for a glass of stout. This would knock me out and give them a peaceful evening, where Walter could eat his bread and dripping, soaked up from a frying pan and flavoured by the crumbs of previous meals.

My nan's friend Rene was also a big influence in my life. She was a source of interest to me because she owned pigeons. I was fascinated by their ability to fly anywhere but to always come home. They were definitely the right kind of pet for Rene, who had only ever once been out of Bridgnorth. The occasion had been the purchase of her wedding dress, and the sickness she'd experienced on the bus home put her off ever entering a vehicle again. Even for her husband Cyril's funeral, Rene's eighty-something-year-old feet took her over five miles to the church at the top end of town and back down to the cemetery, rather than see her in a car. She chain-smoked all the way there and back.

She was a source of my cigarettes when I was a teenager.

All of these wonderful people meant the world to me, but the only corner of my life that brought me pure happiness, such as most children feel on a daily basis, was still my grandparents. In fact, I was only told off by Nan Hayes once in my whole life, and I admit that I deserved it on that occasion. All I felt from them was warmth and, with them, I could feel fed and full and normal.

Nan Hayes' chip butties – doorstep bread with butter spread so thickly that the hot chips sank into it – were to die for. I would eat one as I walked up the path to Mum's car, trying to finish it before I got in, for fear of 'getting grease everywhere'. It was enough that I was chastised for being greedy again, for pestering for food…again. These butties symbolized Nan's quiet subversion, her understanding of my needs, a silent and unwitting two-fingered salute on my behalf to the woman who seemed to always hold things back from me, mainly nourishment.

Nan managed to toe the line with my mum all the time except once, when I was around four or five years old. Then she came out to battle for me – she simply couldn't help it.

We were all at Nan's house, in the front room. I loved Nan's house, loved it especially when the fire was lit, flames dancing and cracking, gobbling up coal, wood, any old rubbish thrown on. I was mesmerized when Nan and Granddad fed the fire with their bare hands. My wonderful nan was properly grandma-shaped, round for good cuddles and infectious belly laughs, and my granddad's arms were solid from his years working down the mines.

Judith and I were winding our way in and out of legs, checking on the fire, occasionally looking up at glass cabinets with their range of dusted ornaments, and waiting, almost patiently, to be allowed to pull items from the buffet onto a paper plate. I was not yet school age and was so small that the world of adults appeared giant-like to me. I didn't even think they could hear us chatting, as they were so busy discussing important matters above us.

So, when I needed an expression for something being utterly awful, I uttered the word *pup* – a local phrase similar to *shit* – in a sentence to my sister, in the middle of a room where several other conversations were happening out of my range. It was bad luck that my mum caught it and that she was close enough to me to smash her hand across my face before her anger could subside.

'Margie! No! What did he do?' Nan was there within seconds, reaching out her arms to me instinctively, to calm my howling, make me better, protect me from further harm.

But my mum pulled me out of her reach and, with one look, warned my nan not to interfere.

'He has a foul mouth and needs to learn a lesson!'

'What on earth did he say?'

'Pup!'

Through my vision blurred by tears, I saw Nan's face, soon joined by my Aunty Hilda. They both looked horrified by what they had seen. The other guests fell silent and, maybe feeling awkward at the family drama unfolding before them, focused a little too intently on their drinks.

'Margie, that's nothing! We used that word! Did you really

have to hit him as hard at that? Let me see him!'

But my mum wouldn't let anyone comfort me. I was left to cry, and bitter tears ran over my stinging cheek. My nan could only look at me, her eyes full of sympathy, desperate to pull me to her. Meanwhile my dad said nothing to defend me and muttered words that aligned him with my mum. I was not allowed to go out and play. I needed to learn manners and I needed to learn that words like 'pup' had no place in polite society and certainly not in Nan's front room.

Worse still, the beautiful, enticing, magical sandwich spread was restricted. I was not allowed to take my fill, enjoy the choosing and the tasting at leisure.

Observers might have thought this was part of my punishment, but it was my everyday. The punishment was not restriction of my normal intake of food, which was already strictly limited; it was seeing that there was more available and being unable to have it.

Despite the odd occasion when summary justice – and sometimes injustice – was meted out, my pre-school years seemed fairly happy. My parents, and particularly my mum, helped me to get ahead, so that I was no stranger to the three 'R's when I started school. This meant I was a good representative of the family. Appearances were so important.

Unfortunately for appearances, I allowed the school see-saw to wallop me in the mouth very early on and it dislodged my four front teeth. This did not reflect on the family's moral and social standing, but still…

It really hurt. I cried a lot. My face and head did suffer when I was little, one way or another.

My mum was sent for and it was serious enough for the Head to reassure me that she was coming to get me. Apart from the pain, there was so much blood and I must have looked a mess. This time Mum wasn't cross, she just took me to Mr Robertson, the dentist. He distracted me with his false hand that moved at the back of one of the cabinets, injected me to help the pain, and scraped out the final shards and roots of my front baby teeth.

I spent the next few years with whistling gaps, waiting patiently for my adult teeth to fill them.

I didn't let that bother me. Instead I enjoyed the whole school experience, with its 'play and learn' ethos. Teachers with exotic names like 'Mrs Ramone' took us, wellies squeaking against each other, to explore the science and nature of the woods, gathering up damsons to make pie, sending us home with purple lips and a full tummy – always welcome.

I must have been the son my mum especially wanted at that time: she had nudged and taught and moulded me until I held the much-coveted title of 'cleverest in the class'. Speaking to adults was also an easy skill and earned me remarks such as 'Neil will make Prime Minister one day!'

Of course, despite all this promise of greatness and intelligence, I couldn't help being a young boy who enjoyed hurling himself about dangerously, without regard for his own safety. Thus, when caught balancing upright on the top of the school climbing frame and told to get down by anxious dinner ladies, I thought nothing of leaping the five or six feet to the concrete below.

Looking back, I am surprised those dinner ladies didn't have seizures.

I would leave the relative freedom of school, where science and maths and language were learnt through so many games and fun activities, where I could use up some of my unspent energy and competitive spirit, and go back to my mum. If I hadn't scuffed my shoes or appeared looking scruffier than the others, she had time to ask me about the school day and my victories and would be pleased to hear when I had been better and cleverer and faster than anyone else. I had to account for my friends and was steered away from anyone or anything that might jeopardize my chances of success or the family reputation.

So far I was doing well.

But things were about to change.

Chapter 2

The moment that separates my two views of the world is now lost. I just know that, at some stage, my place in my mum's world shifted inexorably and I have never understood why. For me, our Sunday evening routine came to symbolise this change.

The world was full of children enjoying their Sunday evening bath: bubbles and warm water and the last fun of the weekend before school the next day. Clean towels, mums mopping up water from tousled hair, brushing gently, unknotting strands carefully, playfully brushing through with the dryer on a low heat. It could be a time to chat and cuddle before the school week commenced and 'together time' took second place to our busy lives.

My hair was bright ginger – I was the only one with ginger hair in my family. I liked it long and my parents let me keep it that way. I just needed a bit of help with it after my bath, so mum would blow-dry it for me, styling it for me with her bright orange Moulinex hairdryer, shaped like a gun.

There must have been a time when I sat down innocently and expected my mum to dry my hair delicately, maybe even lovingly, but I don't recall.

She would appear with the hairdryer in one hand and a hard plastic brush in the other. I would sit down and brace myself for the torture to come. The hairdryer would burst into life and she would hold it so close to my head that the hot air had no place to go but directly into my skin. I could feel my skull burning and so I would yelp and pull away.

It didn't matter that I cried or screamed or pulled away; in fact, that only made it worse, for my mum would then tell me to stop moving, to stop being a baby, and hit my head sharply with the back of the hard plastic hairbrush, cracking my skull in the same place she had just scalded.

I dreaded Sunday evenings but soon learnt that keeping very still and biting my lips kept tears and cries at bay and brought the whole horrible process to as speedy an end as possible.

I kept this all to myself. I didn't understand it but soon learned to deal with my mum carefully, so as not to antagonize her and make my world more uncomfortable. It was slowly dawning on me that I could never choose my friends and I could not choose my personality. I was being moulded to an unspoken plan.

In between Sunday evenings, however, the week was dotted with chances to be away from home. My friends and I flew about the estate on our bikes. For most of this time, I had no front teeth, so with nothing more to lose, I didn't think. I was fearless.

The edges of the estate unfurled themselves on building sites, which, lacking in partition walls, offered us so many opportunities. Scaffolding was to be climbed, all the better to hurl ourselves into sand piles, our legs buckling as we landed, bones straining to stay whole.

Someone had the bright idea of riding our bikes off the scaffolding, and we perfected the art of positioning ourselves just right so that we and our bikes could part company mid-air, landing separately in the sand.

Brilliant!

Barry Sheen was a big hero of the day. He made skidding an aspiration, and we developed the skill of setting our tyres just right to avoid rupturing them completely – my father was always mending punctures! One of my friends, Frank, was particularly good at this activity. We spent a long time together as he was clear of my mum's radar, and what she didn't know, she couldn't spoil! We stuck a number 7 sticker onto our bikes and pegged a playing card to our back wheel so that we roared along the road. If I didn't look down at my scrawny legs or catch sight of myself, freewheeling my second-hand Raleigh bike past suburban windows, my bright ginger hair sticking out at all angles, I became Barry Sheen.

On one particular day my younger neighbour Daz and I were 'bombing it' round the roads, the card being hammered by the spokes, weaving along the middle of the road with no care whatsoever for our own safety or anyone else's. I was free and immortal and no one was hurting me or making me be what I was not.

We both stood up to push down with more strength on the pedals, gaining speed, our backsides bobbing from side to side, dancing with the saddle. We hurtled towards a hill on a bend and, when we were breathless with the exertion, we freewheeled down the hill, on the wrong side of the road, seeing just enough of the road ahead to stay upright. The air raced past me, plastering my t-shirt to my skinny chest, the edges flapping in the force of the wind.

The car appeared at the same time as the noise of screaming brakes. A collage of sights rapidly imprinted on my mind: a woman's face, horrified, Daz's bike twisting round in his effort to keep alive, my own hands gripping the handlebars.

We came to a halt within centimetres of each other. The woman flung open the door and screeched at us, 'What do you think you're doing? You could have been killed! What idiots! What on earth were you thinking?'

We stared at her, then at the girl who had climbed out of the car's passenger seat. They were both clearly shaken. We expected the woman to carry on yelling, but instead her words turned to wails and her hands flew to her face to hide the tears and push back the sobs. Her daughter burst into tears, a little mirror of her bawling mum.

Daz and I looked at each other and our faces screwed up too. With laughter. Before the driver could recover from her shock and tie us into a tiresome conversation about road safety, we rode away down the rest of the hill.

Round the corner, we stopped again to laugh, catch our breath and laugh again. It didn't bother me that I had wet my pants. This happened every now and then, when I was with my friends and we were laughing hard about some daft, childish, unimportant thing, bent double, stomachs hurting with it. It wasn't a sign of fear, even if I had nearly hit a car.

We stayed out as late as we dared or until we got really hungry, often altering our watches as a ready excuse for being late. Only once did I push the boundaries so far that my parents came out looking for me!

When I had to go home, when I knew I had pushed my freedom as far as I dared, I felt a weight descend on me again. This happened every time I had to go back; my freedom was rarer than for others my age. But this night, the night of the car that nearly hit me, the night of the laughing hard and the damp pants…this night was worse than normal.

I tried to dry myself off before I got home, but it didn't quite work. It didn't worry me what my friends thought, if they even noticed; we all need that amount of laughter in our lives.

My mum didn't feel the same.

As soon as I got in, she grabbed hold of my arm with one hand and clutched at my shorts with the other. When she felt the dampness, she leant in and hissed, 'You are a dirty boy! You are disgusting…maybe even that baby next door is too old for you to play with?' Then she pulled off my shorts and pants and threw them in the washing machine, while I was left to scramble up the stairs to my room, half-naked and ashamed of the fun I had had.

This grabbing and sneering and humiliating became our special routine. Affection, understanding and fun was also in short supply at home, like food – I rarely stopped being hungry. The portions she gave me were insufficient for the energy I expended and there was no room for fat in my life. I was at best skinny, at worst skeletal, and this look was like a sign round my neck labeled 'victim', 'poor', 'unnurtured'.

This is why I loved parties: for the greater chance of filling myself up, and maybe gaining some weight to be as strong and as tall as my classmates. I had learnt how to avoid detection, as long as I was in a crowd. Mum could not watch me all the time and there were often other kids who would fetch me an extra sandwich if she were on guard at the buffet table. Her biggest fear was getting fat like both my grandmas, and apparently this extended to me and Judith getting fat too.

I was once enjoying such a party round at Aunty Karen's. It was for her daughters, Anne and Jane. I was eating and drinking with the other children, away from the adults with their boring conversations, when one thing led to another and I forgot myself and had fun.

The warmth spread across my crotch and was just starting to make its way towards my knees when the wall of adult bodies seemed to part, revealing my mum's grim expression. I looked down at the patch of wet spreading across my trousers and back up at her face.

The cold fingers of dread clutched at my insides.

'Come here, Neil!' she demanded, her voice a low growl, as she battled to retain control of her anger before all these people.

I walked slowly, felt myself start to tremble a little. All eyes were on me.

When I was close enough to feel her ragged breath on my face and see her pinprick pupils in her cold eyes, I whimpered something of an apology, but it was ineffective and no barrier to her cruel hands, which grabbed and hurt and whipped away my trousers, leaving me exposed to the guests. I covered my crotch with my little hands, which now smelt of pee, and ran to a corner, where I could still hear her tirade against me, complaining to all the adults there about my dirty, stupid ways and her embarrassment. The other children there no longer wanted to play with me, either because I stank or because I was a 'baby' or for both reasons.

When I was around seven years old, we moved into a house with a huge front window. I cannot pinpoint an exact time when it all started, but bit by bit this window afforded my mum many extra opportunities for my humiliation. It was a particularly useful window when it was dark and we had the light on. Passersby could watch all sorts of tragedies unfold on our floodlit stage.

And I was the hero of many plays, tortured mentally, forced to stand – for all to see – without trousers, vulnerable, questioning my hopelessness, wondering why my mum did not help me conquer this affliction. Only the settee afforded me some comfort, some shelter, when I was permitted to use it.

And from 'stage left', my sister would enter and laugh at me, either because I was naked, or because I was still unformed, unmanly, stick-thin, or maybe because it put her on my mum's side and endowed her with protection from the same treatment.

This particular routine would persist for the next five years. Within me, I looked for an escape.

Chapter 3

My mum's approval or disapproval continued to affect her mood and hence our happiness. Judith and I adapted our behaviour, folding ourselves up in a corner, making ourselves as invisible as possible, wearing certain clothes, even if we hated them or they were uncomfortable, all so we didn't aggravate her. Judith was more successful at this game than I was, or so it seemed. Our mum always seemed to have a headache and, as we were rarely allowed out of the house, our childish games were soon replaced by reading, or watching TV on its lowest volume.

At first I accepted my mum's frailties. At least I was not the only person to pain her. My father managed it quite a lot too.

He was once late home. My mum paced and muttered and checked up on the oven, which was slowly ruining the dinner she had prepared. She seemed cross he was late, rather than worried.

She turned the oven down to a low setting and packed me into the car to fetch Judith from gymnastics. When we got home, she opened the oven door again, sighed, slammed it closed and took up her angry tirade once more.

Her muttering and grumbling had been going on for a while when the phone rang. Judith and I looked up from our books, having buried our noses in them to keep out of Mum's firing line.

'Hello?'

Distant words, too faint to decipher.

'What did you do that for, you idiot? Your dinner's ruined!'

More words, a soothing tone this time.

'What a stupid thing to do! Hurry up...if your tea is burnt, it's burnt!'

And she put the phone down and bustled back into the kitchen.

Judith was brave enough to ask why Dad was late. Had he worked late? Bumped into friends? Had the car broken down?

'He's gone and had a car accident! What a fool!'

I hoped Dad was not injured but dared not ask after him. When he came home quite a while later, he looked shaken and exhausted. He slipped into the house ready to appease his wife and apologise for being delayed. Even at my young age, I thought it would have been nice for him to have had a hug, and maybe even a freshly made sandwich.

She was just as scathing of my father when, on another occasion, he broke his leg slipping on ice in a car park ('Idiot!'). She was so affected by her headaches that I thought they must be horrific, but as I got older I dared to challenge their constancy, their intensity, and it was then I found out that it was all my fault. On the one hand I was relieved to learn that my mum did not have the brain tumour I was starting to suspect; on the other hand I discovered I had the power to cause constant pain to someone who was meant to love me unconditionally.

As I grew, so did my appetite. I would arrive home thinking of food, my stomach growling and more than ready. From the road I could hear the sound of my mum's fingers hammering her electric typewriter with its golf ball of numbers moving across the top. She knelt for hours, page after page crawling over the back of it, transformed into some document before being replaced by a blank sheet again. The racket filled the house and, even if Judith and I had been interested enough in each other to chat, we would not have been able to hear ourselves talk.

Without looking up from her typing, she would call me over so she could feel if I was damp. She wasn't gentle and her grasping fingers made me wince.

'Don't worry, Neil. I'll get you some clean trousers. You'll soon grow out of it…it happens to lots of children.'

That would have been a comfort, wouldn't it?

Instead she said, 'Dirty boy! No wonder people don't like you!'

I did once ask if there was something wrong with me; how did she know that wasn't the case? But she explained that I was just dirty, not ill.

This ritual was not even abandoned on the rare occasions I had a friend with me, and our mutual embarrassment formed yet one more barrier between me and a normal childhood.

So, after a day at school, I was welcomed by noise, humiliation and a long wait for an insufficient and tasteless meal.

I fell into a rhythm to help me cope. When I was at home or out with the family, I had to take on the shape of the boy my mum wanted, work carefully around my mum's unpredictable, fickle, damning temperament, lose the spontaneity of childhood, and plan my sentences and my actions to minimise their impact on the equilibrium.

Permission to go on a bike ride became a dazzling gift. These sorties gave me the freedom I needed to claw some enjoyment out of life. School became a greater refuge, where I could be myself. I dreamed of joining the army, like Granddad Obbard. I saw it as my escape, but when I dared mention this to my mum, she told me I would certainly not join the army and that I would grow out of that idea.

We would see.

My youthful energy soaked up physical activity. Outside of school I learnt to swim, and I was very soon training at Northgate Swimming Club, competing in galas and representing the county. My parents took me and Judith every Saturday, first to Madeley in Telford, then Bridgnorth Leisure Centre. I spent four or five years at this club, during which time I learned to accept the cutting comments about my poor physique from those who were bigger and faster than me.

Other activities I was allowed to do included ballroom dancing at the 'St James Old Time and Modern Sequence Dance Club' down the road at St James in the Grove. I was dragged there on occasion until my early teens by my mum, who used to take Nan and Granddad Hayes.

I was also made to attend confirmation classes, despite hating it, not believing in it, and having a developing sense that the whole lot of those churchgoers were hypocrites who preached one thing and did something else!

Pie in the sky!

I sat through my lessons just to ease any tension at home, but every word sounded like pure 'pup' as far as I was concerned.

Of course I never said any of this out loud, but no one could stop me thinking it.

I met Andy the first year of junior school when we were both Miss May's class. Every day was a collection of lessons and exercises we tolerated just for the sheer delight of being together, having fun, seeing the daftness in everything. We pulled faces at each other until one of us could not move for laughing; we ran out the door before the bell for playtime had stopped ringing and raced each other to the top of the climbing frame. We only really worked when Miss May was standing over us or we had been threatened with no playtime.

The world was amazing with Andy in it, and I loved having a best friend. He stayed at school for lunch, whereas I used to have to go home. He would slip me some of his pocket money and I would pick up some gobstoppers for a penny or halfpenny on the way back to school. We squeezed fun out of the last few minutes of the lunch hour, charging around, unable to talk because our teeth were stuck together or our mouths full to bursting.

Sadly, we made the mistake of thinking that our friendship would be allowed to exist outside of school too.

I was upstairs, pulling on some shorts that my mum approved of, when I saw Andy and another boy coming up the road on their bikes. I waved out the bedroom window and ran to the stairs, slamming my bedroom door behind me. My scrawny legs could not get down the stairs fast enough and I even grabbed the banister with my left hand, pushed the wall with my right and took four steps at once.

But I was still too slow. She had already opened the door.

I could see Andy standing next to his bike, holding the

handlebars, looking up at my mum. The other boy had waited near the gate and turned his bike to face the road, ready for our getaway.

'Can Neil come out to play?'

I moved further down the stairs, standing near my mum, who was holding the door open, ready to let me break free of this house, ride away with my friend, enjoy a day of childish exhilaration.

'No.'

Andy and I both looked up at Mum. He looked confused and I looked pleading.

'No,' she said again, firmly. 'Neil is not going out to play with you because I don't like you.'

Andy looked stunned. He stared at her, searching for words that never came. She stood in the aperture of the doorway, blocking my freedom, cutting me off from one part of my life that gave me happiness.

I understood straightaway.

I had been wrong to have a best friend I had chosen myself.

Andy finally rode off, with a slight wobble, looking back only briefly.

He never called for me again, and from that day on, I was less and less included by any of the local boys in anything outside of school. Very soon, my mum's reach would extend even there, for she demanded I be in a different class to Andy.

This shift coincided with a new phase in my life – one that would last for years. I started to punch walls and doors. I imagined they were my mum, who was so stubborn and rigid and unyielding and unforgiving. She positioned herself, like an unbreachable wall, between me and our neighbours, between me and my schoolfriends, between me and anyone who fell short of her unachievable standards.

She turned people against her.

She turned us into an island.

The mixture of self-harm and the release of tension helped me survive.

Of course, Andy and I still got together every chance we

could, each dashing to find the other at break and lunch times, which we filled with as much fun and friendship as we could manage. All these times I could pretend to be a normal child with a normal mum.

With Dad, it was different. I wanted so much to be like him. Every now and then he would go into a secret place in the garage and appear with his sheath knife for me to look at in wonder. I was allowed to touch the handle and, as I did so, my imagination conjured up stories of brave acts, where my father saved lives and where his very appearance, wielding this knife, sent baddies scuttling in fear and trepidation. When he told me he had been a Cub, and all about his exciting camping trips, I immediately wanted to be one too.

I was allowed to join the local Cubs and, despite my disappointment that we were not, apparently, allowed to carry sabres, I had the time of my life!

Akela and Baloo (in their everyday lives they sported the less exotic names of Daisy and Graham) led our troop with enthusiasm. We would all meet up at the Dingle, a piece of woodland at the top of the road near the leisure centre. We met in a hut that sat on breeze blocks on top of a steep bank. This mound cradled a tunnel over a disused railway line. The tunnel was massive and very long, stretching through town as far as the Severn Valley Railway. Of course, it was cut off from us by a fence, but this was easily wrecked for access to the shadiness beyond. We would turn up early to Cubs and hang around in the half darkness, learning how to smoke from the older boys who knew enough about things to hide their habits.

When Akela and Baloo turned up, we continued to maraud in the Dingle, but now it was legitimized by our quest for badges. We set fires and tracked down promising sticks, setting about them with blunt penknives until they were sharp enough to stab sausages for us to hold over the flames. These squirmed and twisted and finally burst from their skin and, when we had checked they were hot all the way through, we ate them up and replaced them with marshmallows. For me, these outdoor meals were a godsend, bringing my day's calorific total more in line with everyone else my age.

Then we were allowed to play boyish games and practise being superheroes, chasing around, imagining we were soldiers, capturing flags, laughing, daring each other to climb the bank and stand on top of the tunnel, laughing some more and forgetting our home lives.

I never did get to go camping. There were no explanations for this beyond a simple lack of trust in me. Judith was luckier, or rather, more trustworthy.

I never did get to go camping and I never did get to understand why.

I was allowed on the odd day trip, though, especially if it was educational and/or a badge was to be gained from it. One that sticks out in my mind for all the wrong reasons was a trip to Slimbridge Wildlife Trust.

We spent a pleasant enough day there, crossing bridges over waterways, spotting birds and other wildlife. Of course the trip to the shop was the top of everyone's list of things to do and I had a few pence for some sweets.

Michael Adams, however, had at least two pounds to spend on whatever he wanted, and what he wanted was no less than six mint chocolate chip ice lollies.

The rest of us were naturally envious, standing around watching him devour one lolly after the other, discarding one, two, three, four, five, six sticks...but we were vindicated on the trip home.

'Sit down quickly, boys!' Baloo was in a rush to set off. The bus had been waiting for us in the heat and the plastic seats were hot to the touch. The sooner we started off, the sooner some kind of air would filter in through the two roof vents. Air-con was a luxury for the future; no one was used to it in those days.

'It's too hot, Baloo!' someone whinged. Baloo almost snapped but controlled himself in time.

'Get sat down, then, and we can get going!'

'I don't feel well!' This was Michael. He was sitting across the aisle from me.

Akela looked at him sharply. 'Take your jumper off then.'

But he didn't, and Akela's attention was taken up by the driver, who wanted to know something about the journey back.

Once we were settled and promised not to move around too much, the engine sprang to life and moved us slowly out of the car park. We gasped in the heat and willed the bus to speed up so that some more air would be stirred up to relieve us.

I looked across at Michael Adams. He was bright red and looked most unwell. His head leant against the windowpane and his mouth was open, revealing a green tongue. As I watched him, he groaned in discomfort and shouted down the bus, 'Akela!'

Something in his tone brought Akela up the bus faster than I would ever have thought possible. In the blink of an eye she was there, barking orders at Michael: 'Sit up! Jumper off! Hands in the air!'

We all sat up and watched as the jumper was turned inside out over Michael's head and he flayed on the seat, both arms caught up in the jumper, his back exposed as his t-shirt was pulled up inside the jumper, his head lost in all of this, emitting groans and cries of discomfort.

Akela's worldly experience and heightened senses kicked in and, with one last yank, the jumper flew off, Michael's arms flopped to his sides and Akela's hand slapped down over his mouth, just as he vomited.

The stink of half-digested mint chocolate chip lollies permeated the stuffy atmosphere of the bus and we all yelled in disgust, plastering our hands over our noses and staring at Akela's hand, which served as an unsuccessful dam to the bright green liquid being expelled from Michael's stomach. It squeezed through Akela's fingers and down Michael's chin, and any that failed by that route burst from his nostrils, spraying the plastic seat in front.

And in the midst of the mayhem, Akela did not move. She simply bellowed three words up the bus: 'Graham! Plastic bag!!'

On that stifling hot bus, even with the stench of vomit in our nostrils, we knew this would be a source of amusement for a long, long time.

Chapter 4

My transition into secondary school age was a victory for my mum.

The preliminary battle took me unawares. I was excited about my fresh start at secondary school, hoping to be able to spend more time with Andy, relishing the thought of stepping into a new environment. Maybe I would make new friends coming from other primary schools? This was going to be good!

Then she came home with a package.

'That's for you, Neil.'

I should have known better, but I approached it with happy anticipation. I pulled back the wrappings and revealed an instrument of psychological torture: a briefcase.

My shoulders sagged. I didn't say thank you or look thrilled.

'What's the matter, Neil? Aren't you going to say thank you?'

'Is this for school?' I knew, but I was stalling. How could I deal with this? My mind was racing. If I kicked off, she would say I was ungrateful. If I cried, she would say I was a baby. If I accepted it wordlessly, I would be a laughing stock at school.

'Of course it's for school!'

I turned to her and tried a new approach.

'Mum, I'm worried about something.'

If I explained how afraid I was, she would surely take it back to the shop and swap it for an Adidas sports bag or something? I couldn't possibly go to my new school with that!

'What?!' she snapped.

I persevered. 'Everyone is getting a sports bag, Mum. If I take this, they'll laugh at me!'

There was a moment when I thought it might be all right,

that she might be hit by a wave of understanding, compassion even, that she might wrap the briefcase back up and swap it for a sports bag.

I was wrong.

'Don't be ridiculous, Neil. I've bought it now, so be thankful you have it!'

That was the moment dread replaced excitement. I no longer looked forward to my new school.

I wandered through the school with that blasted briefcase on my first day, a minority of one in a throng of brand new trendy Adidas bags. This, alongside my finely coiffed and bright ginger hair, set me apart, labeled me 'victim' and set the standard for the rest of my school days.

My mum had seen to it that I didn't have any friends at all outside of school, and almost all of the few I had in school then started to tease and make fun of me. My hair was still being styled by my mum. I had tried to tell her how much I disliked it and how I was being teased because of it, but she just replied, 'Well, *I* like it!' It would be a little while longer before my style would be my own.

I had long since taken up smoking, either to be like my dad or to cock a very secret snook at my mum. (Imagine what people would think! Maybe Aunty Rene slipping me the odd cigarette was also evidence she was putting two fingers up at my mum?!) My starting to smoke was certainly not due to peer pressure, as none of my peers cared what I did or did not do. I could count my proper friends with the fingers of one hand.

My lonely existence meant she was now able to impose her will on me with little resistance.

'Sit down and get on with your homework.'

I did exactly that. At school I had become the freak with no friends. This role involved me generally being the butt of everyone's joke and picked on. Although Andy was a constant friend, we were each disliked by the other's mum, so contact was very limited. In addition, one person could not counteract the swarms of bullies that took their pleasure from my distress every day. I learnt the entire thesaurus entry for 'ginger' and every insult known to man. My answer was to offer some kind of clever retort and leg it before they could wallop me.

So sitting down and doing my homework became the norm. What else could I do?

'Do that piece again, more neatly, Neil!'

'You must write a few more paragraphs, Neil.'

'Redo that exercise, Neil!'

Some nights I was at the dining room table from the moment I walked through the door until bedtime. If I had looked out of the huge window, I might have seen Andy and the local lads spinning past, doing wheelies or riding hands-free.

My dazzling gifts of occasional freedom dwindled to almost none, and without the interaction of friendship, I had to amuse myself. Having learnt one day that magnets can be charged with electricity, I lay in bed wondering about that very fact and mentally concocting a range of experimental activities. Inspired, I got up, rummaged around for the necessary items and wrapped a magnet and two prongs of a plug in wire before pushing it all into a live wall socket.

There was a loud bang, a shooting flame and the rallying cry of my sister from the next room: 'Daaaaaaaad! Neil's done something!'

There ensued the battering of my childhood, accompanied by yells and reminders of how stupid I was, to put my life and that of my family at risk with this ridiculous experimentation. All my punishments have become a blur. Sometimes I was belted with the sole of a pretty hard slipper, sometimes with the flat palm of an angry hand. This incident was more prolonged and painful than any before, but, as I had almost set the house on fire, I accepted the punishment and never did it again.

There were endless arguments, mainly about homework. It was rarely done to my mum's satisfaction, her standards being at some unachievable level, way above mine or even my teachers'. She stood over me as I worked, querying, suggesting, commanding, and I worked slowly to accomplish her perfection or reworked exercises with her guidance; but sometimes the anger and frustration in me burst out and I slammed a door or hit my fist against a wall until it bled.

I soon learned to lie about homework in an attempt to alleviate the intense pressure I was put under at home. School matched the torture of my home life. I was called a swot for being up to date with homework and watched as any friends I'd clung to grew apart from me, either because their relationship to me would make their lives harder with the cool crowd, or because my mum and her insane schedule had seen them off.

At school, I experimented when I could, laughing at the gossip about the French teacher, Miss Ellis, who reputedly owned a wooden tit. I laughed with the rest of the class whenever she asked, '...wouldn't it?' and tried to share a complicit look with the others, as we stifled our giggles. I rarely managed it, though, as they were all looking at their friends and not me.

Even food did not afford me any release, due to Mum's lingering, persistent dread of obesity. The hours of homework were therefore barely alleviated by my break for tea. I had so little on my plate that even chewing slowly could not afford me enough time to refresh myself, and so term-time became a fresh hell.

An unexpected escape was, ironically, paid work. When I was about 12 I got a paper round at the local shop. I got myself up at 6am every morning, bar Sunday, and dragged myself sleepily out of the house, whatever the weather. I grabbed my bike and set off for the shop, where I stood with the other paper boys, smoking the singles the owner, Geoff, had sold or given to us.

The round wasn't difficult and I was fit enough to cope with it easily. Only the belligerent dogs were an issue for me, but I dealt with that with a quick thwack on the nose with their owners' rolled-up paper; on some occasions, I just threw the paper over the fence. If the owners didn't like it, they would have to make sure their pooch was locked away, that's all!

One morning, I opened the door to a sheet of torrential rain. I was about to step through it to get my bike, when I heard Dad behind me.

'Hold on a minute, Neil. You can't go out in this. Let me get my shoes on and I'll take you in the car.'

Whenever the weather was really bad like that, Dad would drive me to the shop, wait whilst I collected my bag, checked off the papers for my round and ran back to the car. He would then drive my round, idling the engine at the end of every driveway, watching me as I ran up the drive, shoved the paper into the letterbox, and ran back, jumping back into the car.

It was an act of rare kindness in my childhood and I loved it! It was great!

Throughout my childhood, holidays away from home had been average events. We stayed in the UK, often Wales, and engaged in activities which were both unremarkable and lacking in extravagance. Nan Hayes came with us on one occasion and renewed my image of holidaying adults by actually playing football with me on the beach. The love of football in a grandma was a rare occurrence in those days. She'd played the sport as a girl and loved to watch it on TV.

From this sea of mediocre, pleasant enough holidays, two stand out: Devon and France.

Nan O's was a haven for me. She and Granddad Obbard lived near the beach in Exmouth, so there was always the promise of games and sand and swimming. Much more exciting than all that, though, my Nan O was a fantastic and generous cook and my granddad was my hero.

Orphaned by the gasses of the Somme, Granddad Obbard had walked to school on his first day in his bare feet. He'd muddled his way through his poor childhood, finding his place in the adult world as a grocer's boy, moving into the trade one exam at a time. The advent of the Second World War found him married to Betty and the father to Lewis: Nan O and my dad. Taking his responsibilities to his family seriously, he volunteered for service, rather than wait to be conscripted, to get the best deal. From what I could gather, Granddad spent some of the war wielding an anti-aircraft gun in the ditches of southern England. Otherwise he was part of the battle for Europe.

As soon as we had done the settling-in thing down at his and Nan O's house that summer, I went to sit by him to ask about my favourite story of all: the day my granddad had defeated a Messerschmitt pilot. He smiled indulgently at me and started his story.

'The plane came towards me and I positioned my gun...'

Granddad crouched down in his chair, his hands holding an imaginary aircraft gun, squinting up at the ceiling. I looked up too and the ceiling fell away until I was there with my granddad in that ditch, protecting everyone from Nazi invasion.

'I shot at the plane and it banked away from me. I thought I had seen him off, but he turned and came back. I shot again and again...'

His arms shook as he fought the German. I was grinning with delight. What a story!

'I hit the plane and, when he turned away, I thought that was definitely the last of him. But he came back, so low that I could actually see his face. He was aiming for me. I was going to die unless I acted fast...'

Granddad Obbard, looking up at the ceiling/sky, his imaginary anti-aircraft gun to one side, leaned in to me conspiratorially and delivered the punchline to the story.

'As he bore down on me, his determination to end me then and there in his eyes, I threw myself into the ditch, ripping my clothes, tearing my skin on the branches of the bushes. I waited, sore, scarred and afraid, until the sound of that Messerschmitt engine faded and I knew I was safe.'

When my mum came in, she caught us in a moment of adoration and pride. My grandfather must surely have loved his role in my life and I certainly loved him. He was amazing! I wanted to join the army and be just like him!

'Neil! Come away from Granddad, stop bothering him!'

Granddad and I both jumped as we returned to the present day. Granddad tried to tell my mum that I was not bothering him, but it served her purpose to ignore him and I had to come away.

I went into the spare bedroom where Judith and I were going to be sleeping. She wasn't in there at the time, so I could sit on the edge of the double bed and look through the bookshelves. They were mainly books my father used to read.

In the other part of the house, I could hear the voices of the adults, low murmurs, the odd polite laughter, the unwelcome interjection of my mum's voice. Judith was probably with them, knowing to keep quiet when Mum was talking, knowing to smile and laugh when it worked in our mum's favour.

I was drawn immediately to one book. It was in hardback, brightly coloured with red and gold, its front cover sporting three horses – black, brown, white – all wearing ceremonial bridles, rearing up in unison, their riders straight-backed and proud.

The 1952 Empire Youth Manual with its promise of adventure.

If I was going to be sidelined, forbidden to talk to Granddad, at least I could lose myself in this book. The men in my family were all brave adventurers who conquered the enemy and wielded knives. I wanted to grow up like them, so I flicked through the book, scanning the contents to find exciting stories to help me to be like that too.

Just then, Judith came in. She looked from me to the book with a disparaging expression before muttering, 'Tea's ready!' and disappearing again. I put the book on the bedside table nearest the door, as Judith had already put her things on the other side, and went through to the kitchen/dining room, my stomach, as usual, rumbling.

Nan O's table was heaving with plates, piled high with meats and vegetables and Yorkshire puddings, jugs of thick, rich gravy and shining cutlery. The dessert spoons pledged hidden delights.

I was ecstatic. My mum's cooking had not improved and, as the years went on and I glimpsed and coveted and tasted other people's food, I realised that her cooking was no less than dreadful. So, when faced with such a succulent feast, I tucked in with gusto.

'That's enough, Neil!'

Of course, it was my mum. I had put a slice of meat, some

carrots and a roast potato on my plate, and had been reaching for another when she put a stop to my fun.

I felt my shoulders sag and I lowered my eyes to my plate, knowing it was useless to argue. 'But I am starving!' may have been medically true but it would have had no impact on her. Instead Granddad and Nan O took up the sword.

'He's all right, Margie! There's plenty!'

'He's a growing boy! He needs his food!'

Both were glared into submission. 'He's just being greedy. He has enough!'

I didn't have enough. I never had enough. I was always hungry, never strong. How would I ever be able to stand up to the friends who were, one by one, turning into my tormentors? How would I ever be able to fight enemies or wield knives like my father and grandfather? However would I get strong enough to join the army?

We ate in silence for a few minutes. I watched enviously as Granddad Obbard piled potatoes onto his plate and splashed steaming gravy over them. I ate slowly to make it last and thought a lot about pudding.

Just as most of us were sliding our knives and forks together on our empty plates and swallowing the last of our meal, Granddad Obbard groaned apologetically, picked up his plate and pushed the gravy-bedecked potatoes onto my own plate with the back of his knife.

'My eyes were bigger than my belly! Do Granddad a favour, Neil, and eat those up, would you?'

Still ravenous, I obliged, taking care not to look at Mum, who must have had a face like thunder.

It was soon bedtime and, as I pulled on my pyjamas, I was struck by two thoughts: I could not recall ever going to bed full before, and the Empire Youth Manual.

I slid into bed, grabbing the book off the bedside table on my way. I settled back on the pillows and opened it, flicking through and finally settling on an article about the White Park Bay in Northern Ireland, a National Trust site in County Antrim.

I could hear Judith saying goodnight to the grown-ups

before entering our room. She got changed over in the corner. I didn't take any notice; I was too engrossed in my book with its images of rocks and foam and cliffs and its ancient legends.

Judith got into bed and unsettled my position, but I carried on anyway, turning to another article about the navy.

My boyish mind made me believe I could be anything, go anywhere, do anything.

That moment I was free. I was happy. I was a boy like any other. I slept happily, full from my meal, full of possibilities.

When I woke up the next morning, the book was still on the bedspread. I was reaching for it when Judith opened her eyes. I didn't recognise the look on her face, but it surprised me enough to pay attention to her as she started to speak, to share her thoughts, to draw me into her world.

I didn't want to be there, I didn't want to know any of the things on her mind, to share what she wanted to share, do what she wanted to do…I just wanted to go back to my book and the unknowing me from the night before.

At some point, the Empire Youth Annual slid quietly onto the floor.

I hated it. I tried to stop her, but she would not let me run away from this. She told me she would tell everyone I had been naughty if I did not give her my full attention and do as she asked.

I was the most confused, the most afraid and the most in need of being rescued that I had ever been.

The room closed in on me, stealing air from my lungs, until I heard a noise in the hallway.

'That must be Nan O and Granddad!'

Judith moved away sharply and I was finally given silent permission to leave the room and slip out to the toilet.

I stayed in there as long as I could. I washed myself and thought about the time, minutes or eons ago, when I was happy and innocent and full of dreams.

As I returned to the bedroom, I passed closed doors, hiding adults who would never believe me, who would probably punish me.

My side of the bed looked rumpled. Judith now had her back to me.

Before I got back into bed and waited to be called for breakfast, I picked up the Empire Youth Annual and slipped it back onto the bookshelf.

I never read it again.

We left a couple of days later, after more 'secrets' I was not interested in. My self-esteem and faith in family had been eroded, my memories of Nan O's house tarnished, overwhelmed by new tortures in my life.

I never wanted to go back there again with my sister, dreaded ever having to share a room with her again. By chance, it was the last time we did stay over, as, for some reason, we only went for the day from then on – until I could drive myself, and then I became a regular visitor.

Our next holiday was to France. Judith and I were squashed, with the other baggage, into the car and we all endured hours of travelling, via a family room in a hotel in Reims, to the south coast: Fréjus.

For most of the journey I sat in silence, weighing up the probability of new hazards. Every space I found myself in, every conversation I was engaged in, every action I performed, all these things had the potential to spin my world into fresh depths of hell if I was not careful.

My life had become a desert with indiscriminate expanses of quicksand.

One anxiety threatening to paralyse me was, thankfully, quieted as soon as we got to the caravan.

'I am not sleeping in the same room as *him*!' Judith whined, pointing at me with her finger. 'He might want to *touch* me!'

I looked sharply at my parents, but they did not register any emotion, just let Judith choose where to sleep, and I was more than relieved that she would be too far away from me to take me to that place I so dreaded.

We embarked on our holiday. The language barrier should not have been too bad, as my mum spoke a bit of French. However, she was also timid in these situations and so she dispatched my father to do anything requiring interaction with the locals.

'What do I say?' Dad hovered nervously, ready to memorise the sentence and dispatch himself without delay to the shop, before he forgot it.

She sighed. Having an incompetent husband must have been a trial.

'Je voudrais huit petits pains, s'il vous plait!'

'What?'

'It means you want eight bread rolls! Crikey, Lewis, do you really need telling that?…Zhe voodray wheat petee pan, si voo play!!'

He trundled off, repeating the phrase under his breath, returning with a baguette.

'Why have you got that? What did they say?'

My father just shrugged and placed the loaf down, as some kind of ineffective offering to appease my mum, who was almost apoplectic.

'For goodness' sake, Lewis! Can't you do one simple thing?'

She was furious with him and, now that he had helped me so many times with my paper round, I felt a closer bond to him and this emboldened me to speak up.

'Why don't you go, instead of just sending Dad?'

That was the wrong thing to say! I was told that I didn't know everything and to mind my own business. It was my later experiences with people that taught me she must have been terrified of speaking French to natives. Later, when I was learning French at school, the role of family spokesperson fell to me. I did a good job of it but my bravery and talent did not win me any praise.

In contrast to our British holidays, the weather was hot enough for us to spend the whole day at the beach. Warmed by the Riviera sunshine and soothed by the breeze coming off the Mediterranean Sea, I played the whole day, alternately enjoying the sand and the refreshing water on my feet.

Returning to the caravan, I started to think this might be

okay; I might be able to enjoy life undisturbed, as long as I was careful what I said and how loud I said it.

I had hoped too soon.

I awoke around midnight, feeling nauseous and in excruciating pain. I staggered through the caravan to my mum, pulling at her arm, murmuring 'Mum! Mum!' before I collapsed on the floor next to her bed.

Of course, it was sunstroke. My back was one large, painful blister where the sun had burnt me as I played, oblivious to its intentions. I managed to get through the night until my parents took me to the local pharmacist. I didn't understand a word he said, but his facial expression and body language said it all: my parents were selfish and idiotic for taking a ginger boy with pale skin to the beach without protection.

In spite of that, we were back at the beach within the hour, my mum fulfilling her one wish – to sunbathe; Dad pleasing her; Judith playing; and me in a T-shirt, huddled under an umbrella, watching the world.

This was the way of our holidays from then on – one hour's play in the sea, wearing a T-shirt, paid for by hours under a brolly, watching the fun happen around me.

This may have been sufferable had I been allowed on school trips. The mundaneness of everyday school life was punctuated by opportunities to break out into the wider world, free of parental control. My classmates looked forward to their escape to Arthog, Wales, Windermere...

I was repeatedly told '"No."'

Judith, of course, went on several trips, including the third-year trip to France. In her wake, I was riding the promise of my first trip abroad without Mum and Dad. I told them all at school, proudly. I would be able to join in at last, maybe even be one of the gang, leaving my briefcase at home, free of homework, hundreds of miles from my mum's reach. Judith had been. They had said I could go too and I was so excited.

No. No I could not.

'Have you paid your deposit for France, Neil?'

'No. I'm not going. I'm not allowed.'

The voices took on a whining edge, mocking.

'Neil can't leave his mummy!'

'Neil is such a baby!'

They knew what she was like, could see her standing at the big window, waiting for me when I was due home. She never closed the curtains, preferring the light, the openness, the feeling of exposure. I, on the other hand, shut the curtains whenever I could.

'Why is your mum constantly looking out of that window, Neil?'

'I have no idea!'

'Your mum's a weirdo, Neil.'

I knew that already. Whenever I was allowed out, set free, I saw that normal people closed their curtains, did not allow the outside to see them, laid bare. No one else's mum watched out for them from the window, analysing, overseeing, judging. Her shadow over my life, with its grasping, prodding fingers, destroyed my confidence, which had ebbed away to nothing. I was abused at home, bullied at school, and any friends I had dwindled to almost none when I stopped being able to take part in any normal teenage activities due to my mum's rigid routines and her expectations of behaviour and standards.

Judith and I shared much that was unpleasant, but she was better at adapting to our mum's whims than I and was rewarded with a greater semblance to a normal childhood. I watched as Judith enjoyed a party when she became a teenager; when she reached sixteen; then at eighteen, when she achieved her dream of getting engaged. I had been allowed to invite whomever I wanted for birthday teas when I was small, but my very last party was on my twelfth birthday. Two friends joined me to see *Pete's Dragon* at the cinema, followed by tea at home.

I can't remember details. These faded with the years, overshadowed by my confusion, my wondering what I had done wrong, why I was being punished.

Even then I thanked my lucky stars for Andy and another lad, Luke Woods, stalwarts who stood by me in spite of it all. If I was ever released, they accepted me back unquestioningly, and we sought out scraps of spare land and discarded materials (mainly blue rope, for some reason) and created, amongst other things, our own form of extreme sport, entitled 'Death Slide'.

A gang of us, including Andy, Luke, and William Allison, were playing on the old railway track at the bottom of the steep slope at the Dingle. Between the tracks were stones and rocks and general sharp and harmful rubbish. We came, quite fortuitously, upon a roll of thick steel cable, discarded by some workman, no doubt. We stood around looking at it, our brains working on a use for it, when Andy uttered the words, 'We can make a Death Slide!'

We didn't know what that would consist of at first, but we were at the foot of a steep slope, with trees at the bottom and at the top, we had steel cabling…it was bound to be awesome!

'Yeah! Brilliant!'

Before we knew it, we had unwound the steel cable and were in the process of stretching it from a tree at the foot of the old railway to one of the trees at the top when I spotted an old milk crate and the idea moved onto a whole new level.

A couple of us proceeded to clamber up the slope, me gripping the end of the steel cable, until we reached the trees at the top.

The others brought the crate up, dragging it with the help of some blue nylon rope. The crate was made with wire, some of which was curled up to make a handle. Once we, the crate and the end of the steel cable were all together at the top of the slope, we threaded the steel cable through the handle, tightening the wires as we went.

Then we wound the steel cable round a tree and all of us pulled on the end to make it as taut as possible. It took almost all our energy, but the results were worth it.

The milk crate was swinging slightly from the cable at the top of the slope, over the railway track. At its highest point, it would be 10 metres above ground level.

We had created a Death Slide.

I don't remember checking for safety that day, or ever, to be fair. We'd all found it hilarious the time a blue rope swing we had fashioned snapped when Andy was mid-flight above a bed of nettles; incidents like this did not improve our attention to safety! We hurried back up the slope to the crate at the top.

'You go first, Neil!'

I knew it would be me. It usually was! I had the advantage of being both intrepid and the lightest one of us all. Both of these qualities were necessary to be 'the tester', and when we had created something as dangerous as the Death Slide, no one else was keen to be the first.

As I hung onto the crate and kicked off from the tree, I was pleased and nervous in equal measures. The gang cheered, as it was clear the Death Slide had been engineered perfectly for a speedy descent. I felt the wind in my face, forcing my T-shirt flat against my ribcage, as the velocity picked up and the sound of my friends receded.

Eventually the Death Slide deposited me at its base and I waved to the others, victorious. After that, we all vied to take turns and we spent the morning clambering up the slope, pulling the crate back with the help of blue rope, and hurtling down again.

It was all the most incredible fun, brought to a halt only when William Allison got stuck at the highest level. The cable had become gradually a little slacker and movement was therefore inhibited. William hung, helpless, from the crate, his legs thrusting, trying to gain invisible purchase. The rest of us stood below him, laughing and waiting for his arms to tire and for him to drop down onto the stones, old railway lines and other bits of individual, unreceptive items which formed the bed below. None of us thought about helping him – it was all just too funny.

Eventually, William had no choice but to let go and let gravity do its thing. He dropped like a stone, and by some luck, and with no help from us, he landed alright and was not injured, just ridiculed. It was the end of the Death Slide, however.

The grandly titled Stanley Lane Industrial Estate Rubbish

Dump was our preferred place for target practice. Armed with our catapults, either a Strike 9 or a Black Widow, a far cry from the forked twig catapults favoured by cartoonists at the time, we set up ranges, and nearby windows were only broken occasionally.

One day I was heading home with my catapult. I had stashed my bike at Andy's house but had decided to leave it there and go home for what I loosely called 'tea'. I was nearly at the road behind the school field, just negotiating the Landslide, a slope about 80 metres long, shored up by rocks in oversized metal mesh between the field and the road, when a light blue Mercedes drew up and the middle-aged driver opened his window.

'Oi! You!'

I looked up but didn't take more notice than that. I was concentrating on my footwork.

'You, boy! At the top of the Landslide!'

This time, I stopped and looked properly.

'What?'

'What have you got in your hand?'

I held my catapult behind my back with one hand and waved the free hand at him.

'Nothing!'

'No! The other hand!'

I bent my free arm behind me and slid the catapult to my free hand, then showed him my other hand, now empty.

'Nothing!'

Maybe it was my annoying grin or my bare-faced cheek, but he was not happy. His face screwed up angrily and he spat out orders, insults, condemnations. I ended up telling him to f**k off before retracing my steps, gingerly but speedily stepping down from the Landslide and heading over the school field to Andy's.

I would get my bike after all!

I had retrieved my getaway vehicle and was cycling up the main road to my estate, Queensbury Drive, gripping the handlebars to steady myself as cars overtook me. I had wedged my catapult down the back of my trousers, hidden by my T-shirt, so Mum wouldn't spot it as I rode up.

Suddenly I noticed that no cars had overtaken me for a few minutes, but I sensed one behind me, close to my tail. I glanced over my shoulder.

A light blue Mercedes.

It was him!

I picked up speed and, when I reached the T-junction at the top of Queensbury drive, I turned right.

So did he.

I continued a little way, my mind racing, until I saw the cut-through, and darted down it, jumping off my bike and walking. Cars couldn't come down here, so maybe I had shaken him off.

But the car was waiting for me at the other end, so I pulled back and waited, pressed against a fence, just out of his view, my heart thumping against my chest wall. If he followed me home and told my mum what I had said, my life would not be worth living!

He must have thought he'd missed me, for I heard the screech of tyres on asphalt as he drove away at speed. I jumped back on my bike and pedaled like crazy to my house. I shot up the drive and round the back, depositing the bike away from street view. I ran upstairs to my bedroom and peered out of the window, holding myself well out of sight.

For almost 15 minutes, he drove up and down the road, slowly, menacingly.

I changed my T-shirt, by way of disguise, and took my place at the tea table. I hoped I had done enough that he would not recognise me, should he look through the huge window.

I got away with it. He left. My heart rate returned to normal, but I was on edge for days, checking the cars whenever I went out.

Luckily there were plenty of spots away from roads where we could spend time. One of our favourites was Tramp's Cave, a few miles over the fields surrounding Bridgnorth, not far from the industrial estate. It was secluded enough and we were able to harvest blue rope, which was particularly useful for making swings, as long as we had an old tyre or a substantial plank. One of our creations took us 15-20 metres up into the sky – the more of us that pushed on it, the higher we would go.

My entire childhood seemed to be made up of an unhealthy imprisonment or bursts of freedom where I was reckless and fearless and tireless. All of this made my one ambition, to join the army, a given. My aims in this regard never faltered and kept some spirit in me alive. At a school careers interview I stated my ambition to join up.

I felt quite the grown-up, discussing my future with someone who was taking me seriously. The interview took place in a small office. The careers officer sat on one side of the desk and I sat on the other. He asked me about my likes and dislikes, my hobbies and what I was like at school. When I mentioned the army, he nodded and wrote something down, then put his pen down and smiled, wishing me luck. I dawdled back to lessons but I was satisfied with myself, my plans. It had been nice to talk about Neil Obbard for a change.

My mum told me I had wasted the careers interview, as I was not allowed to go into the RAF or Army or Marines and they would make sure I would not. It would never matter how old I was. They would find a way to thwart my plans, even if I were 18 and didn't need them to sign the papers.

I really hated her. I had one dream and she was not allowing it.

In desperation, I started to lie in order to be able to do what I wanted. For months she thought I was going to swimming lessons when, in fact, I was paying an ex-kata world champion, Michael, to teach me wado-ryu karate. I had asked, of course, but the answer had been no. Their excuse was that I might use it on Judith.

Judith and I rarely breathed the same air these days, let alone talked. Why I would randomly unleash my newly acquired martial arts on her, ninja-style, for no reason whatsoever, was beyond me.

I made my way to O Levels: Maths, English Language and Literature, French, German, Physics and Controlled Technology

(Electronics), in which I fashioned a fully functional burglar alarm. Throughout all this period, my work was supervised by my mum, who was only happy when I was studying at home, at school, or enhancing my prospects through swimming or doing my paper round. Other excursions were tolerated and probably only permitted when she could not bear me in the house, due to her headaches.

The one good thing about this period of my life was a decent set of results. I looked forward to the next chapter, when I would be old enough to achieve my dream – to join the army and be rid of my family.

If only I had known.

Chapter 5

I had turned sixteen in the spring, given up my paper round, sat my exams, and stopped weeing myself when I laughed, so now was a good time to join the army, maybe become a pilot in the army air corps.

'I want to join the army, Mum! I've always wanted to!'

'No, Neil!'

'Dad?'

But it was useless to ask him, once Mum had spoken. His life would not be worth living. In fact, both of them were firm on this issue – they were having none of it, and without their signatures on the consent forms, I would have to wait until I was eighteen. Meanwhile my mum held aspirations for me, mainly banking or quantity surveying. Judith had a successful boyfriend who worked in a bank, so that would be the least I should achieve.

So, I prepared myself for a couple more years of doing my mum's will, seeking out the odd activity she knew nothing about.

We argued. I slammed doors, belted walls, yelled.

She won.

The summer of 1986 was enhanced by an unconscientious off-licence manager who didn't care how old we were. Andy, Luke Woods, Julian Milson and I used to buy a couple of cans of Tenants Super lager. At 9.5% it didn't matter how horrible we found the taste, we just threw our heads back and took huge gulps to get as drunk as we could, as fast as we could. Drinking helped me to cope, to forget all the crap in my life. We tried all sorts, venturing onto Thunderbird cider, but rejecting Woodpecker for its inability to inebriate. We wandered round

Bridgnorth, sometimes round the walls of the castle, with its bins, whose contents were so beautifully flammable. We always ended up on a slow walk home, sucking on mints to disguise our activities to parents who might care.

Most of our sessions happened behind the town library, but we were not averse to visiting the leisure centre and using the climbing wall round the back to access the roof, where we sat, legs swinging, drinking and chatting about all kinds of stuff. From there, we could look past the school, joined to the centre by a covered walkway, to the school field beyond and the Landslide.

Using the leisure centre roof as a viewing point or drinking den was not allowed, of course, and that made it more fun. The staff of the leisure centre couldn't see us, but others could, especially the inhabitants of the house next to the school.

When we saw their shadowy figures reaching for the phone, we called them 'Nosy Old Bats!' or 'Interfering Gits!' for spoiling our fun. However, we leapt up, headed over the walkway and the school roof, clambered down the other side and legged it over the field, the leisure centre manager and staff in hot pursuit.

We found out later that people had climbed onto the roof with the express purpose of peeking into the skylights above the women's changing rooms. This had never even occurred to us and we would definitely have tried that out, if we had realised!

When I went for a job interview there, to work on the reception, the manager (Stephen Batch, a nice guy who had taught me how to swim) made me promise he would not need to chase me off the roof ever again. As it was good money and a step up from delivering newspapers, I agreed.

Also at this time Andy and I started training a lot more. Near us was the High Rock – a big sandstone cliff. There we would tie the ubiquitous blue rope around trees up at the top, jog down to the bottom and climb up the cliffs, the blue rope hanging comfortably in our reach. Once I trod in a sand wasp nest. The inhabitants swarmed round my legs and crotch, so I used the blue rope for the first time to rescue myself. I climbed up 20 metres to the top of the cliff, pulled myself over the edge, and whipped off my trousers. Luckily, I was only stung seven or so times, but that was painful enough.

Swimming in the river was another welcome activity. We stripped off, slid on a spare pair of pants brought for the occasion, and dived in. On returning to the house, I would have to smuggle the wet undies into the airing cupboard, where they dried nicely at the back of the hot water cylinder.

Despite all this fitness training, my friends and I still met up for drinking. Girls had started to become a bigger part of our lives. Luke was with a girl called Tina and I was with her best friend, Andrea Crossley.

Andrea was nice enough, but looking back, she didn't flick my switch. It was convenient, at a time when having a girlfriend was the done thing, the sign of progressing to the next stage in your life. Andrea's affiliation to me was akin to my first beer or my first cigarette: a sign of progress towards adulthood without any momentum. It was the same for all of us, as we played at being adult without emotional complications.

The four of us went to the cinema one night to watch *Pretty in Pink*, that big 80's blockbuster. Six boys on 50cc mopeds and other scrambler-type bikes roared past us. One of them spotted us and did a double take, just as I remembered that Andrea had gone out with someone in a moped gang before I had allowed her to transfer her vague loyalties to me.

I watched the group until it reached the corner of the street and started to arc round in a U-turn, readjusting their sights on us.

'You should go, Neil! They're coming to get you!' Tina yelled.

I turned to run. Luke joined me. We tacked right as fast as we could, through the Auction, hurdling over barriers intended for cattle. Behind us the bikers had been forced to a halt, but they revved up threateningly and branched back to catch us out further round.

The chase was on, but I knew Bridgnorth's escape routes and hiding places better than anyone. Luke and I twisted and turned, pelted, checked, hid, caught our breath and pelted again with the sound of angry engines. Eventually the gang deemed revenge for Andrea duly executed, or they got bored. Either way, we were left alone to find our girls again.

As the summer merged into autumn, Friday and Saturday evenings at Severn Park became the main social events, watching boy racers screech around, cans in our hands, our girls loosely with us, pockets full of Polos for the walk home. The effects of the beer were quicker to wear off than the smell.

By now I had been reluctantly shepherded into A Level courses: Physics, Computer Science, Law. These were split between school and Bridgnorth College, a couple of miles down the road. Although I had chosen the courses, they were of little interest to me. I soon fell into a lazy routine, doing very little work, even missing classes. The walk to the college with David Melton was more often than not interrupted by a trip to the Hare and Hounds, virtually opposite Aunty Rene's house. Dave and I had a good laugh, downing pints and eating pies in our schoolwear! My whole sixth-form experience was a farce. The one redeeming feature was that they took me out from under my mum's feet and, whilst I was doing her bidding, there was less for her to moan about.

The cycle of laziness, boredom, drinking and fooling around might have lasted forever, but I fell out of a tree one night and discovered my wife.

Andy and I were perched in some branches in Severn Park. We each had a can in one hand, two discarded onto the grass below.

We slurred words at each other, making complete sense to no one but ourselves, no doubt. My Aunty Hilda had just died, and I had finished things with Andrea, whatever 'things' were. I hated A Levels, wanted to join the army, despised my mum. Maybe Andy knew all of this and maybe he didn't. When you were sixteen and lads, you certainly didn't discuss feelings. We just met up every Friday night and spent time together, making my life tolerable, as ever.

As we talked, two girls wandered along the path that led

past our tree. I twisted myself to one side to see who it was, but felt myself falling. Even with a can and a half of Tenants in me, I knew I would land in the river or onto the girls. In a fraction of a second I decided to avoid getting wet and engineered my fall away from the water.

Luckily for Tina, I landed next to her, barely touching her on my descent. She looked startled at first; then we all found it funny. Andy joined us, climbing out of the tree in a more dignified manner, and we hung out together for the rest of the night. The conversation was light, easy. I hadn't spoken very much to Tina before like this, and as I watched her speak, I felt the shift of a new emotion in me.

Tina was beautiful. She was kind, she made me laugh, she listened to me. She was one of the good ones – the complete package. She not only made me feel as if I were finally worth something, she made me want to deserve her.

We started going steady a week later, when I cemented the start of things with a kiss. It can't have been dreadful, because she smiled at me afterwards, and I felt real and unqualified and undemanding love for the first time.

Luke was my friend and Tina's boyfriend. Our new relationship coincided with the gradual breakup of our group, and his feelings about the matter were unclear. As far as Tina was concerned, her relationship with Luke was not serious, and I couldn't have cared less then. However, we have been together for over thirty years now, so we are hoping he has forgiven us!

Tina was in the year below me. She lived out of town and I had not learnt to drive yet, so lunchtimes at school were fairly precious. The bus on Saturday allowed us two and a half hours, dropping her off outside Woolies at ten and gathering her back up at half past twelve. We hung around, we chatted, we laughed, we learned about each other.

I kept quiet about Tina at home. I knew exactly what they would think. Tina lived in a council house and her sister had got herself pregnant at the age of sixteen. I could hear my mum's voice, dripping in hypocrisy, blocking out her own council house heritage, ignoring her own parents' council home.

'They are not nice people, Neil!'

Nice people were those called Simon who worked in banks, whose sister had married a farmer. Nice people were called Jones, not Roberts.

I didn't get it at all.

Tina's family lived in Neenton, a decent cycle ride away from Bridgnorth. Seven easy miles brought me to Tina's house, which soon became a haven to me.

The house was always thick with smoke, laughter or open and honest grumblings. In the middle of it all was Tina's Dad, Edward. He was really down to earth. He worked in a shelving factory in Telford, where he represented the rights of his colleagues, but his real heart had been given to the TA over thirty years earlier. I don't know why he didn't join the regular army; I am sure he regretted that.

One of eight children, Edward had been born of the fiery Granny Roberts and her lovely husband Bill. Granny Roberts had been a housemistress at a boarding school and was not averse to whacking naughty children in the street. Edward was hugely respected and liked by his enormous circle of friends and acquaintances. He handled two things remarkably: His Austin Maxi, which he maintained with the help of a spare bought for the purpose, and Tina's mum, Edith, winding her up for his and our entertainment when her default grumpiness threatened the atmosphere.

I absolutely loved it there. Tina was my world, but being accepted by her family gave me indescribable joy. I was not only welcomed – in spite of my reputation and lack of any discernable future prospects – I was Edward's kindred spirit.

Tina already knew a bit about my family life through school gossip. She had picked up on how little I ate at home, how controlling my mum was, and when she told me how much she hated that I could never do anything right for my mum, it made me happy.

Tina got me. She understood me through and through. She even supported my ambition to join the army, because she came from an army family and knew it was a good life.

When I told my parents about Tina, about two months into our relationship, it led to an inevitable argument.

'Tina Roberts? No, Neil! I'm not happy with you mixing with her at all!'

This wound me up. I didn't hold back. I glared at her, raising my voice. 'I don't get what your problem is!'

'But Neil, they are just not a nice family!'

'How the hell do you know?!'

This caused Dad to intervene. He sat up from the settee and twisted round.

'Don't speak to your mum like that!'

I shrugged and left the room. There was no way I was giving Tina up. Never. She was the one good thing in my life and I would never let her or her family go. They thought my family were stuck up. My family thought they were rough and unscrupulous.

I knew which side I was on!

One particular day sums up how the Roberts family worked. We were all snowed in for a few days. I had completely relaxed into this family life, well used to the arguments that flared up and were resolved easily, without recrimination. I relished the easy swearing, permission to say what we wanted, be ourselves. I could experience life, for the first time, without the fear of judgement. I envied Tina's childhood and was glad she had not known even one day like mine.

Edward and Edith were smoking on the settee. Tina and I were slouching against the window ledge, lazily watching the snowploughs shooting snow off the roads and over the fields, aiming to bring movement back to the traffic that had been halted. They were so far away, down the hill, that we couldn't hear the engines, and could only imagine the conversations when abandoned cars impeded the process.

Sophie, Tina's six-year-old niece, wandered over the field to the house. Her coat and gloves were dripping with snow, her little nose and cheeks bright red from the cold. She was holding one ear.

She disappeared from view down the side of the house; then we heard her open the kitchen door and shout for Edith.

'Nan?'

Edith went into the kitchen.

'Nan! My ear hurts!' Sophie sounded like she might start to cry, but Edith was not sympathetic.

'It's your own fault! If you go up there playing in the snow, what do you expect?!'

Edward let out a sound that was part laughter, part contempt. 'Edith! You miserable cow! If there had been shops up there, you'd have been there too, like a shot!' And he bellowed with laughter, a deep, smoky cough, then looked over at us and winked conspiratorially. Tina and I smiled at each other and looked back at the snowploughs, leaning on each other.

Edith came back in, cuddling Sophie and threw some comment back at her husband before settling down again, content just being together.

Yep.

I loved it there.

Another favourite place was the Dolphin fish and chip shop, owned by Mick Stones, ex-SAS. We lads (Andy, Luke and I) often ended up there to soak up our beer and we naturally got talking.

Mick started helping us with our fitness training, ironic for a chip shop owner. We used to go to the Friars' Sports Field next to the river and do pull-ups, chin-ups and dips from one end to the other of the field on the steel cricket net frame. We put weight into a Bergen rucksack and ran with it. With all that, and the swimming, I was developing my strength and fitness and knew I would be grateful for it when I finally joined up.

'You are obsessed by your fitness!' moaned my mum.

My father gave me cigarettes and beer. 'You aren't training again, are you?' he would groan. Honestly, they were so negative, it was as if I had taken up drugs or ballet or had joined a neo-Nazi group or something. They didn't realise that training myself, pushing myself to my limit, drew my tension away from its cause – them!

By early 1987 Judith was pretty serious about her banker boyfriend Simon and had set her mind to getting married. He was clearly a good catch – I knew that because my parents wanted me to follow in his footsteps – but they still wanted Judith to wait a while.

Whenever I was at home, life for me was still difficult. I could not be left in peace. On one occasion, when I was trying to ignore my mum's relentless bullying, niggling demands for a response, she tried to stop me shutting my room door by putting her hand in the way. I pushed against the door and trapped her hand. I couldn't help feeling glad.

Judith's attempts to sway my parents' opinion and the ensuing arguments on the matter gave me some respite from the usual emotional battering. However, verbal tactics clearly weren't working, so Judith adopted plan B.

I was enjoying some solitude in my room, drinking tea and looking forward to a scheduled phone call with Tina, when Judith came into my room to tell me something. We barely spoke to one another, kind of co-existed, so this was unusual. She shut the door behind her and leant against the wall. I looked at her questioningly. 'What do you want?'

Judith showed me a small plastic container and slurred, 'I've taken these.'

I sipped my tea. 'What the hell do you want me to do about it?'

She shrugged, dropped the container and stumbled out of the room. I groaned and finished my tea. I could do without this. Tina was ringing me soon.

But after a few minutes, I thought I'd better do something. I swept up the container, walked downstairs and went into the living room where Mum and Dad were watching TV. I placed the pill tub on the arm of Dad's chair and said calmly, 'Judith's taken these.'

Both of them shot upstairs and, within a couple of minutes, Judith had been led to the car and Dad was driving off to the hospital. Mum stayed behind. Her face was drawn and pale, but she held it together whilst she was in full view of the neighbours.

As she came back into the house, the phone rang. I picked it up, but before I could speak, Mum grabbed the receiver off me and spoke to Tina.

'Hello, Tina! Neil might not be himself for a while. It's not due to you or to anything you've done, so don't worry. Okay?'

I heard Tina murmur something in return and then I was allowed to speak to her myself.

'What on earth is going on, Neil?'

'Judith's taken an overdose,' I said, watching my mum's face stiffen with anger.

Judith's stomach was pumped, but she got what she wanted, and the wedding date was set for that summer. She married the perfect man. So perfect that, a few years later, he left Judith and their two children when he thought she might have a debilitating illness. This can't have been in my parents' plans, and I did enjoy asking them if they still wanted me to be like him. Judith married again, twice more.

The wedding was a chance for me to show off my Tina to Nan O and Granddad Obbard, who had travelled up for the wedding, staying with Nan and Granddad Hayes. Of all the guests, I was the one with the least interaction with the bride, but I suppose etiquette and appearances dictated I had to be invited too! It wasn't too bad. I spent much of the day being bought beers by Granddad Obbard, who gave me the money, then whispered, 'Get me a whisky too, lad!'

I enjoyed being with people who loved me for who I was.

One day Tina and I were knocking about on the Crown Meadow, another of Bridgnorth's parks, quite near where I lived. We were a bit old for the swings, but it was a lazy day and no one else was around, with or without children. At first we sat on the swings, suspended between childhood and adulthood, facing the rest of our lives together. It was always so easy talking to Tina. She knew all about me and was still here. After so long trying to measure up to my mum's ideals and coming up short, Tina's unconditional acceptance of me was like a warm bath on a cold day. On this day something inside me felt that love and appreciation.

This day took on a significance for us when, after a normal start, hanging out chatting, I acted out of character and was…

Romantic.

I took Tina's hand and led her over to sit on the grass near the slides. 'Tina?'

Tina looked at me, waiting for what was to come. Did she know?

'I can't see me being with anyone else, ever…'

Tina smiled and told me she felt exactly the same. She was 16 and I was 17 and this was it.

Forever.

In the coming weeks, I saved up almost £200 from my earnings at the leisure centre and we chose a ring together in Kidderminster: a small diamond, surrounded by sapphires, with two more diamonds on the shoulders. The jewellery was not important but its significance to us both was. For Tina it represented security and commitment. For me it represented the start of my own family with someone who actually loved me for who I was. I put the ring on Tina's wedding finger and we were committed to each other.

Returning home, I closed the front door behind me and was overcome by the familiar sense of oppression. With a mixture of excitement and dread, one borne of my new status, 'engaged', another borne of having to interact with my parents on such a sensitive issue, I entered the front room.

They were on the settee, watching television. Dad looked up at me briefly and muttered 'Hello, Neil.' Mum didn't seem to have noticed me.

I waited for a few minutes, but no natural pause in the programme's storyline presented itself, so I made my way to the hearth rug and faced them, making my announcement. 'I got engaged to Tina today!'

The only thing that moved in that room was my mum's head as she leaned to one side. 'Get out of the way of the telly, Neil!'

They hadn't heard, hadn't listened, so I slipped out of the room and went upstairs.

Sod 'em.

Chapter 6

The next academic year was upon me and I trudged back to school with less enthusiasm than the year before. My propensity for boredom was not even shaken by a Physics trip to a conference on GKN Technology in Material Science with Mr Duncan. He was not my favourite teacher and I was certainly not his favourite pupil. He worked in vats of sarcasm, and I was a 'dick' – a lethal combination. On arrival, I looked at the invitation, and the day brightened…as the conference was mainly for people in industry, there was a complimentary bar.

A complimentary bar!

Three hours later I was still there – the only one there – and this did not marry with the school's ethos. After that, the staff refused to teach me and I was excluded from school. Mr Duncan got into trouble, which was an added bonus.

Naturally the school informed my parents of the incident. An official typed letter on headed notepaper was sealed in a stamped envelope and dispatched via Royal Mail. It fell through our door and straight into my hands, so I was able to give it a quick read myself and then destroy it. My parents never knew.

Miss Ellis, who had known me all my school life and taught me five years of French, was Head of sixth form. I really respected her and she always seemed to take pity on me and, because I was upfront and did not try to hide behind lies, she supported me. She was a heavy smoker, a bit of a dragon to many (not to me), and had come through rumours about her wooden breast unscathed. Because of her, I was allowed to take my exams at school and continue to attend the college. Even a letter home would not be necessary, all of which suggested she knew what my mum was like. I spent the next year and a half on a partial timetable, leaving home for 'school' and wasting my time. I have no idea to this day how it remained a secret for so long!

Any thoughts of taking that opportunity to join the army were soon dismissed. I could not sign on, so I applied for various jobs. My parents drove me to evening classes in Shrewsbury, where their efforts were eventually rewarded with one bare pass and one fail in Economics and Computer Science.

I learnt to drive and was able to use Mum's blue Ford Fiesta to visit Tina and practise handbrake turns, or scare Dave Melton half to death when taking him to college.

These were the wilderness years. I achieved nothing.

But my big chance was imminent.

Chapter 7

Finally, in January 1990, I joined the army. I had wasted enough time and I no longer needed parental consent. Tina was really pleased. The army was in her blood; she came from a long line of soldiers and knew this would be a good life for us.

Even so, they tried to sabotage my decision. Under orders from Mum, Dad went into the Army Careers Office and spat out a whole host of lies about my health to prevent me from being accepted. The only affliction there was any truth about was hay fever and, as far as I know, a runny nose never prevented any man defending his country.

I passed basic training and was throwing myself into my new life, with its structure and its freedom from the torturous comments and needling of my family.

I trained hard, mostly with Corporal Steve Waterman. He was an ex-SAS attached guy, well over six foot. His love of karate appealed to me and we fought in training a lot, either in the gym or off camp, in town.

I was beginning to turn into a real fighting machine. I proved myself when on guard one night. A fire had started in the NAAFI and soon took hold. Steve Waterman and I ran in and dragged out some of our fellow soldiers who had been drinking and dowsed the flames. We ended up with smoke poisoning and a good story to tell!

I'd like to say I was the hero, loved by my superiors, respected by my section, even my platoon. I'd like to say that saving the lives of my fellow soldiers boosted my military career and proved my parents wrong about me and army life...but I can't.

I was a total idiot.

I was so heady with my release from home life that I drank as often as I could and picked as many fights as I could and gradually alienated anyone in a position to support me.

Once, when training with Steve, he approached me with bare feet, adopting a fighting stance and aiming to kick me. The idea of smashing his foot occurred to me, so I did. There was a sickening crunch as I broke his toes, and my friend was limping for weeks.

The PT instructor hated my arrogance. I was better than everyone, even him, thanks to my training with Paul and Andy back at home. One day, when passing the gym on my way off camp to the bars, I spotted him weight training with a guy named Bob. These were both massive guys who clearly lifted weights a lot. They were both sweating, taking time out before going back to their bench presses.

I swerved inside, the guys I was with following me unquestioningly.

'What you lifting?'

The instructor did not look pleased to see me and took my interest in the way it had been intended. I walked to the bench, slid under the bar and lifted it once. It was easy. As I slid out again, standing up and smoothing down my clothes, I riled the instructor: 'Nah! Too easy! Nowhere near hard enough! I'm going out on the lash!'

Bob and my guys laughed, but the PT Instructor jumped up and lost no time in positioning his snarling face right up to mine, so I could feel his breath on me.

'You're a dick! Get out!'

I laughed in his face and swaggered out, looking forward to a night on the booze, maybe taking in a couple of fights.

The local town, Ashford, was full of young men wanting to get one over on the squaddies. The dangerous time was after closing, when we were all tanked up. The kebab house was a kind of meeting point for anyone with a lot of pent-up tension. On one occasion, mine was released by throwing a local through a nearby clothes shop window.

One night, we said goodbye to Sue, a very nice barmaid

from the Swan. It was pub closing time, but we weren't ready to go back to camp or give up drinking, so we headed for the Zodiac Club, despite it being out of bounds, as announced in the Part One Orders on camp.

There were four or five of us, including my mate Taff, a great laugh when we were out drinking, and Ronnie, famed for being a biter ('I just love the rush of blood through my teeth!'). What our intentions were as we walked in, I don't recall. However, as soon as we were all inside, and the door had separated us from the outside world, it all kicked off.

The battle cry 'Who do you think you are?' spilled out of someone's mouth and heralded a fight. A fast sequence of still frames ran like a film before me: flying and flaying arms and legs, angry faces, shocked looks, eyes full of bitter retribution, furniture hurled with ease through the air. It was twenty locals on us few.

Suddenly a bottle was smashed and its neck held in a furious hand, the sharp, jagged glass bearing down onto my throat. I grabbed the wrist with one hand and bore into my assailant's arm with the elbow of my other arm. He yelled and dropped the bottle as his arm was broken, bone forced in the opposite direction to the one nature intended.

We were going through the crowd, one sorry individual at a time. I kicked one man in the knee, making sure to lift the kneecap with the toe of my boot until he slumped to the ground and I could kick his head in. As a bit of variety, the next idiot to fall before me was kneed in the face and stomped on as he lay on the ground in agony, and I moved onto the next person.

We were victorious. We were strong and trained and at the zenith of our fitness and manhood. As the crowd fell, I became aware of others in the shadows and imagined a siren in the distance.

'Come on! It's time to go!' I barely noticed any bruising on me. Really…this had been too easy!

We had to drag Ronnie off someone's neck. He turned to go, their blood dripping down his chin whilst they writhed on the floor whimpering.

'Shit! Ronnie!! Are you a f**king vampire or something?'

We made it back to barracks. My worst injury throughout all these scraps was a broken nose or a black eye. I was good at fighting and could take it. Luckily, we faced no repercussions whatsoever, for this or any other fracas. Sometimes Sergeant May would even ask us if we'd won. We had 'Crown Immunity', a phrase banded about by the barrack room lawyers whenever anyone wondered if we would ever be arrested and actually made to pay for the damage we had inflicted.

I was such an idiot. Apart from the fights and the drink, I was also the best clown in camp. Maybe it was my desire to be accepted, a distant memory of the boy with the briefcase, but if anyone challenged me, I did it without a second thought.

'Neil, I bet you can't…'

'Neil, why not…'

Therefore it seemed like an excellent idea, on the way back to barracks one night, to carry out someone's ingenious suggestion and steal the four Nissan flags from the forecourt of a showroom.

I shimmied up each flagpole in turn, unraveling and unclipping each flag to the laughter and admiration of my crew. It was not sensible. I had been drinking beer, shots and anything I could get hold of, and I was now hanging off a metal structure to amuse my friends.

The next morning, more laughter awoke me and I remembered I had stashed one of the flags in my personal locker as a memento. The sense of pride in an accepted and successful challenge gave way to regret as I realised what everyone was laughing at.

'Oh shit!' I put my head back under the pillow.

Outside, fluttering high above the parade ground, were three Nissan flags on our military flagpoles.

'Ah, Neil! That was brilliant!'

'You legend, Neil!'

I may have been a legend and I may have won some acceptance, but the officers hated me.

If someone had taken me to one side and had a word, maybe

it would have helped. As it was, my only redeeming feature was fitness, and I was pushing myself so hard that I ended up damaging my knee. The pressure to retain soldiers had disappeared with the Berlin Wall and 'Options for Change', which was reducing the army, so there was no question of nurturing talent, and physio care for my knee was non-existent. I watched as men left, many to join the Territorial Army.

If I had been medically discharged, I would not have been allowed back in. So I left of my own accord, happy to know that I could be accepted again but aware that my behaviour would need adjusting when I went back.

I had disappointed Tina and proved my parents right.

For now, I would need to go back to the house with the big window.

Chapter 8

I moved back home again, where my parents thought the army was out of my system and made no mention of it. I was thoroughly fed up and mentally drained. It was exhausting being a dickhead 24/7! To save myself getting too bogged down in regret and to avoid being under my mum's feet again, I looked for work immediately.

Tim's restaurant employed me full-time as a general dogsbody. I worked the bar, set up the restaurant and waited on tables. Tina worked there too at weekends, when she wasn't studying Hotel Catering and Institutional Management at the Birmingham College of Food.

The owner was Michael Smith. His daughter, Chloe, had a crush on me, which was awkward. They made us wait on the family at Sunday lunch, once the restaurant clients had all left. It was humiliating enough that I didn't have any qualms skimming money off the bar. In fact, I was surprised to hear that takings were up since I had arrived and could only wonder how much the last employee had made on the side!

This arrangement lasted for a few weeks until Michael phoned me up one morning to complain that the cutlery I had put out in the restaurant was smeared.

'That's not my job, Michael! My job is to set the tables, not wash up!'

He disagreed, so I slammed the phone down and, in a rage, went to sort it all out face to face.

Unfortunately Michael didn't see my point of view, even when I attacked him verbally and held him up against the wall by his throat.

He relieved me of my employment and, when Tina turned

up that night to start her shift, she found she had been sacked too. The restaurant wanted a clean slate, severing all ties to me. I did get good references, though.

The next person of dubious perception to employ me was Brian, owner of a joinery company specialising in fencing and stables. I worked alongside Jim. Well, work might be too strong a term for it. Jim was a strong guy, good at his job. I was his sidekick, there to help him. Basically, I couldn't be bothered with any of it and found anything else entertaining to do. Holding panels, which blew in the wind, made me laugh as I staggered about with them. Andy came to work there at one point, which was not good news. Apart from lazy pub lunches, Jim, Andy and I worked out how to manipulate the guard on the nail guns, and tumbled around nailing each other's clothes to pallets. Brian never knew, and I was 'let go' due to financial pressures and totally unrelated to my violation of Health and Safety rules.

By now Tina was working on the reception of the Telford Holiday Inn, so I looked for a job in that area. As soon as I secured a job for a security firm, we bought a house together and I was able to throw off my mum's nagging and manipulating, swapping it all for the responsibility of a mortgage. The house was on Bishopdale Road, a repossession job which needed a thorough clean and makeover to be habitable.

Around this time, I followed a poster advertising a kickboxing class back in Bridgnorth Leisure Centre. Ed Davies, from Northern Ireland, was used to street fighting. He was a complete fighter, a black belt in Kyu Shin Kai, a mixture of traditional katas and kickboxing. He later ran classes in Telford, Brookside too. He knew his stuff and helped me to draw on all my previous training, pull it all together and hone my talents. I ended up doing three or four classes a week and he trained me to combine my raw rage, my ability to see the whole fight and my techniques to guarantee success. We became good friends.

My new job's hours were horrendous. I worked from 5pm to almost 8am, five or six days in a row, with travel on top of that.

I wrote three cars off in as many months due to fatigue. First my own black Metro, then my boss's car, which he had kindly lent me to enable me to get to work. I pulled the bumper away from the tyres and carried on driving. Finally there was an Austin Maestro. In the last accident, I came round to find the car wrapped round a concrete pillar. I escaped injury in all three accidents.

The work was unpleasant. Local Indian restaurateurs in Sparkbrook paid for my security to patrol the streets, as a deterrent to criminals who had taken to stealing from the cars of clients. This sounded fairly straightforward but led to all sorts of hassle I could do without. The thieves, thwarted by our presence, took solace in trying to thrash us. Even casual passersby paused their journey to have a go. It was like we were wearing T-shirts with 'If you can't beat me up, you're a pussy!' plastered all over them.

One night I had the chance to practise my newly refined skills for real. I was checking on a building site when I disturbed some thieves breaking in. I stopped them and used some clever moves, learned from Ed, to fill a couple of them in before they managed to get away.

I felt powerful and strong and invincible. Beating other human beings up did as much for me as my violent outbursts or my drinking. I needed it to cope.

The next day, I told the builders, an Irish gang. I enjoyed the telling, knowing that this was my only chance, as Tina would not want to hear it.

They seemed pretty impressed.

'I didn't bother with the police, just filled 'em in good and proper. They won't be back. No point in telling the coppers now, when I would just land myself in it for taking the law into my own hands!'

I noticed one or two of them glance at each other, sealing a silent agreement.

'You like a fight, do you?' Accent thick with an Irish lilt. Where was this going?

'Yes...?'

'If you fancy making an extra few quid, we might know how you can do that.'

They ran a fight club in the shells of bourgeoning supermarkets or multi-storey car parks. Between 50 and 100 men scurried in under cover of night and jostled each other to place bets or find a good spot.

The first night, I eyed up my opponent with interest. I was nervous but my training and fitness had not let me down yet. We circled each other, increasing in daring and momentum as the crowd jeered and yelled. I went in first, administering fists, heels of my hand to the face, another old favourite, smashing my elbow into him, stamping the back of his heels as he fell, yelping for his ruptured Achilles tendon.

It was an easy £200. Sometimes I even bet on myself. Tina never knew at the time; I admitted it much later. It wasn't difficult to hide, as my injuries were too few to betray me. I quit before anything could go wrong. One opponent's head had swelled up so much after a fight, I feared I would be done for manslaughter. Sometimes knives appeared. No, it was time to finish this, despite the welcome extra funds.

One good thing that came of this lousy job was my two dogs, Clicker, a male, and Khan, female, both German Shepherds. Clicker had been mistreated by a security firm, but I gained his trust and he and Khan settled well with me and Tina. Tina found some comfort in the fact that the dogs came with me to work, giving me extra protection, even though I could handle myself. Khan and Clicker settled with us so well, in fact, that they started their own family with us, bringing upon our household an element of nurturing I felt good at.

Tina and I had to help feed the pups, as poor Khan was exhausted. I was enjoying sitting there with my new family, Clicker lazily watching us all, acting out the role of a traditional father, Tina feeding a pup with a syringe, when the watchful, protective Khan stood up and wandered over to Tina, grabbed the pup in her mouth and brought her over to my lap.

I laughed at Tina's offended expression and smiled at Khan and the pup in turn, cradling it carefully. I was actually moved by that moment of trust in me.

One day, a few months after this, Clicker took advantage of the gate being left open by neighbouring kids and took himself off. We didn't know about it straightaway, because he came back and hung around in the garden, like butter wouldn't melt! However, he had gone for a pregnant woman as she got out of her car.

I had no choice. The lady Clicker had attacked was fine, but I couldn't risk it. I took him to the vet to have him put down.

The vet was someone I could have easily filled in. The low-life took a long time to deal with Clicker. At one point, when I thought Clicker had finally gone, he chirped, 'I could bring him back now, if I wanted!' I told him to get on with it, not at all impressed by his god-syndrome. If he had known what I was capable of and how I felt at that moment, I dare say he would have kept his mouth firmly closed!

Fortunately for him, I just went home to Tina and Khan. A sad day for us.

My wages were lousy, but it was legal and helped pay the mortgage. Once the fights were a thing of the past, the best I could do to save money was ask the foreman to get me cheap materials off-site so I could do up my house cheaply. I had spent much of my childhood watching Dad redo various parts of the house. It was like the painting of the Forth Bridge – always something to do, under my mum's watchful eye, so I was well versed in DIY! Despite this help, it was still a stretch, even with both of us earning; so, nudged by Tina's dad, I joined him in the Territorial Army to top up our income.

The training was easy, as I knew it would be. I enjoyed the exercises, was proud to be doing something useful again. Edward had done this for decades, but it wasn't a permanent solution for me. It would do for now, though, for a couple of years or so. The wilderness years were behind me. I was drifting away from parents whose feelings were symbolized by a family portrait of everyone but me, to another family, which accepted me as I was and even liked me.

Eventually I was to rejoin the British Army, which would

not only set me more challenges, it would also give me an even greater sense of self-worth, banishing the awkward boy and the reckless teenager forever.

One Shot Part 2 – Manhood

Chapter 1 – Basic Training

I turned my back on my earlier career and lifestyle choices and embarked on my army career, for real this time. Tina was supportive, as ever, sending me ahead to forge a life for us in my chosen regiment – The Light Infantry, an amalgamation of The Somerset and Cornwall Light Infantry, The King's Shropshire Light Infantry, King's Own Yorkshire Light Infantry and Durham Light Infantry. The Shropshires (part of the Light Division) had been my county regiment, famous for its bugle-shaped cap badge, producing the world's first elite troops, and being amongst the first to wear camouflage.

I was to see out the summer of 1994 in Winchester in an Army Training Regiment. A platoon of about forty of us called one block home, and our section of ten became our family.

The first day, we circled one another, ostensibly sorting out our bed space, checking out the block. In reality, we were assessing one another and comparing ourselves, working out where we stood in the unspoken ranking system.

Although we didn't get the 'steers and queers' treatment, meeting the platoon sergeant and section commander for the first time on that first day intimidated the others. Not me. I could see through their rhetoric and mind-games, read their body language, and knew it was all designed to start the process of breaking down our facades and rebuilding us as a team. I knew enough not to show this in front of them, of course. Cocksure crows were not popular with anyone, least of all officers.

When we were left alone again, one or two laughed it all off, making out they hadn't been scared. I could see straight through the false bravado, and any nerves I'd suppressed dissipated altogether. I knew I was at the top of the food chain, but I still needed to work the others out properly, so I set about getting to know them in earnest over the coming weeks.

Some of them had always wanted to be in the army, some were following their father's trail, and the rest, like me, were here as a last resort.

We soon fell into a routine, or rather were beaten into one by rigorous army standards. We were up at 5am every morning, one hour ahead of reveille (ironically, French for waking up). Before breakfast, one of us would donate a blanket to lay out on the floor. This served the dual purpose of protecting the floor from our muck and buffing up the surface as we walked with it, shuffling along. We also had to ensure our bed space was up to the high standard set, to be in with a chance of being left alone and avoiding re-inspection later that day.

Every locker in the ten-man dorm had to be choreographed so that folds, lines and buttons were all at exactly the same angle, distance and direction as everyone else's. Most of this would have been done the night before, but in the morning we had to create a 'bed block' on our mattresses – basically a pile of folded bedding, with the largest item at the bottom, working up like a pyramid, with a uniform distance from the edge of one item to the next, all the way around that item. Even ironed creases had to match! Again, the same on every bed. This was made almost impossible by the orange and red stripes on the counterpane. However, more often than not, I set the pattern, completing my area first so that everyone was forced to match me and I could relax without having to tweak and refold to suit someone else.

Making the bed up later in the day was equally challenging: hospital corners, bottom sheet, blankets…it was not unknown for men to sleep on the floor rather than have to alter their bedding to suit the next due inspection.

We had two sets of belongings such as toiletries: one set for show and one we actually used. Our personal locker housed shaving brushes, toothpaste, and deodorant, which were comfortably used and discarded until needed again. Our bed space locker displayed the products as new, with no hint of human use whatsoever. All very well until the personal locker was inspected too!

Once the dorm and bed space were 'inspection ready', we shaved and washed in a separate room, with its rows of basins and toilet stalls which afforded us only a modicum of privacy. (When I said I wanted to get to know my section, I hadn't counted on bowel movements being part of that!) Then, after a final check of personal effects, the whole platoon congregated outside with a knife, fork, spoon and mug, forming three ranks and facing the section commander, Corporal Mackie, whom I came to like and respect.

Mackie marched us to breakfast at the cookhouse. We had exactly fifteen minutes to collect and gulp down our fry-up, cereal and large mug of tea. We were allowed one rasher of bacon, one sausage, one egg, one piece of fried bread and some tomatoes and beans. We were always ravenous, not only because we were men at our peak, but also because we virtually never stopped; we were always on the go. So, if we were lucky enough and the chef turned his back for a few seconds, we could load up our plates with bacon or sausages and hide the contraband under the beans or tomatoes – or eat it before we got to the end of the queue, which was a good idea, given the short time we had before moving back to the block.

At 6:30 we headed back to prepare for the 7:30 block inspection. All forty in the platoon spread about the block and washed, rinsed, buffed toilets, basins, floors, skirting boards, tops of doors, stairs, banisters. The stairs were blackened by shoe polish, in sections, so that men using the stairs had to filter past those doing the work. When it was all completed, we checked our bed blocks again and looked forward to putting the next inspection behind us.

For men who dreamed of military action and testing ourselves in battle, we spent a lot of time cleaning, folding, measuring and also ironing bedclothes-sometimes even ironing bedding on the bed itself! Our range of attitudes reflected our backgrounds – how houseproud our families were or how lazy, maybe where our priorities lay. Yet, this attention to detail was starting to form minds and thought processes we could rely on in war zones, and also conditioned us to accept the army's rules without question. I dare say it set a few on the path to crippling OCD as well!

We stood to attention when our superiors came to inspect us. They moved around the dorm, scrutinizing, moving fingers along shelves and ledges to check for dirt, measuring, assessing, and imparting very little in the way of praise for weeks. If something was found that deviated from the acceptable, we knew about it, and our hearts sank at the thought of having to do the show-parade at 6pm for violations in the personal bed space. This sometimes meant dragging our beds and lockers to the guard house and setting up in front of it, recreating the space in the dorm, redoing all the measurements in the hope of passing and not having to redo the inspection at 10pm that night. The re-inspection of the block would be at 8pm and there was a special kind of hell reserved for those who failed both inspections.

At some point I learnt to let it flow over me, realising early on that they would find something wrong even in a perfect bed space, if it meant moulding our characters in their image. As we stood awaiting pronouncements on our fate, we would stare straight ahead, often into the eyes of the guy opposite us, and, in this case, the challenge was to pull a face quickly enough not to be noticed by the officers, whilst making that person laugh.

In between inspections we attended classes on Drill, Nuclear, Biological and Chemical Warfare, Rifle and Weapon, Fieldcraft PT, Map-Reading and Health and Hygiene. I found most of it fascinating – especially learning about nuclear blasts and how we could survive as little as 200 metres away if we avoided the blast by laying low in a trench. Running six miles a day tabbing – carrying weight – was easy for me, as my fitness levels had been honed by swimming, kickboxing and the Territorial Army. I won the Best at PT award, fixing my physical supremacy in the group.

With all these classes, we had little time to doss around. We had to launder our own kit, watching over it in case it got lost or stolen and we would have to replace it by signing away some of our wages. Ripping or shrinking an item was better, as they would be exchanged for free at the Quartermaster Stores.

If we had any free time, we went straight to the NAAFI for food. I became very fond of strawberry Yazoo milkshakes. If we ever got off camp, such as on the first weekend, when we were allowed to go and buy personal stuff, we headed straight to the pub for a few beers. It wasn't what the army wanted, but we were young men in our twenties and drinking beer whenever we could was some kind of badge of manhood then. Not that I needed anything else to prove myself. I was the fittest, most confident, most experienced, and was looked up to and respected by a few of the section in particular. These were Wardy, Crabby, Woody, Logi, Cocky and Easty.

Woody was slightly taller than me, brown-haired and quite thin. His soft-spoken voice, inflected by Battersea, belied the dense nature of his thinking.

'Woody! You need to iron your waterproofs, mate!'

'Oh, okay! Cheers, Neil!'

It took a few minutes and the smell of burning to alert Woody to the fact that you don't iron waterproofs due to their being made of plastics.

Another time, as we were preparing to go out in the field, packing our rucksacks, the chatter lively, I told Woody we needed an ironing board. He actually carried one out of the barracks with him, much to the amusement of the rest of the platoon.

Once, Woody accepted my help to check his bed space ahead of a re-inspection. It was well-known that my preparation was excellent even if I had been drinking.

I looked over his bed, shelves and wardrobe. It was perfect, but I still moved in closer and, one item at a time, threw the uniform and kit over my shoulder, where they unfurled and landed in a pile on the floor. Each item was declared 'Not acceptable!'

When I turned round, Woody was staring at his belongings in despair and the rest of the section were watching and laughing.

Cocky was broad Cornish and was handicapped by his lack of general fitness. This didn't bother me until we were out on a run. When we finished, we had to do press-ups until the last person had caught us up. With this in mind, Wardy and I would encourage him by saying 'Keep up, you knob!' 'Hurry up or we'll get beasted cos of you!' or 'chinning' him (thumping him in the face) as he lumbered around the course.

And when Easty slowed right down on one run and we had to carry him on a stretcher, we managed to kick him as we ran. Once we finally arrived at the end of the course, we threw him off the stretcher, head first, where he landed four or five metres away.

These were the activities that kept us laughing. These days it would be called bullying. No one challenged me, not one of them. No one dared. My childhood had clothed me in an impenetrable armour, which bled empathy. Meanwhile, I was the alpha male, afraid of nothing; and, for the first time in my adult life, I felt good at something.

We were marched everywhere: from lesson to block, from block to canteen, from canteen to block, from block to lesson. One day we were slouching around town centres, hands in pockets, shoulders hunched; the next we were swinging our arms back and forth to shoulder height, thumbs down tight against our fists, our legs hurled up, parallel to the ground, heels slamming down in rhythm with 39 other men.

'At ease! Fall out!'

'Go!' We ran into the block, grabbed our towels and leapt into the shower. Two at a time.

That's right. One day we were enjoying hot showers, taking our time, appreciating the peace and quiet of a locked room; the next we were jostling for space, elbowing each other as we tried to wash away the sweat of a heavy PT session. Barely dry, we dressed and were outside within five minutes, ready to march off to our next slot.

'What is the point?' someone grumbled, his damp trousers clinging to his legs.

Learning to work under pressure? Pushing our patience to its limit? Those who hated it, couldn't cope, were the first to be weeded out, sent back to their family.

Of course, the speedy turnaround between classes was just one trial.

Drill meant another kind of inspection, and the one area to look out for was the dreaded tramlines in our 'lightweights' – green trousers which needed one crease down the front. If you got two, it would take an aeon to put it right! If we failed an inspection, we could expect a 'beasting'. This was usually a physical trial, such as maintaining a stress position.

'Plank! Hold!'

'Press-up! Halfway! Hold!'

'Platoon, mark time! Knees hip high! Bring the thighs parallel to the ground! All together now! Left, right, left, right!'

Any deviation from perfection would end up with one or more of us grimacing, willing time to evaporate and end our agony. Even a perfect turn-out could lead to this, if the NCO or officer in charge happened to feel like inflicting humiliation or pain on anyone, either because they had taken a personal dislike to that person or just because they could.

We looked forward to the late afternoon and evening sessions. These were labeled 'downtime' but they were mainly anything but! From 5 to 6 or 6 to 7pm I would be in one of several very long queues, impatiently crawling nearer to the phone boxes to spend a few minutes on the phone to Tina.

Then there were the visits to the laundry room to stare at my clothes swirling around in a washing machine, guarding them from practical jokes or confusion about ownership. Then came more ironing, tidying, cleaning, preparing for another inspection and endeavouring to pass it with distinction, or at least avoid being beasted.

One night, we were all in the NAAFI (Navy Army and Air Force Institution...or No Ambition and F**k All Interest), enjoying a rare period of downtime without any jobs to do and with enough beer to make us brash enough for dares.

Someone set the challenge: 'I bet none of you dares iron a load of tramlines in their lightweights for tomorrow! You're all too scared!'

We laughed at the idea and swigged our beer, but it was Wardy who took up the mantle of 'platoon goon'. Wardy was an easy companion, funny, with an amicable enough competitiveness, so we were soon back in the block, watching as he ironed several creases into his trousers, our boozy breath encouraging him with hoots and jeers.

If he regretted it the next morning, it was well hidden by bravado and his sense of heroism. On this particular morning, the platoon got away with several minor infractions of the dress code, as they were all overshadowed by Wardy and his beautifully pleated trousers!

Training for Nuclear, Biological and Chemical Warfare provided us with another trial, which some found worse than the beastings: the CS gas chamber.

The NBC gear encased our whole body, keeping all dangers out and all sweat in. We had to perform PT in it, in order to strengthen our mobility in such an attack. As we thundered round, all we could hear was the sound of our shallow, rasping breathing in the respirator, as we produced more sweat.

The CS gas chamber was a room approximately three metres square and fitted 10 to 15 of us nicely. We were shepherded up to the door, watching as the officer in charge threw in little smoking pellets. We trotted inside in a line, following each other round the walls until the order to stop came. The door was slammed as quickly as possible to halt the escape of the gas, which turned in on us instead.

Claustrophobia kicked in. We were in a small room, made smaller by the fog arising from the pellets, trapped within our suits. The order to remove our mask came to us one at a time and we were told to recite our name, rank and number.

'PRIVATE OBBARD 24837684!' I screamed as fast as I could, the gas clawing at my throat, tightening my airways so that my lungs screamed for air. My eyes felt like they were on fire as the sweat on my skin fought the CS gas; the pain was blistering. They may have asked me more questions about my platoon, section, section commander, and if I answered, I did so without awareness. Every inch of me wanted to get out.

Luckily I had gained enough respect from the officers to be allowed out without them blocking the door. I hurled myself outside and leant against the wall, gasping. I raised my hands to my face.

'Don't rub your eyes!'

The advice reached my brain just in time. I turned my face against the direction of the wind and opened my eyes as wide as I could bear, gulping down the fresh air, waiting for my lungs to be filled with it.

It took a while but eventually all of us had been processed by the CS chamber, spewed out physically weaker, but mentally stronger.

The gas had a debilitating effect, constricting our airways, stinging our eyes, reacting with the sweat and burning our skin. The threat was real and the ability to remember basic details and communicate them clearly was severely tested. We screeched out our personal details, trying not to breathe in at all, words and numbers falling out of our mouths, one on top of another, our eyes screwed shut or blinking rapidly. Once we were cleared to leave, we shot out of the chamber and recovered against the wall, gasping, drawing in the fresh air desperately.

If we were ever attacked by a nuclear, biological or chemical weapon, other needs could take precedence over self-identification, so we learnt how to eat and drink.

The procedure was simple: open decontamination pouch, remove water bottle and straw, insert said straw into the bottle, deep breath, remove mask, insert straw into mouth, suck and put mask back on before needing to breathe again. All this was seen as even more successful if our thirst was quenched without getting any black shoe polish, applied to pass an inspection, on our faces. It was even better if we managed to wash the container out properly!

The filter was the key. It was our main defence against nerve agents but only lasted 6-24 hours, depending on the circumstances. A liquid agent attack would only buy us six hours, for example.

The DKP II (decontamination pack) was a pad filled with Fuller's Earth, which absorbs all evils. We had to learn to clean our kit without those evils finishing us off.

'Blot, bang, rub!'

Somehow, with huge, ungainly rubber gloves on, I undid the DKP (Decontamination Kit Personal) packaging and slid the pad over two of my fingers, blotting the chemicals off my protective gear. I turned the same pad inside out and replaced it on my hand to bang it all over my hands and arms, releasing white powder. I banged and rubbed until my gloves had a complete covering of the white powder. Finally I took my puffer bottle from its secure place in my webbing, unscrewed the cap and squeezed it all over to soak up excess liquid contaminants.

'Blot, bang, rub!' Webbing pouch. Remove canister from the webbing pouch on the other side. Unscrew the old canister and replace with the new one.

Deep breath, eyes closed, I felt for the hole on the S10 respirator, lined up the canister and screwed it back in. Furious breath out, to blast away any contaminants caught up in the new filter. 45-60 seconds of internal panic and outward calm. I usually managed it, but others weren't so lucky. They panted, shallow, anxious breaths, desperately trying not to breathe but unable to help themselves.

Speed was of the essence as we decontaminated our skin, staving off blisters and burns by rubbing more decontamination powder into our hands like surgeons preparing for surgery.

'Blot, bang, rub!'

The pitfalls of practising this process included having to remove all the powder in time for inspections and the inevitable practical jokes. Hence we learnt to air our suits on lines and check the Fuller's Earth had not been replaced by grit that would get into our eyes and cause untold damage whilst simultaneously amusing the rest of the section.

Of paramount importance was our 'skill at arms' training. We used the SA80 assault rifle, and our dependence on it in times of war meant we had to know it inside and out – literally!

I came to know the name and function of every part, its capabilities, how to strip it, how to re-assemble it, how to care for it, how to maintain it. I came to know the complexities of using its sling, how to shoot it and deal with stoppage. I knew to turn the rifle to the left to look at its right side, exposing the parts. With my left hand, I would forward assist and give a short tap on the cock and handle, controlling the pistol grip with my right hand.

If the rifle still failed, we had to move it back over to the right, pull the cock and handle to the rear, engage the hold and opening catch, tilt it back to see inside to the rounds in the magazine and chamber, and check the magazine housing by pushing up a bit until we heard a click and knew it was correctly seated. Finally we engaged the bolt release. Most failures were down to problems with the gas supply, such as when residue built up round the holes, but in the field other issues, like sand, could be responsible.

The gas propelled the bullet forward, some going out at the end, the rest diverted by a gas block and plug. We could choose normal setting or excessive with the flick of a switch. There was a series of gas parts whose purpose was to cock the rifle for us. The gas strikes the face of the bolt block, grips the base of the bullet, pushes to the right and picks up a round from the top of the magazine – all in one move.

We learnt all about this in class, complete with weapons handling tests, before going out onto the range.

During the course of these lessons and practices, we managed to improve our six-packs, as any mistakes resulted in press-ups! The first person to mess up had to do five press-ups, the second ten and so on. In one particularly sloppy lesson we got up to one hundred! Someone failed to keep the weapon parallel, someone else turned theirs around, names of parts eluded one, the correct order of the drill another, incorrectly positioned hand guards, undone webbing pouches...

One cause for frustration was the sling. Alone or in pairs, we had to practise how to fit it. This mainly started with a Section Commander NCO throwing it out of the window, meaning a quick run out to find it. It was always more fun if you found your own sling and then had time to throw someone else's deeper into the shrubbery before running back in, and double points for knobbling someone on the way to or from the collection of the sling!

It didn't take me long to master the series of buckles and loops and have the rifle correctly dressed and attached to my side. It was then a great source of entertainment to watch the others standing up, only to find their rifle dropping at one end or even landing on the floor.

Fieldcraft was all about living and operating outside 'in the field'. We had lessons on this virtually every day and each one started with us jumping up and down to check we could move soundlessly. Announcing our arrival to the enemy by clattering a spoon against a mess tin was not advised!

We enjoyed demonstrations about camouflage, watching various soldiers parading in front of us in various states of dress. One wore virtually just his underwear and would have been seen miles away, his skin was so dazzling. Another seemed to have half a tree strapped to his body, with leaves and even small branches appearing from every loop in his uniform.

The ideal camouflage consisted of a moderate mix of green and brown face paint and a small amount of foliage held on by black elastic attached to the webbing.

We soon set about sourcing this useful black elastic to accessorize our DPM (Disruptive Pattern Material), allowing the insertion of grasses and the resulting invisibility.

Once we were made up, we had one minute to run out onto Flowerdown, a training area/scrubland next to the barracks, and hide.

As I ran, scouting for the perfect hiding place, happy memories of being a Cub in the Dingle flooded back to me. I loved it! I settled in some bushes and waited it out without moving. I watched as training instructors set about trying to spot us and a 'walker' with a walkie-talkie strutted round, darting looks around the undergrowth, pulling back branches, checking heathers, revealing one of my peers after another until only I was left. I was the winner!

In Fieldcraft, we met ration packs and practised cooking and eating them. Our first exercise was at night. We had to erect a poncho basha, a basic shelter in olive green or DPM. We chose a Battle Buddy (mine was Logi) and we set up our tent, manipulating bungees and tarpaulin until it was erected to military satisfaction. Logi and I managed to do well enough that we and our kit were waterproofed, all except Logi's feet, which hung out the end of the tent.

To eat, we dug little holes in the ground and used firelighters to create the heat necessary to boil our ration packs without the wind destroying the heat and without being seen from a distance. Over the low fire, we erected a hexy (a block of hexamine, a solid fuel), then put our mess tins on top, filled with water.

The ration packs were tastier than they looked, although we were always hungry, so maybe we were not the best to judge them. Once we had eaten we had to clean them so that they were inspection ready. The easiest way to clean them was to wipe them on the grass. We then moved on, removing all rubbish and any other signs we had been there. Later we would learn how to dispose of our own waste, but for now, we had Portaloos.

Skills began with the basics. What is a map? How do you fold a map? What are grid references? What do the symbols mean? What is the difference between a civilian and an army compass? How do you use a compass? How does a compass relate to a map? We learnt useful mnemonics such as 'mag to grid get rid' and 'grid to mag add' and adjusted our readings accordingly. Before long I could find my way to a 6-figure reading and proved myself in a theoretical and practical test, where I had to navigate to 3 or 4 points within 5K squared.

Historically, the British Army has lost more men to a lack of hygiene and the resultant disease than in battle. We had to be able to wash ourselves properly in the field without the luxury of showers. Armpits, groins and feet were designated 'vital areas to keep clean and dry'. Trenchfoot was literally a crippler and I didn't fancy anything that could go wrong under my arms or in my pants, so I listened very carefully. Also, being young men with young men's needs, we were reminded of the existence and usefulness of condoms, when considering unwanted pregnancies and STIs.

I enjoyed all these skills immensely. I was comfortable with the kit, unafraid to cook or sew for myself, happy outdoors. The whole army thing was one hundred per cent for me. For someone who had grown up the object of derision, mistreatment and abuse, I was hardened enough to avoid being affected by army rules and terms of behaviour and determined enough to be top of the tree in my section. There was no way I was going to be the Neil of my childhood, even if it meant stepping over others to escape him.

On the morning of my passing out parade, I checked my appearance in the mirror, brushing away the tiniest of flecks that no one could see and straightening my beret. My hair was cropped close to my head. My uniform was freshly pressed. My boots were shiny enough for reflections. I was ready.

As I looked in the mirror, I could hear the banter from the dorms, low laughter tinged with anticipation, the faraway rumble of vehicles carrying relatives who then had their passes checked and were stewarded into organised spots.

I took a moment to look at myself. This was the culmination of all my work. This was the end of a journey which had seen me turn down dead ends and lose my way. This was my first major success that was not illegal or engineered by my mum. I had done this for me and I had made a good job of it.

The inspecting officer was the Commanding Officer of 5 LI – 5th Battalion Light Infantry – so I was known to him personally, as he was a colleague of Tina's dad. The whole day passed smoothly, and I was awarded 'Best at PT' officially. There was clapping and pride.

I had finally pleased my parents. They attended my passing out parade with Tina, wearing their finest clothes and their proudest smiles. Afterwards, in the 'milling around making small talk' stage, they spoke about me with a new tone to their voices. I hadn't realised until then how my joining the army had been their idea! They'd even put photos of me up in their house. Maybe they were missing me, now I had moved out?

Chapter 2

I progressed onto Phase Two training with around 20 of the men I had passed out with and some others from the same platoon. Still buoyed by our success at basic training and with the clapping and congratulations still fresh in our memories, we made our way to the Infantry Training Battalion at Ouston, Albermare Barracks, on the outskirts of Newcastle. I thought I should make sure Granddad Obbard knew I was there, as it had been instrumental in defending the northeast in the Second World War.

The barracks was a melting pot of a range of different divisions: Queen's, King's, Scots, the Light Division.... We clung to the identities forged in basic training and used up much of our energy and machismo defending them.

For example, at one point during this phase, we had a night off and most of us headed for the Newcastle city centre. Wardy, who was now in my section, had a handy girlfriend, Samantha, with a car to transport us two, Ken, Jamie and Chaz. Wardy and Samantha dropped us off and went their own way, whilst we went on the lash.

A few hours later, we clambered into a taxi, lolling around in the seats until we were poured out back at the barracks. There were plenty of others arriving back at the same time, among them a Scouser called Scouse, from the Royal Green Jackets, who liked a fight.

I made my way straight to one of the phone boxes, thinking Tina would want nothing more at this time of night than a slurry conversation with someone who might not be one hundred per cent clear what he was saying.

Tina was listening patiently to my ramblings when Crabby

ran over to me, pulling at my sleeve. 'Come on, man! There's a fight! We are going to be in so much shit!'

I hastily said goodbye to Tina and put the phone down straightaway. We ran to the block, more or less in a straight line, and assessed the situation as best we could.

The Scots were on the first floor and the Lights on the ground floor. It appeared that our section had piled upstairs to attack the Scots, fuelled as they were by alcohol and idiocy.

We ran upstairs and joined the mêlée. However, to my surprise, instead of throwing a few punches or wielding my elbow, instead of head-butting and kicking, I became the voice of reason, ordering my section to stop this nonsense and go back to their dorm.

One or two listened, and those who didn't I grabbed and threw towards the door until only the Scots remained, grumbling and refocusing, as they had been readying themselves for sleep when they were attacked. I apologised to the Scots on behalf of the Lights, hardly believing the words that came out of my mouth. Who was this?

I had to get things right this time.

I was on my way back down the stairs, wondering whether to call Tina back or just get some kip, when a couple of Scots appeared round the bend, one of them armed with a metal dustbin lid. His expression reflected crazed revenge. Before he could register that I was the enemy and try to crush me with his impromptu weapon, I raised my hands defensively and cried out, 'Whoa! Look, guys! Come on, mate! You don't want to do this, do you? See what I've done?' I pointed behind me, up the stairs. 'I broke up the fight and sent our lot back downstairs!'

The wielder of the dustbin lid was not quick enough to dispense with it, so I tried a different tactic: 'Really? Don't you think you would look daft with a dustbin lid up your arse?'

And I walked right past him, confident that he would not do anything.

Thankfully, I was right.

Back in the dorm, we were all coming down from our high when an NCO from the Scots appeared. Someone must have called him. 'Come on, you lot! In the corridor, you cowards! Attacking men in their sleep!'

That did get my back up. Cowards? You don't call the Lights cowards! They hadn't been asleep anyway! It was just a load of men gobbing off, burning up energy induced by beer. I kept quiet a while longer.

The NCO was on a roll now. His full patriotism had been driven to the fore and his body was puffed up with Scottish pride. He didn't quite sing 'Flower of Scotland', but he did bring up a two-decade-old footballing victory of Scotland over England at Wembley, or as he put it, his finger stabbing the air with each syllable: 'In the heart of your capital!'

I couldn't help myself. I was trying to be good, I really was, but...really? I thought the words and they were out of my mouth before I could stop them. 'Remember Culloden! We took a country!'

His face took on an angry puce as he darted looks from one to the other of us.

'Who said that?!' he roared.

Silence.

He asked again but no one gave me up and I wasn't going to hand myself in. It was in everyone's best interests that he decided not to pursue the issue, and we were allowed to go back to our dorm. Tensions had been so high that further insistence might have ended up with him being attacked, so it was just as well.

Phase Two was all about specialist training, the majority on exercise. Under the supervision of Section Commander Corporal Cheeseman and Platoon Serjeant Al Hewson, we engaged in more range work, working with 51mm mortars (the platoon weapon), learning how to stop drills with mortars, firing on targets. Other weapons used included the 94mm anti-tank launcher. We fired this after stop drills. The disadvantages of this light-weight, portable, single person anti-tank weapon were its incredible noise and its back-blast, which pushed out and sucked back in whatever was in its rear view, meaning we had to build in more safety checks than were normal or interesting.

Normal Safety Precautions, or NSP, engendered the learning of some mnemonics, like NESW – Never Eat Shredded Wheat – designed to help us remember to check the firing pins, remove the end cap, check the wiring, then replace the end cap. The mnemonic Every Dame Loves My Hard Dick was attached to the GPMG, the General Purpose Machine Gun, which was often manned by two firers. To train for this, we stood in two lines, facing one another. The weapon was passed up the line, zig-zagging its way along. We watched and checked the person next to us left, diagonal left, opposite, to the right of us and diagonally right. All of these checked me when it was my turn. We pointed out errors. If we did it wrong, we had to do press-ups. If we didn't pick up on a mistake, we had to do press-ups. The NCO was also in trouble if anyone didn't know what to do, so we learnt quickly.

The northeastern winter battered us with its inclement weather, which seemed to collect over Otterburn or whichever other training ground we happened to be on. By day the sections trained alongside each other, firing blanks at targets, then moving on to live rounds, motivated by competition. We discussed and practised battle formations, checking our spacing, considering the advantages and disadvantages of each one. At night we warmed ourselves up, dried ourselves out and gave way to banter, celebrating our strengths, consolidating our loyalty to our section, with no care for the outsider or thought for the weakest.

By the end of the phase the six battle drills were part of our psyche:

- Prepare for battle
- Reaction to effective enemy fire
- Locating the enemy
- Winning the firefight
- Attack
- Reorg

Prepare for battle

When the orders were given, we went into full protection mode, checking our ammo was loaded in the magazines and that the 2i/c (second in command) had reserves. We oiled our weapons and checked all parts were in working order. Our clothing had to be appropriate to the environment, with webbing, camouflage and waterproofs as needed. We ensured we had water and the special equipment we might need, such as wire cutters and chargers and even a ladder. Two of us would have to carry this, as well as a sledgehammer. There were fun days, smashing in buildings made of corrugated iron in wooden frames to train for urban warfare.

Finally, we checked that all our pouches and pockets were closed and radio frequencies and batteries were checked, if we had to have one.

I hated having the radio, a PRC 349. Luckily I only had it when taking a turn at being 2i/c, the army's way of developing leadership skills and our understanding of responsibility. They could lump it, if it meant having to operate with a crap throat mic and a rubber earpiece held into place by Velcro wrapped round your head. The whole thing was uncomfortable and ended up sweaty and often dirty from the mud. It was as big a joy to hand over to someone else as it was a curse to receive it!

The last element of our preparation was the orders – the briefing, the battalion's instructions, its specific objectives, all noted down by the section commander in his book. The point of exercises was to practise 'quick battle orders', i.e. how to deal with an attack on the way to performing your objective.

Apart from the section commander, we always had a 2i/c, and each of these took charge of half the section and labeled the two halves Charlie Fire Team and Delta Fire Team.

Reaction to Effective Enemy Fire

How do you think you would react to shots fired at you? We were drilled in the arts of Dash, Down, Crawl, Cover, Sights and Return Fire. This was one of the most important reasons for staying fit. (Now it is a case of firing a few shots in a general direction, taking cover and returning appropriate fire.)

Locating the Enemy

An obvious advantage in warfare is knowing where the enemy actually is, so locating the enemy is vital. It is also the hardest thing to do, as you are trying to stay alive and uninjured, dealing with gun smoke, the flash of the weapons, the natural anxiety within. However, once located, another acronym kicked in: GRIT, a Fire Control Order.

- Group – say who in your section should return fire
- Range – give the distance in metres and use the clock face, as learnt in Fieldcraft
- Indication – describe the enemy location explicitly to everyone in your group
- Type of fire – say what kind of firing

So, once alerted to enemy positions, the section commander would have to say something like: 'Section, 150m two o'clock, tree base, RAPID FIRE!' All of this clearly, loudly, given as an order, with a pause in between each detail, to allow his voice to carry and thoughts to be processed without fear of misunderstanding. The 'rapid fire' was delivered by a light supporting weapon, the ammunition fed through, making it more accurate.

Winning the Firefight

This entails putting more rounds into them than them into us, or at least keeping their heads down long enough to allow us freedom to manoeuvre.

Attack

- This is split into three phases:
- Approach

- Assault
- Fight through

It is up to the section commander or 2i/c to decide whether to engage left or right flanking, or go straight up the middle with bags of smoke, and also what cover to use.

Re-org

Once we heard 'Position Clear!', the whole section was to move to a position 20-30m from the cleared enemy position, following the path made by the first troops. At this point, we took stock of the situation, using the following guidelines:

- Protection – ensure we were safe from all angles.
- Ammunition – 2i/c had to check how many magazines we had used, how many were left, and replenish our stocks.
- Casualties – once we knew we were safe and had what was needed to protect ourselves if the situation changed, we could check out and help anyone injured.
- Equipment – we checked whether we had dropped anything and assessed whether anything lost was worth the risk of returning. Bergens were cast off in battle, for example.
- Searches – someone was sent to check the enemy killed by our section. Were they dead? Did they have anything useful? Intelligence?
- Sit Rep, or situation report – signaller sent an update.
- Dig in – in case of enemy counter attack.
- Orders – there was no time to relax; we prepared ourselves for the next stage.

Apart from the six battle drills, we learnt patrol techniques: fighting patrol (obvious), standing patrol (observation), clearance patrol (checking the ground for signs of the enemy so we could sleep easy in the harbour area, for example). We practised a range of formations as a section, then as a platoon, finally as a company, which constituted all three platoons: Scots Division, Light Division and regiments from the King's and Queen's Divisions. All formations had their advantages: arrowhead, file, staggered file, extended line and so on.

Bayonet training needed a certain mindset, and the army engineered this by beasting us for a whole day and withholding our freedom in the evening. They woke us up by throwing icy water over us, turned over our beds, trashed our lockers, forced us to do so much physical exercise we almost passed out... all of this designed to make us so angry, to build up so much frustration in us, that we would readily engage in stabbings.

Wardy and I spent the day laughing, which probably irritated the officers as they attempted to quash our enjoyment and replace it with anger. They ordered us all to march on the spot, chanting, 'Kill! Kill! Kill!'

So, we all charged at sacks with our bayonets, releasing pent-up anger, which was immediately replenished when the officers sprayed us with fire hoses. We ran again, yelling at the top of our voices, grunting with that final thrust, twisting the bayonet and hoping that it would be that easy in a real-life situation.

Family life went on in a parallel universe and would soon move on to a new stage. At the end of November, I found out I was going to be stationed in Germany. I had an idea whilst on guard one night and called Tina. 'I'm off to Germany, Tina. If you want to come with me, we have to get married!'

Tina knew what I was like. I was not into all that romantic crap. The nearest I had got to that was in the park when we were sixteen. She agreed to marry me, as it was sensible and practical. We thought Christmas R&R would be a good time.

'What about booking a church, Neil?'

'We don't need to get married in a church, Tina!'"

I hoped she wasn't going to insist on that. I couldn't bear the thought. I knew she used to go to church, but she hadn't been very often for years and I was hoping she had grown out of it.

'Why not?'

'It's all a load of crap. You know I can't stand all that bloody nonsense!'

'Okay, okay!' Tina soothed me. She knew there was no winning this one. 'Okay, Neil. I'll book the registry office. I won't worry about the church wedding, as long as...'

My heart sank. 'What?'

'...as long as you agree to letting me baptise any kids we have.'

I had no problem with that.

I wouldn't need to go.

We had our non-fancy, small wedding at the registry office in Wellington, Telford on 28th December, with a reception at Parlor's Hall Hotel, Bridgnorth. Guests included my best man Ed Davies, parents, siblings and their children only, apart from Jonesy, who left training for the day to attend our wedding. I appreciated this.

Tina wasn't bothered about a huge, over-indulgent wedding: her dress was £35 off the market. I was lucky enough to get away with my uniform and the three bridesmaids (our nieces Sophie, Isabel and Lydia) looked lovely in their BHS Christmas dresses. Just a couple of rings and we were good to go!

Tina's nervousness was exacerbated by her sister's lack of punctuality. She almost had a panic attack in the car to the church, which may have put a dampener on events.

In the end, all went smoothly. We stood in that little room, all scrubbed up, both sides of the family pretending they liked each other for the occasion. Tina being kind to my mum, despite hating what she was like to me, my mum being polite for appearances' sake, despite her as-yet-undeveloped liking for Tina. The children were oblivious to the politics in the room, just swirled in their dresses and looked forward to the buffet.

Our wedding was followed by a few nights in the Holiday Inn in Cambridge. To top off the non-fancy theme, we drove there in the yellow BT van I had driven around in with my dogs when

I was working security. Once my R&R was over, I returned Tina home and went back up north to take up my training again, leaving Tina to organise the house and the packing. I was relieved that Edward had volunteered to take Khan in.

At the end of Phase Two, all but two of us underwent a final two-week exercise, to put into practice all these new skills. It was early 1995.

At the start of the exercise, Willie was found shaking on his bed. He had been a para and I had known him from the 5LI TA, so I knew he was a tough one and this surprised me enough to ask him if he was okay.

He said no and burst into tears. 'I can't breathe!'

It turned out he had pneumonia, so he was whisked away to be put right and rejoined with another intake at a later date.

Logi tried to leave the army on purpose, but they just moved him to another platoon. Bad move! They hated him and beasted him constantly. We heard he'd had to run round the drill square, holding his gun above his head and chanting, 'I love the army and I don't want to leave!' until his attitude was sufficiently adjusted.

The rest of us were 'enjoying' the winter in Otterburn, where the snow was over our knees. On one particular day, I was 2i/c. It was virtually a white-out. I kept counting heads but I wasn't overly worried about losing someone, because the Scots were behind us to scoop up any trailing behind.

It was a challenging few hours. The snow made moving difficult, and the cold was taking over one miserable centimetre at a time, starting with our feet, hands and faces. It was starting to get darker and colder when shots were fired at the back of me. Instinctively, I counted my section again.

Someone was missing.

I yelled for us all to stop. Who was it?

The section huddled up and established that it was Liam who was absent. I ran over to the Scots. 'We're a man down. Have you seen him?'

'Yeah!' said one of them. 'We saw him fall down a bank back there!'

He looked back and pointed through the pure white haze to a slope we had passed earlier but which was now invisible. As he turned back, pleased with himself for throwing some light on our mystery, his face met with the butt of my gun.

Whether this was revenge for the raid on their dorm or not, I don't know, but I was incensed. Luckily, the Scots' NCO was as annoyed as we were about it.

We all went to look for Liam, shouting his name, flashing torches in the face of the relentless snow. Eventually we found him, drenched through but not injured. Relief all round, not least for those who had watched him fall and not reported it.

The NCOs found a hut full of hay bales and ushered us all in to shelter from the winter storm. We were told that no one had to be on guard duty. We climbed into sleeping bags, wet clothes and all, and slept until 10am, by which time our clothes had mostly dried out. Then we were allowed to take our time over breakfast, drinking endless mugs of tea (the main sustenance of the private – kept us going in every situation!) and sitting around, eating and enjoying the unusual rest.

Of course, we all knew that this was a sweetener from the NCOs, who had cocked up bringing us out in this weather!

Phase Two was completed. I performed well and was the only one to pass the Combat Infantryman's APWT (Annual Personal Weapons Test) first time. The afternoon I did this, at one of the Catterick ranges, it was pissing it down with rain and the wind sent the rain sideways, so not only were we drenched, but our performance was sorely tested. If we could hit a target in this, we could do it in any circumstances!

I hit it first time, every time and enjoyed the treat of getting warm and dry in the range hut whilst the rest of them struggled on.

So, my official title was 'Best Combat Infantryman'. First out of all the platoons put together – about 150 men. I couldn't wait to tell my Tina. I was certainly not doing too badly for a scrawny ginger from Bridgnorth! I had never really felt I could please my mum, but a few days later, at the Passing Out Parade, she and Dad smiled proudly at me.

This was a new sensation for me and I loved it!

Chapter 3

The Family Office, specifically Serjeant Riley, helped our transition to Paderborn, Germany, in early 1995.

We flew over all together, mainly guys I had done Phase Two with; then we peeled off, most on buses to the barracks, Tina and I with a member of the Family Office, to be taken to our new home.

Our new address was Lahrkampstrasse 23/3 – a huge flat with a balcony, in a well-maintained 1960s block, all off base but within walking distance of the NAAFI. It would have been perfect had I been based at Sennelager, a few metres from our flat. Instead I was based at Allenbrooke Barracks, Paderborn, a bus ride away!

Tina and I had one week to settle in before I was on duty again. We acclimatised together, trying out the buses from the quarters to the barracks, checking out local shops and amenities, although we would rarely use them and would not see the locals a lot. Tina found a job in the NAAFI and we were grateful for the extra income and for something to keep Tina busy when I inevitably was called away.

I met Timmy Outhwaite, ex 2LI, at the bus stop on my first day. We got chatting and he offered to show us around.

Tim knew a lot and it was a comfort to us to be looked after by someone like him. He explained things as we went along, pointing out roads and places we might need, explaining a bit about procedure and so on. This help extended to outside working hours and, as it was Tina's first ever time abroad, this kind of personal touch really helped.

Bit by bit we got to know people. The other families in the block were friendly enough and we enjoyed a social life with them, the summer sun offering up plenty of BBQs, for instance.

It sometimes feels that even the happiest of times must carry with them some kind of burden. Around this time, our old neighbour from Bishopdale Road called us about a parcel that had been left at his house. A veritable can of worms had been opened, revealing fraud and theft committed in our names by the current occupiers. There followed letters and calls and finally Tina's journey to court in the UK to clear our names.

In my army role, I was more responsible now. I was in a position to advise others. As such, some of the lads turned to me for help as we settled in. Seb Topham was one of these. He was further out of his comfort zone than the rest of us. Someone must have helped him set up his bank account at home, for he seemed totally clueless, even without the language barrier.

'What do I say?' His accent was broad Yorkshire.

I tried to be patient. 'See the pay officer for your details, then go into the bank and hand them over. Then you say you want to open a bank account before saying (and I said this phonetically), "*Al us clar*?"'

To be honest, I didn't think I needed to point out that 'al us clar' (Alles klar) was German for is everything clear? Who couldn't work that out?

'Is that the name of the person in charge of accounts, then?'

I was baffled. 'Is *what* the name of the person in charge of accounts?'

'Alice Clar! You said I need to ask Alice Clar!'

Sometimes I felt like frigging Einstein.

I liked it here in Paderborn. I was older, more experienced, married…why not have it all? Tina was grounded, and dealing with the move and the fraud case without drama, so we decided to throw something else into the mix and dispensed with her contraceptive pills, leaving our fate to Mother Nature, fully expecting a few months' wait and lots of fun along the way.

The morning of my first day in A Company, Second Platoon, I said goodbye to Tina and set off on a bus to my base. I should have been apprehensive, as new lads could expect some kind of bullying, but I was confident. Maybe I could thank my childhood for that, at least.

I met Serjeant Richie Benson, a great guy who liked a beer, especially when under pressure, and off I went! A proper soldier of the British Army!

The early days were spent working on the Warrior Armoured Personnel Carriers alongside Corporal Grant (Cary), the APC commander, and Timmy, the 2i/c of the section. Cary was mad keen, always encouraging and diligent. He would be both a good role model and highly irritating first thing in the morning, which is not my best time.

I fell into base life easily, as if I was born to it. What was not to like? I was being paid for doing what I enjoyed and had a lovely wife to go home to.

Within a week or two, two life-changing events occurred: Tina fell pregnant and I was asked to do sniper training. (What can I say? I was always a good aim!)

Tina was 'late' and took herself off to the doctor's for the pregnancy to be confirmed. We had a laugh about the speed at which it had happened and settled in for the wait.

Meanwhile Richie Benson had contacted Al Hewson to recommend me for the course. There were six of us in total out of 500 soldiers. Some of the older guys were peed off I had been asked, as I had only just arrived. I was told this by some of the guys who liked me and had supported me. Apparently I was 'alright', 'a nice guy', 'fit', and 'professional', all of which was quite a compliment. The fact that Richie had put his faith in me meant a great deal and I was made to feel that I could have a real future in the army. In fact, the decision to do this course was a pivotal moment in my career.

I rocked up for the training only to find it wasn't quite a done deal. We were assessed straight away for physical suitability and some poor guy with glasses was sent on his way. We ended up with seven or eight soldiers, Dicko, Brez, Dagger, Coley and Seb, all nice people, instructed by Terry Sandford.

We were all happy enough that day, but each of us has since found ourselves the centre of our own story – a hit and run, drugs, physical injury, and so on – jettisoning us from the path we had envisaged that day.

During the sniper training course, we concentrated on the seven basic sniper skills. All of these were simply concentrated versions of the basic infantry skills, with the exception of air photography and stalking.

'Sniper Knowledge' entailed understanding the complete weapon system (The L16 Sniper Rifle) and how to manage it by taking external factors into consideration, such as wind. We also learnt how to calculate range and to sketch the panorama from an observation post (OP). Close Observation Platoon, with a camera, came later.

From the 'Map Reading and Air Photography' section of the course, I came to hone my map-reading ability and was capable of pin-pointing someone using an eight-figure grid reference, i.e. to within 10 metres.

I had to be able to navigate, pin-point features from a map, and read, grid and scale air photographs, marrying them to a map. This would allow me to plan any task and navigate to and from the area of operations. We were trained in the use of the stereoscope – placing two photographs together accurately to then zoom out to 3D – so we could better visualize the target area and plan an operation.

'Concealment' was a fun course. We were taught to conceal ourselves quickly and efficiently, with the obvious aim of remaining undetected and in a position to engage the enemy. We practised the art of disguise with a ghillie suit. Using a hot glue gun or good old-fashioned needle and thread, I fashioned a suit fusing strips from an old jacket, building up layers of thickness. Metres and metres of black elastic was added all over my DPM jacket, trousers and hat or hood, which would support branches and large twigs and enable me to sit in bushes, undetectable.

One advantage of the ghillie suit was that it was meant to smell earthy, so we didn't have to wash it or polish our shoes or anything. This would one day help me to avoid detection by dogs in a live situation.

Concealment involved considering the front screen and the backdrop and learning how to use trapped shadow. If you know how this all works, you can blend in anywhere! How useful would this be?

'Observation' – Snipers are taught intelligence-gathering through scanning, observation, and logging everything. Minor details become relevant, as they might help us to spot our target and can certainly enhance any report back to the battalion. At the start of the day's training, every day of the course, we played the memory game 'Kim's Game'. No one ever did ask who Kim was.

I was instructed in the art of 'Stalking', how to choose the best route to the target and the selection of the best position from which to fire. It was the culmination of all other skills put together.

There are many methods of 'Judging Distances', which is vital if our 'one shot' is to be accurate, hitting first time without giving any warning whatsoever. Judging distance could be done by sight, by knowing the ground, using the terrain and common indicators, such as the heights of vehicles. We could also use 'binos', or binoculars, as long as we knew what military gratical pattern to put in them. We had to learn the 'Sniper's telephone number,' 223435678, the amount of clicks between each distance setting.

'Shooting' – sniping consists of 80% observation and 20% action. Obviously judgements are made before shooting and there is a range of conventional and unconventional shooting positions to choose from. Also, wind speed and direction need to be taken into account. Choosing wisely increases the probability of a first round kill. We engaged our SAA – Skills at Arms – learnt on basic training: the position and hold must be firm enough to support the weapon. This must point naturally at the target without any undue physical effort. The sight alignment (i.e. aiming) must be correct and the shot must be released and followed through without undue disturbance to the position.

All this was made easy with the L96; it was a beautiful

weapon and quite different from the normal infantryman's rifle.

The success of our training was assessed. For one test we had to navigate to a grid reference, locate the target and take the shot, all without being seen. Walkers were out being directed to movement by the OP target. They confirmed you could actually see the target by having you report via radio the letter the target held up for a few seconds. Then you had to extract yourself without being detected.

Each of the seven sniper skills was assessed to the same degree, but one assessment stands out more than the rest.

We were given a grid reference for our OP and we found it and set ourselves up, concealed, to observe. Brez thought outside the box and hid up a tree. The walkers were sent to find us, looking, no doubt, for the black circle which marked the barrel of our gun. (I later spotted a sniper in our Bosnia training. This annoyed the trainers and made Richie Benson quite proud!) One of them was the instructor, Terry Sandford, and we could hear his radioed conversations. He had reached the grid reference and was looking for us, repeating the phrase 'I can't see him' over and over again.

Eventually Brez received the command to take his gloves off and wave at the target in the OP. He did, of course, and Terry looked around, expecting to see Brez appear from the undergrowth.

'He's waving at you!'

'Where? I can't see him! Are you sure?!'

'He's 7-8 metres away!'

'!!!'

'Look up!'

When Terry saw Brez sitting on a branch, waving, a huge triumphant grin on his face, he declared his disappointment at being caught out with a few choice expletives.

It was a while before Brez and I stopped chuckling at that!

Chapter 4

Travelling with the Army is either amazing or torturous. They either get you there in the shortest possible time or you are the lowest of all low priorities. Our journey to Canada to undertake a six-week training session, in the spring of 1995, fell into the latter category.

We started out fairly positive. We were heading for BATUS Suffield Camp, into which all other British Army bases would fit comfortably, making it by far the biggest in the world. We would be as near to real-life battle situations as possible, without it being real. What was not to like?

We had a meal before we set off and settled ourselves into snug seats. These seats turned cramped very quickly, probably about the time hunger started to make itself felt.

Hour after hour of numbness, fatigue, stomach cramps and weary conversations melted into fitful attempts to sleep.

Finally, we landed...and stayed exactly where we were for three hours, until the plane was refueled. We were only in Newfoundland! Still more of this horrendous journey to go! Still no food! I was beyond ravenous. My best hope was sleep; that would discount me from the ever-tetchier conversations, the banter which was taking a nasty turn.

As the plane made its final descent into Calgary, Alberta, I made an effort to look out of a window. My first glimpse yielded a patchwork, which, as we flew down, revealed itself to be blocks of houses, perfectly aligned, perfectly symmetrical and quite fascinating.

Removing myself from that seat, that plane, was magical. The ability to move, breathe fresh air and know that food and drink could not be far in the future, these were all truly appreciated.

We went over to collect our luggage from the conveyor belts. I took one look and decided to stretch my legs some more before collecting my belongings. Every bag on there was the same size and colour, differentiated only by its tag: A Company, blue wooden triangle; B Company, a square; and C Company, a circle. Once you found the right shape, you had to bend over and read the name, all of this whilst the bag was sailing past you!

I went to the loo and walked around a bit, watching the others from a distance. They were jubilant when they found their bags and rushed off to the buses, leaving me to find my own bag easily, there were so few left. I figured the buses wouldn't go without us all on them!

I was virtually the last on board. The excitement of landing had been replaced by something more depressing: still no food and another four-hour journey to go.

I slumped into my seat and somehow found the stamina to tolerate the situation, but the view didn't help: mile upon mile of straight roads edged by endless prairies to each side of us. The only distraction was the noises from my stomach, crying out for food.

When the buses drew to a halt and we knew we had finally and really arrived, we poured out with renewed enthusiasm. Surely they would feed us now?

'Come this way!'

We did just that. Personally I was hoping for bacon sandwiches or a chicken stew. I think my mouth even started to water, though my belly was silent in anticipation. Maybe behind that door?

We were ushered in and shepherded down rows of hard chairs, all facing the officer at the front. I listened for the clink of plates or the noise of food being ladled onto dishes, waited for the smell of something to reach my eager nostrils...

'Come in, come in! Sit down! Shut up! Listen!'

Wow.

I only heard the start of sentences. I would perk up when I heard the word *food*.

'Don't...'

'Don't...'

'Don't...'

Really?

'Welcome to BATUS...'

'...cup of tea...'

Bingo!

After the tea, we were lodged in a huge dorm. I threw down my stuff and we went directly to the canteen, where I was delighted to see it was stew. Not bad!

I was so eager to grab my dish and shove the contents down my throat as fast as possible, I neglected to assess the looks on others' faces. It was a mixture of acceptance, disgust and disappointment.

The stew was dreadful but it held some nutrition, I presumed, and needed to be eaten for the purposes of keeping me alive. It was nowhere near Nan O's standards, but that couldn't be helped.

Hunger pangs abated, only sleep eluded me. We returned to the dorm, flung a few things into a locker, which we had to share with two or three others, and eyed up the damage caused by previous squaddies, before collapsing on the bed.

I lay there, observing the high ceiling, trying to find a position which would keep me cool on this hot night, listening to the sounds of almost one hundred men snoring, or at best wheezing, around me. I almost laughed; Wardy would have seen the funny side of this. He hadn't come because he had damaged his hand when he got it stuck in a door. Rumour had it his wife didn't want him to come and he had done it on purpose to get out of the trip. I don't know. All I know is all the doors back in Paderborn were slow in closing, so it would have been quite something to have had time to stand there, hand held out, until the door dawdled its way to crush said hand.

The next morning we had enough fry-ups, cereals and tea to make us feel properly human again, and ready to crack on with the business of training for war. We went off to the tank park to prepare the vehicles.

I got a fair bit of exercise that day, due either to dehydration from the heat on my fair skin and ginger hair, or the change in water. The poetic name would be the 'shits', sending me, sweating in the intense heat, back and forth between the toilet block and the tank park.

Between bouts of diarrhoea, I helped my less than sympathetic team to prepare our Warrior Armoured Personnel Carrier and the kit to go inside it. We would need to be confident it would not break down and that we would have whatever we needed to survive comfortably out in the field. We collected and checked mugs, lids, cutlery, dishes, the boiling vessel and various personal items, setting it all up in the back of the APC, held in place by bungees. The whole process took most of the first two days, with evenings set aside for personal downtime.

Personal downtime to men our age always involved alcohol and generally 'having a crack' or pratting about. The main aim was always to get hammered.

The construction of the NAAFI didn't help. It was held together using high steel beams which offered a new challenge to buying beer. Why walk to the bar when you could shimmy across high beams instead, accompanied by encouraging yells from the sea of drunken faces below?

The first night, I went to bed early, exhausted after the shits. The beer had hit me harder too, so it wasn't long before I was ready for bed and had drifted into a deep sleep.

'ARE YOU OKAY?' I had been grabbed by my shoulders and shaken. The shock of being woken up so violently caused synapses to fire in my brain, and images and fears flashed through my head until I was able to focus on the face before me.

'What's happened?'

As he spoke, the reek of his breath, infused with beer, washed over my face.

'Just checking you weren't dead, or in a coma or something!'

I was incensed. 'Cheers, mate, but can you f**k off?!' And I rolled over to the sound of laughter.

In the morning, I got up as soon as my eyes opened, hoping to avoid the big queues at the phone boxes. It was just before 6am. If I called now, Tina would still be up. I clattered around dramatically, looking for my phone card in several noisy places, before 'finding' it. The buggers who had found it so hilarious to wake me up last night groaned. I guessed we were quits. For the time being!

One advantage of an early morning call was that I wasn't drunk. I was a sloppy drunk with a penchant for singing *Blue Moon* and telling Tina I loved her. This way, I was more reserved but made more sense.

The third morning, we got our battle orders. By now we had fully recovered from our long journey and our APC was ready to go.

There was a full briefing. We would exercise battle drills as a section (about ten men), building up to working as a platoon (three sections), before the company worked together (three platoons and Company Headquarters) and on to the whole battalion (four companies and the Battalion Headquarters) and finally, and most spectacularly, the Battle Group, which included all the tanks and artillery.

We drank in the briefing notes. We would use blanks first, then live rounds. Safety would be paramount. We learnt about the dos and don'ts of the tanks, the use of the phone in the back to respond and co-ordinate. We were told not to sleep under APCs, in case they sank onto us in soft ground, and to sleep on the right of them, if we had to. As they were NATO vehicles, all overtaking would be to the left, thus avoiding running over slumbering soldiers.

We checked out the capabilities of the AS90, which was fairly new at this point. It was a big self-propelled artillery gun. We went through the fire missions. It was powerful stuff.

I enjoyed my first time in the Warrior, engaging in armoured warfare. The scale of the exercise was impressive. We would speed up to enemy positions at 40-50 mph, the commander and gunner on top, the gunner firing. In the back, we were subject to swaying and jolting as we moved over rough terrain. Sometimes the vehicle would lift off the ground when crossing a hill at this speed, and we felt it in our stomachs. Luckily, with the usual five of us in the back, plus our kit, things were snug, even though we favoured chest and rig webbing, rather than waist webbing, to try and save space. It was hard to imagine how seven would fit in, which was how many the Warrior was built for!

When we were close to target, the commander would radio back to whichever of us was 2i/c. He, in turn, would press his hand over his earpiece for better hearing and yell, 'Get ready! Three, two, one!' Then the hydraulic door opened, announced by the driver, and we jumped out, carried by the momentum of the vehicle as it was thrust back after braking sharply. We peeled away, avoiding all the injuries the Warrior could cause, and moved into position. Careless of my own vulnerability, I was usually the first out, which meant I took up the position the furthest away. I would place my gun on automatic before exiting the vehicle, to be ready.

The Warriors all took up position, their incumbents pouring out and scattering to create fan-like, finely choreographed shapes on the battlefield, facing the target. This was just like real war, except the various Warrior crews were competing for the best, most accurate attack.

The safety crew was never far away, and changing from blanks to live rounds and back again was taken very seriously indeed. Whenever we swapped from live rounds back to blanks, all artillery had to be stripped down, all kit had to be checked and people inspected, to be absolutely sure that not one single live round remained. The British Army had learnt from mistakes and its safety measures were the result of lessons learnt the hard way. They weren't so good at man-management, but on the ball with health and safety! Ade Farmer, for example, got shot in the leg when clearing a trench. His nerve endings were damaged beyond repair but, silver lining, he was able to use his leg to put his cigarette out.

We learnt to clear trenches (more successfully than Ade Farmer), various defence techniques and how to advance to contact with tanks. When the artillery, tanks and air support were all performing together, the noise ran through our very bones. It was intimidating and empowering at the same time.

A guy called Sheff and I were practising firing 94 mil portable rocket launchers. We were being nudged into position by the safety staff, who had a better overview than we did of the lines of fire on the field.

'You're first!' they called to Sheff. I moved behind him to get a good view.

'Have you got your ear defenders on?'

'Yes,' he replied, settling the rocket launcher onto his shoulder and firing.

He was too quick to fire, not because he missed the target, but because he had failed to check his back blast area, where I was watching whilst simultaneously putting on my own ear defenders.

The blast caught me unawares, knocking me off balance, the noise tearing through my ears and displacing air, so that I could only hear the doosh-doosh of my heart pumping my blood round. It felt like the air around me had been sucked away. I swallowed, blinked a lot, swallowed again, tried to yawn, to clear my ears. He was mouthing something at me and I tried mouthing something back, but it was just as well he couldn't hear.

The safety guy seemed to be telling me it was my turn now, or at any rate, that is what I presumed. I removed the straps, aimed and hit the target, not forgetting to check my back blast area, like a good soldier.

Afterwards, when we could hear again, Sheff and I had a laugh about it.

Another day, we were manoeuvring as a company across the softly undulating prairies, whose grass was almost as short as that of a football pitch, when and Seb and I were called away to hone our sniper skills.

We decided on positions, camouflaged ourselves according

to the environment and settled in for the long haul.

Eventually an APC made its way into our vicinity and we watched through our sights as it rumbled closer, came to a clumsy standstill and spat out some soldiers, watching out for us. They climbed on top of the APC and rotated round, perusing the landscape with their binoculars.

They simply did not spot us, even when a curious deer wandered over to us and Seb muttered to it to go away in his broad Yorkshire accent.

We were just wondering how much longer we could remain hidden when some instructors rocked up, shouting out that we should let ourselves be seen so they could bring us water.

As we stood up, grateful for the refreshment in the relentless heat, the personnel on the APC groaned and pointed. All this time, we had only been a few metres away! They must have been gutted!

Fresh food rations were provided every three to four days, when the battalions took it in turns to defend each other, giving cover to approach 'replen'. Each Warrior in turn moved through the camp, opening the top hatch to allow the rations to be passed down.

These were anticipated with enthusiasm, but often army choices were quite random.

'A gâteau? What do we do with this?' I asked the CQMS (Company Quartermaster Sergeant in charge of stores). He grumbled some obscenity in reply.

Other delights included four loaves of bread, squishy enough to fit in all sorts of nooks and crannies in the Warrior, and a tray of eggs.

More often than not, we ate the fresh rations on the first day, taking it in turns to be cook. With fresh cream cakes and eggs, it was the sensible option. One of our favourite meals was Egg Banjos, so called because, once we bit into it, yolk usually spurted down our fronts and the ensuing wiping away with one hand resembled playing a banjo.

Otherwise we managed on Boil in the Bag or tinned rations for ten men, where we got away with it, or for eight men if the

CQMS was being more vigilant or tight. 'But you never gave us enough rations. Can't we have some more?'

Water was provided daily in jerry cans, swapped out for empties. I personally drank a whole jerry can a day to myself, due to the heat and body armour, which was meant to hold us together in the event of an attack, until a medic could do his thing. However, as a general rule, it acted as a conduit for the vast amount of sweat which rolled off me. The one advantage of this was that I rarely needed to wee.

The exercise was full-on, but we did manage a little down time after 'replen'. and this was usually a good time to take a shit.

There were poles and 'mushrooms' for the ends of the poles and camouflaged netting to go over the mushrooms and poles for the provision of privacy when dumping our waste. This rarely worked out, so we ended up grabbing a shovel, going for a recce and doing the whole 'Hole, shit, cover, return' thing.

TESEX was like a ginormous game of Laser Quest. We were kitted out with sensors, which emitted a series of quick beeps if we were 'injured' (called a 'near miss') and a 'flatline' sound if we had been 'killed' or injured so badly we were out of action. Any 'injury' allowed us to open an envelope, which gave us its nature.

If a Warrior was hit, everyone inside was deemed to be out of action too. Sometimes this would be a relief, because it meant we got some time out in the casualty area. In all my exercises, I was only ever a 'near miss' in a hit vehicle.

I was once sitting in the back of a Warrior with Insane Kane, or Chris Kane, as his parents had named him. He was a sniper, just like me. He loved being a soldier and his enthusiasm was infectious.

As we were being briefed, we heard the beeps which indicated the vehicle had been hit and so we leapt out the back before these could set off our personal detectors and rule us out of the exercise.

We hid nearby and peered out at the opposing force, the Light Dragons, moving quickly past us at around 5-600 metres. We shot at them with our sniper rifles and managed to hit them. When their beeps sounded, the commander yelled in frustration and threw down his helmet. As it bounced off the side of his vehicle, Chris and I laughed, then radioed for pick-up.

When we left the area to meet the vehicle coming to collect us, we moved under cover until a Warrior passed us slowly enough for us to jump on. We climbed on top of it, surfing.

This was Insane Kane's influence, of course. I would never have done anything so dangerous off my own bat!

Another day I was tasked to do an OP – Observation Post. This entailed two of us digging into the side of a hill, taking up a patient position and radioing back all information gleaned from our findings.

The earth removed when creating the hole was shoveled into our Bergens and released well away from where it had been taken, so it would be undetectable by others. If we had had a Warrior nearby, we could have dumped the earth in a quick pile and asked the driver to flatten it for us.

When we were collected from our OP by a Warrior, we were surprised to find that there were already 14 men in the back. Some were sitting down, others were lying over knees, some on top of these. We climbed on top of the general pile, ignored the smell and the groans as we settled, and pulled our feet up out of the way of the door. The journey was long enough to be a form of claustrophobic torture.

The NBC phase of the course lasted 48 hours. We were supposed to don our protective gear and sit in our Warrior and simply wait. As it was 40 degrees, we thought this was a bad idea, so we closed the Warrior door and turned off the engines. That way, when they came to fetch us, they had to hammer on the door and we had time to dress ourselves as the driver fired up the engine so the door could be opened.

The irony was that all of us except poor Timmy Outhwaite smoked, and this was our activity of choice whilst waiting to be called out to simulate a gas attack.

Apart from rare calls home to Tina, I sent and received

'Blueys', letters so-called for their blue lightweight airmail envelopes.

I loved getting these, comforted to hear to hear about Tina and 'Baby Ben' (I didn't mind what sex the baby was, but it never occurred to us to have a girl's name ready), happy to hear from my parents and grandparents, especially Granddad Obbard, who'd once told me how much mail had meant to him in the war.

Tina wrote to me about her dad, Edward. He had suspected lung cancer. Tina was about four months pregnant at this time and I was concerned for her health too. I wrote back using words that were simply not enough to convey my sorrow about Edward and my concern for Tina.

At the end of our mammoth exercise, we rode into base, leaving the rolling prairies behind us. After checking out the wagons and equipment, we were able to relax a bit. Some chose an extended R&R, but I wanted to get back to Tina as soon as possible, so I opted for a couple of nights in the nearest town, Medicine Hat.

Medicine Hat was renowned for its strip joints and bars. Being so close to BATUS was both a blessing and a curse, because that many soldiers could keep afloat the town's businesses or close the whole place down, as had happened a few months earlier for 2-3 days, when an almighty fight had broken out.

We caught the bus from camp in high spirits. The journey took around half an hour, by which time we had whipped ourselves up, all of us anticipating our first beer for weeks, some of the others aiming to find a woman or two.

First stop was a strip club. I headed straight for the bar and ordered a pitcher of beer. Where we were made no difference to me, as I was only interested in drinking. I downed my first jug and asked for another straightaway. Behind me, young women sashayed and writhed, twisted themselves round poles, gyrated hips, thrust breasts, licked lips.

'Another one, please!' I'm sure the bartended thought I was with a group, the pitcher had been emptied so quickly.

When I had drunk enough to enable a slower pace, I turned round and looked at the women and, more entertaining than that, at the men watching the women. Some had the bright idea of heating up coins with a lighter and tossing them in the air for the women to catch in their panties. They yelped in pain and bouncers moved in, removing the offenders. Some of the others laughed and jeered, but we were spending too much money for all of us to be kicked out.

Prostitutes mingled with us, women who knew which buttons to press, what to say, how to invite the most sexually frustrated of us to part with our cash for a quick release. The least brave settled for a lap dance with the strippers. The luckiest found a woman who enjoyed one-night stands.

Barry Black had been one of these. He had arrived in Canada in the wave before us and they had been into Medicine Hat for some R&R as they waited for the rest of us to arrive. He had homed in on a local lady who was not shy. Some of the guys had seen him leave with her and, at the time, didn't think anything of it.

The following day one of the battalion was declared missing. Where was Barry Black?

His mates had looked for him without any luck. In the end they had contacted the local police with a description of the woman he had met in the bar. The police must have recognised her description, because they had gone straight to her house and found Barry, held captive, tied to a bed, naked. She had removed his clothes, disposed of them, fed him, and had her wicked way with him for two days.

As we were arriving at BATUS all those weeks ago, Barry had turned up, accompanied by the local police officers who had rescued him from his alleged sex slavery. To this day, I don't know if he had welcomed his captivity or was truly a victim, but his appearance on camp dressed in one of the woman's nightdresses was one of the comic highlights of our trip. He was divorced by his wife soon after we returned to Germany.

As we drank and watched the social interaction in that strip bar in Medicine Hat, we were still laughing at Barry Black. We had all been along to see him in his frilly nighty.

Not all of us ended up in Medicine Hat. Some of the guys went to Banff instead. Baldy Louie and Denty Head Hughie were two who had chosen Banff. The inventive names came from Louie having no hair and Hughie from the dent in his – you guessed it – head, put there by a sledgehammer at some point as a 'bit of fun'.

These guys were both tough northeasterners, and Denty Head Hughie, in particular, was a total nutter. On the first night of our R&R, they found themselves near a glacier lake with two local girls.

One of the girls told them, 'No one can survive in that lake for more than two minutes!'

Hughie's sense of pride and challenge, mingled with his innate idiocy, prompted his response. 'Wahaay, man! I'm from the northeast! I can do it!'

And he stripped down to his pants, dropping his clothes on the shore, and jumped into the lake and swam.

After a couple of minutes, he turned and waved to Baldy Louie and the two girls, then swam out a bit further. Then he waved again and swam on even further. They could just make out what he was saying: 'Two minutes, my arse!'

This went on, with Hughie swimming, waving, yelling, swimming, yelling, waving, until he was only a dot on the watery landscape.

Finally the dot began to get bigger and bigger as Hughie made his way back, blue, to dry land and dry clothes. The rest of the narrative will be left to our imagination, and we can only wonder how Denty Head Hughie's image and performance was affected by his act of bravery.

Our livers suffered for 48 hours, but we still had a great time. It was so good to let go a bit, forget drills and routines, cast off culinary restrictions, be human again. Eventually we bussed it back to BATUS, lolling around, wasted, on the seats, trying to sleep off whatever we had poured into ourselves. We gathered there from our various chosen R&R venues, each of us with a story to tell, as long as we could remember it.

Once our hangovers had cleared enough, we set about clearing the land, ready for the new batch of rookies, scouring the land for empty cases and anything unexploded, a long line of us, like you see on the news when police searches are going on.

It was a truly uninspiring experience, yielding nothing of any interest at all except a few facts about the names of roads in this part of Canada, indicating that this was a nuclear test site and a Native American graveyard – the Crowfoot tribe. In the usual fashion of British Army soldiers, some plundered this sacred place of feathers and skulls, placed on the graves as we might place flowers, and others, like me, respected it.

Finally, we boarded the buses and braced ourselves for the return journey. This would be tough, but at least I had some downtime, then Tina, waiting for me at the other end.

Chapter 5

The platoon engaged in a drinking session in South Germany entitled 'Adventure Training'. Honestly, it was one long assault on our livers, with the odd bonding activity thrown in. I took part in a watermelon race, canoed on the lakes, leapt off bridges and slept in until late morning.

When I returned home, I had worked hard and played hard and was now ready to face my responsibilities again.

Hugging Tina for the first time in weeks, it felt like her bump had drained her of her energy and vigour. She was thinner everywhere but there and obviously anxious about Edward.

We drove from Allenbrooke Barracks, where the buses from the airport had deposited us, back to the flat we called home, in our Peugeot 205 Diesel. It was good to have a break from the lads and even better for that break to be with Tina. I caught up with news about Edward, noticing a change in Tina. She was really worried.

Talk of postings to Bosnia started to take on a different feel now. Briefings on Bosnia formed part of our weekly schedule, and The First Battalion The Devon and Dorset Regiment came to Paderborn with anecdotes of their time out there. One of their platoons had been taken by some Serbs for about a week. They'd appeared on TV, wearing their Norwegian DPM combats. Tina worked with some of their wives in the NAAFI, so I knew it had been an anxious time, even if we all knew it was a political stunt and their status as POWs should protect them. In fact, they were released, had a weekend off and got back to it.

Once summer leave had died down, training picked up. We honed our physical condition with extra PT in the gym and our firing skills at the ranges. We were also trained by one of the Scottish regiments who had been there before the D&Ds and had up-to-date information. We worked through real-life scenarios to prepare ourselves for what was to come, and tested weapons systems such as the AK47.

I was particularly interested in the Dragunov Sniper Rifle, as this was what most snipers used. Its capabilities were known: it disposed of 7.62 mm steel core bullets, and some models boasted a folding stock or butt.

We prepared the Warriors by bolting a framework on them and attaching the extremely heavy Chobham Armour to it, the true nature of which was top secret. All we were allowed to know was that it would absorb a hit effectively.

Once the armour was in situ, we were tasked with painting the Warrior in UN colours. It was naturally a pain to have to repaint them DPM after the Daytona Agreement!

Around this time we got a new, recently promoted Platoon Warrior Serjeant, Serjeant Strapp (Jock for short). He turned out to be a good man, understood family pulls and let us go home early if we had family, unlike the other knobs who made us stay, no matter what.

We were big on irony in the army, so we called our biggest liar 'Bobby The Truth'. He preferred to stay at work one night rather than have to participate in evening routines with his young kids. So his wife dropped them off with him as he painted another Warrior, saying, 'You can stay at work, as long as you look after these!' Off she went! It was hilarious. We all fell about laughing at Bobby.

Throughout the summer, Tina grew bigger; so far all was well. Even Edward had been told his lungs were in good shape, for a smoker! The problem was in the pipe leading into his lungs, but they were coming up with a plan.

One day, I was called into Major Wim's office. Richie was there, standing to the side of the Major's desk. My mind was racing. Had I done something wrong? I stood to attention and saluted.

'At ease.'

I glanced across at Richie, trying to read his expression. He had said he would mention…

'Your wife is expecting a baby – Tina, isn't it?'

'Yes, sir!'

Major Wim looked thoughtful. 'Go and get me your passport.'

I saluted again, turned and marched out of his office. I was no clearer, but returned home as fast as I could and rifled around in a drawer, all the time explaining to Tina what I was doing. I grabbed my passport, kissed Tina and ran out of the flat. Soon I was in front of Major Wim's desk again, handing him my documents.

The Major opened a drawer and placed my passport inside it, before pushing it closed and straightening up to look me in the eye.

'I hope you are not upset with me, Obbard, but I appear to have lost your passport. This means you will be unable to travel to Bosnia with your battalion. If I find it, which I am sure I will a week or two after your baby is born, I will return it to you and you will be able to re-join your section.'

Richie was smiling at me as I registered what this meant. Major Wim was a family man and understood what it meant for me to be with Tina at this time, to witness the birth of my first child.

'Thank you, sir!' I stammered my gratitude.

'For losing your passport, Obbard?'

That night, when I told Tina, she was so pleased. This meant a great deal to us and I would be forever grateful to the Major. It was a good company to be in. The officers were on side with the family and we knew how to work hard and play hard, laughing with one another more than fighting. Always good!

The autumn air felt even cooler once the other members of my battalion had flown off to Bosnia, along with their pranks and everyday banter. Tina was almost ready to have our baby, so home was filled with excited chatter about the imminent birth. Outside of this haven, I was working alongside the maintenance staff, family officers, resettlement staff, the medically unfit and any other soldiers so close to the end of their contract that they were waiting it out at Paderborn. Needless to say I was assigned tasks that were a real drag, properly tedious. This only served to enhance the pleasure of seeing Tina at the end of each day. It was something I never tired of, nor under-appreciated. We both eagerly anticipated the little person's arrival, the time he or she would burst into our lives, changing us forever. My thoughts sometimes hovered over memories of my own childhood and I wondered what sort of a parent I would be, resolved to be better than my own. I wondered if they had ever, in their early days, resolved to be the best possible when they came to collect me and Judith from the arms of our biological mothers.

The toll of Edward's illness was showing on Tina even more now, so much so that a routine trip to the midwife revealed she had preeclampsia, and she was whisked off to hospital. I was called off the training field to return to Sennelager Medical Centre and from there to accompany Tina in a military vehicle to Rinteln Hospital.

As I arrived, my heart in my mouth, wondering what was happening, the faces of the medical staff looked shocked. 'What are you doing with that?' someone asked.

It was only then that I remembered I had my rifle with me. When I was reprimanded, I just said, 'All I knew was that my wife was in hospital, so what did you expect me to do? I was training when I got the call!'

In the hospital, Tina tried to rest, but increasing boredom and not being at home made her very cross and impatient. I was unable to see her every day, as our car had broken down and the effort and cost of fixing it were both currently beyond us. There was a bus up to Rinteln, but I was expected to continue my training. Richie worked his magic for me, but that was still only twice in the whole week.

I was worried. I was not used to being unable to sort things out myself. I couldn't help Edward. I couldn't help Tina. It didn't take long for Tina to lose patience with the whole situation. She wanted to be home with me.

Eventually, on the Friday, Tina wore the staff down enough that they let her come home for the weekend, as long as she promised to go back on the Monday morning. She spent the weekend resting, doing all she could to avoid having to go back inside. On the Sunday evening, we were slouching on the sofa, huddled up in one corner of our huge flat, watching some forgettable programme or other. I noticed she was fidgeting rather a lot and, when I wasn't trying to keep up with the TV or feeling annoyed that I would have to do a mountain of mindless tasks the next day, I wondered why she was so restless.

'I just can't get comfy, Neil…'

'Are you okay?' I sat upright. What did this mean? 'Shall we go over to the hospital?' The hospital was getting on for two hours away.

'It's okay, Neil. I think it's too early, anyway. Don't worry!'

So I didn't worry and we went to bed as normal.

A couple of hours later, Tina nudged my arm. 'Neil! I keep getting contractions! They're coming fairly regular!'

I rubbed my eyes and nodded. 'Okay. What do you want to do? Go back up to the hospital?'

'I don't think so. It's too early!' Tina gasped and froze, waiting out another gripping pain around her middle. 'How will we get there? Have you forgotten we don't have a working vehicle?'

That was true. We would have to call for transport. Then came an idea, a compromise.

'Why don't we go up to the medical centre instead, then?'

The Medical Centre Talbot Barracks was only up the top of our road, near enough for us to walk. It formed the back entrance to the huge Sennelager Camp. This was the answer. I was calm enough, but I needed the security of medical staff. I expect Tina felt the same, because she agreed at once. 'Okay, Neil, but ring them first.'

I didn't need telling twice. As Tina tried to get herself comfortable, her face tensing as another contraction enveloped her belly, I grabbed the phone and dialed. Someone competent answered, or so I thought.

'Hello! We think my wife is in labour. It's our first!'

The voice said exactly what I had hoped and, seconds later, we were on our way. Tina leaned on me, stopping to withstand the pain when it came.

I was relieved to get to the medical centre and hand over responsibility to the staff there. A guard had been called up to unlock the back entrance, a turnstile gate, which was not the most elegant entrance for a heavily pregnant woman. We were ushered into a small room, like a doctor's waiting room. A very nice lady helped us to settle and asked us when the baby was due.

'Another week!' Tina leant on me and yelled, so that the word 'week' morphed into some primeval scream.

The nice lady smiled serenely, not at all perturbed by what she considered to be Tina's 'display'. 'It's probably just Braxton Hicks, then. It won't be the proper labour!'

The nice lady didn't know Tina well enough to gauge her moods through her expression. I did, and I was happy not to be on the receiving end of *that* look!

We stayed in that room for two or three hours, pacing out a routine, which became steadily faster: walk, sit, brace, scream and repeat. With each cycle, I was becoming more and more agitated. Eventually we missed out the walking part and Tina lay over some chairs, writhing. The nice lady popped her head round the door a few times to see if the Braxton Hicks were settling yet. We looked to her, hoping for some respite, pain relief or guidance. On more than one occasion we asked where the doctor was.

'I can't call the doctor just for Braxton Hicks. It's the middle of the night and the weather is far too bad for her to come out for no reason!' Nice Lady would back this up with a serene smile I wanted to knock off her face.

And so it went on. Help asked for in increasing louder tones. Help denied with increasingly more infuriating serenity. Tina held onto my hand like grim death throughout all of this. Eventually a look came over her I had never experienced at all.

'This baby is really coming, Neil!'

'But she said...'

'I don't care what *she* said… it's bloody coming!!!'

With the next scream Nice Lady came back in. This time, she had the decency to look concerned. I ran with it, fear making me confident: 'My wife says the baby is coming, so, as you clearly have no idea what you're talking about. I suggest you pull your finger out your arse and go and fetch someone who does!'

That did the trick. Nice Lady shot into a nearby office and dialed for help. Ten to fifteen long minutes later the doctor arrived, examined Tina, turned to Nice Lady and said, 'I suggest you wake up the ambulance driver. Do you realise I can see this baby's head?!'

Nice Lady had the good grace to turn pale before she disappeared to do as the doctor asked. We should have been in the English-speaking Rinteln Military Hospital, but it was too far now. Tina was half carried into an ambulance and we sped though the streets of Paderborn to the St Johannesstift Hospital, accompanied by flashing blue lights and a siren. The doctor had called ahead – bless her! – and they were expecting us. Tina was swept in aboard a wheelchair, helped onto a clean bed, examined and promptly told she was too late for pain relief.

Despite Tina's total lack of German and my limited amount, we understood that much. Luckily Mother Nature didn't need an interpreter, and within 30 minutes, at 5:52 on the morning of Monday, 6th November, Ben Obbard spilled out of Tina, who collapsed, spent, red, exhausted and relieved.

A second later I was holding this slippery little creature I had helped to create. His head rested in one palm and I cupped the rest of him in the other hand. His black eyes took in his new world and his mouth took in his first taste of air. I was terrified of dropping him, of letting him down in the first minute of his life, of letting Tina down, who had done such an amazing job of growing him all this time.

Whilst the registrar was sewing Tina back together, the nurse encouraged me to wash Ben. 'Papa bath?'

I stepped over to the sink, praying I would do well, be a good dad. I couldn't call it a thorough wash, as I just flicked some water at him gingerly and then patted him with a towel someone offered me, but he was still alive, which was the main thing.

I was proud of myself and especially of Tina. Ben was a perfect little boy. I had helped Tina through the birth, had been the first to hold our son, I had (kind of) washed him…it was all going so well, but boy! I was relieved to pass him back to Tina! She could take over from here, as I didn't trust myself even to change nappies. She would do a much better job!

The first couple of hours as the Obbard Family were spent marveling at Ben's little hands and tiny toes, grateful that he was healthy, that Tina had coped so well. We were exhausted and both relieved that we were not being turfed out to go home just yet. Ben fed from Tina, then slept, his faint, uncontrolled sounds making us wary, until we started to get used to them and a stillness fell onto us.

When a nurse came and placed Ben into the hospital cot next to Tina's bed, Tina settled herself back deep into the cushions and allowed her eyes to close. I slipped out, checked the nurse knew I was leaving so she would watch my family, and went to a payphone to phone our parents.

'Dad? It's me, Neil!' My dad did not register straightaway that I might have news, as it was too early. 'Dad? Tina's had the baby!' Dad shouted Mum through, they held the receiver between them and their voices were filled with smiles. Ben was their first grandson. It felt good to have made them so proud like this.

I called Edward and Edith too, doing well to know the answers to all of their questions. There was a sadness there, that they couldn't see Ben or Tina straightaway. Next I called my own grandparents, Hayes before Obbard, trying to beat my mum to the news. Finally I called Uncle Les.

Uncle Les worked in southern Germany; he had been to see us a couple of times before. I liked Uncle Les. He was as black a sheep as I was, with a secret profession he kept from his parents (Nan O and Granddad Obbard) all their life. I doubt even my dad knew.

Although a member of the RAF, thus achieving a great deal more than his brother, who had left the RAF under pressure from my mum, Uncle Les had disgraced the family by marrying a German woman. Granddad Obbard had been beside himself. I think he thought all Germans were somehow related to the gunner who had tried to kill him fifty years or so ago. He had redeemed himself a little through divorce but had then, horrifically, decided to stay in Germany permanently.

Uncle Les was a proper adventurer. He had cadged a lift to Vietnam with the US Army, been shot down and was lucky to get away with his life and his job. Most astonishingly, he made extra cash through acting and filming porn.

I have never been terribly interested in porn; my vices were drink and violence, but I enjoyed a little bit of kudos once when I glimpsed a film in passing (if I were to add up all the passing glances over the years, it would amount to hours!), and asked for the scene to be rewound.

'No point, Neil. Nothing happens in this scene!'

Oh, but it did. My uncle's reflection could be seen in a mirror on set, holding the camera on his shoulder.

I couldn't wait to tell him, as I found it hilarious, but he panicked. 'You didn't tell your Nan O and Granddad Obbard, did you?' I reassured him I had not and I never did, but his obsession with sex and his loud advocacy of the art gave rise to my suspicions about the true nature of his sexuality. He used to fill my head with tales of whoring and boozing in Singapore, which was known for its 'Lady Boys', and even in Brighton as a young man, when he was delivering groceries for Granddad Obbard's grocer's shop and delicatessen.

'I used to "deliver" what the ladies needed!' he would whisper, a twinkle in his eye, then he would repeat names of actresses and wives of racing drivers.

My uncle, the playboy! It made me smile to think how my parents would take that news! To quote Uncle Les – 'Never turn down sex or money!'

None of this matters a jot, of course, and it mattered even less the day Ben was born, because Uncle Les dropped everything, left his work on the US airbase and came straight up to help us. He visited Tina, met the baby, translated for us when the army liaison translator failed to materialise. He was present when the Nice Lady turned up to apologise to us in the morning. Apparently she was a SSAFA social worker with no idea of midwifery.

In the spirit of the day and because we were simply relieved Ben was healthy, Tina and I accepted her apology and Uncle Les and I celebrated the whole event by drinking ourselves stupid in Sennelager.

It was a great night. We found a great little bar and Uncle Les persuaded the bar staff to stay open longer. I had been awake for about 40 hours, but this was my first child and I would soon be in Bosnia, so I went for it! He even told me he would come and fetch me from Bosnia if Tina needed me – and I believed he could. A few days later he managed to secure a good deal with a local garage to ensure we had a viable vehicle, his knowledge of German and the minds of mechanics saving us from being ripped off.

Tina seemed stronger each time I visited and we trundled up to the 'Goldfish Bowl', where all the babies were kept together, labeled. They all wore the same colour, and the colour changed each day: a German strategy designed to check they had fresh clothes on.

Ben lay there, in the colour of the day, beneath a huge pillow-shaped quilt. We took him out and cuddled him. I became more confident at this and soon stopped worrying so much about dropping him.

The family office sent us flowers and baby-grows and, after a week, contacted the unit out in Bosnia. Major Wim suddenly remembered where he had lost my passport and directed someone to collect it from his desk drawer.

In the run-up to re-joining my section, I tidied around Tina and held the baby when she needed to do any jobs, or just rest. Full-on, modern 21st-century fatherhood had not quite reached me, but I did all right.

Chapter 6

I flew to Bosnia from RAF Brüggen. I was very unhappy to leave my family, but I had to go. The day after, Tina intended parcelling up our new son and driving him all the way back to Neenton to spend time with her parents and show him off to all his relatives in the UK. She would get him christened without me, as we had agreed. At some point when I was settling in Bosnia, my son was welcomed into the church I despised and named Benjamin Lewis Obbard, after my father. Of course, Edward's illness cast a shadow over us all and I was pleased Tina aimed to spend time with him in my absence. They would look after each other.

I had been trained by experts and had read every book and guide recommended. Now, on route to Split on an RAF Tristar, I ran through everything I knew.

I was ready.

In Split, we mustered at the site of some large white tents before going up country. It was a farce, to say the least. Someone indicated the food and told me to report back in one hour. I dumped my bag in an ISO container and was issued with my weapon, an SA80, packaged in Germany and zeroed to my personal settings.

To establish the optimum settings for my rifle, I had to spend 20 rounds, creating a group of bullet holes. The smaller the grouping, the more accurate you were. From this, the correct zeroing point was ascertained, which basically meant I could hit any target accurately.

I will admit it; sometimes I relied on SWAG…Scientific Wild Arse Guess. Other than that, I counted out the ammo and loaded up the magazines, replacing them when spent.

All done. Now for the NAAFI.

The next day we left the warmth of Split to join my section in the wintry north. Our brief was to patrol and dominate the local area. The town was Kislejak, but we preferred to call it 'The Mud Factory', since the mud crawled over our feet, up our legs and over the tops of our gaiters with every step.

We did patrol. We did dominate the local area. We also got drunk most nights with the French Foreign Legion, whose macho culture suited us.

Richie was delighted to see me and showed me off to our new friends whenever he had drunk too much (most nights when we were out, especially in Bosnia).

'This man,' he would slur, slapping me on the back and making sure he had

the attention of our new colleagues, 'this man is a brilliant kickboxer!'

This was the cue for a fight with anyone available from the Foreign Legion.

This was mainly stage-managed, of course. I was gentle with them, accepting victory by their submission rather than beating them to a pulp.

The Daytona Agreement was signed on 14 December 1995 and sealed our transition from UN to NATO forces.

We spent a miserable time patrolling in snow and the cold that reached -10 or -20 degrees. Even the toilets conspired against us, freezing over, so our shit piled up on top of the ice, on display for the next poor sod who needed to relieve himself. We were envious of the Royal Engineers, who had their own toilet block, the knobbers. They had installed their own heating, so no frozen piles of crap for them!

One day I became so incensed at this injustice that I followed an engineer to his bed, climbed on it, pulled down my trousers and squatted to dump on it.

'What the hell are you doing?'

'Where else can I go?'

'You f**king shit! I will get you!'

He lunged at me but I got away with it. I suppose I should be grateful for small mercies, though. One member of the Foreign Legion was forced to clean under the rim of our loos with his fingers after he had stolen something. Apparently he was Japanese and they make electronics with their nimble fingers, so it was a fitting punishment! When he wasn't scraping out dried or frozen shit, he was locked up in a cell made of sandbags, with water and food in a dog's bowl.

You've got to love the Foreign Legion! Despite their different angle on life, we got on better with them than with the Engineers, due to the whole 'we have better toilets than you' thing. We even had snowball fights!

Another source of mutual bonding was the lazyman boilers, which provided us with hot water. Basically they were metal bins holding a tube, one end of which hit the bottom, curled round and exited at the side for the kerosene. There was a little tank for the kerosene on top, which we turned slightly, allowing it to drip down, causing a fire hazard to the imperceptive eye.

My time in the TA had taught me a few things, but none were as satisfying as how to rig the boiler so that Engineers would light them innocently, unwittingly cause a mini explosion and emerge with a blackened face, minus their eyebrows.

We moved from village to village. By now we were camped out in a shop in a village somewhere outside of a Bosnian-Serb checkpoint. As usual, we had installed our purloined log burners and generators, and Jock, who was a star with electronics, set us up with lighting, stripped from elsewhere. It was bleak, cold and remote, all of this made so much worse by the snow. Our days were spent patrolling and undertaking recces, either in a vehicle or on foot.

The ceasefire had eased tensions only to introduce a new uncertainty. The local population was quite friendly and keen to ingratiate themselves with us. They regularly offered us their hospitality, often in the form of Slivovitz, a drink that was truly terrible and barely acceptable as a chaser. Sadly, we were duty-bound to accept, in the name of public relations, so we spent a lot of time under the influence.

The mix of alcohol and weaponry could have been lethal. I was leaning against the Warrior, holding my SA80, when gunshots rang out behind me. I spun round, cocked my weapon, and aimed, finding the enemy in my sights.

A grandma laughing. Next to her, a bride and groom, radiant in the winter sunshine. Beyond them, guests smiling, holding the AK47s they had just fired into the air, a tradition at weddings in this region. The weapons had probably been bought from some of our guys.

December slid by, each day giving way to the promise of a miserable Christmas.

Christmas 1995 crept towards us, with its promise of comfort and family to excite and soothe other people in a luckier world. We watched the dark, unable to combat the ice-cold air as it wound round our legs and froze our boots to the ground. Our fairy lights were the bright tracers of sharpshooters' guns, accompanied by a beat unheard of in any carols. The only baby I thought of was my son, and how I was missing his first Christmas.

Tina had travelled home to the UK with Samantha, who was seven months pregnant. Samantha was Wardy's wife. She had no common sense but was very intelligent. She could work out maths like Einstein, but couldn't work out how ducks got into a tree.

Tina had dropped Samantha off at a Kent railway station and continued her journey alone. She was so tired her eyes had started to droop and the road was blurring before her. Thankfully she had had the good sense to pull over and call Edward. 'Go to Rosie's. That'll save you an hour. Come over tomorrow!'

I thought often of Tina and Ben, and, of course, Edward. The medical staff had led him from a diagnosis of lung cancer in October through to recovery procedures without the operation he really needed. The family was spending Christmas with uncertainty hovering in every corner. Ben's first Christmas was without his father, and with his mum worrying deeply about her own father. I knew Tina would visit my parents and I wondered what they would make of my perfect little son. I had not been able to call since arriving in Bosnia, but I heard later that they doted on him and I wondered what he would have to do for that to stop.

Christmas Day brought me some unexpected treats. It began with a drink, heralded by celebratory gunfire, and ended with a drink. In fact, I cannot remember one minute of that day without a drink in my hand. It was crap, but it did the trick. Suffice to say I was pissed. However, through my gentle, sweet fog (if we had been attacked, this sweet fog would not have protected me), I understood that we were near a signals section, which meant I could call home. We had a 353 rigged copper antennae, but the signals section had the mother of all systems, linked to a nearby house. It stood there, surrounded by mines, our link to the world.

When it's Christmas and you're away from your loved ones, you call them.

When it's Christmas and you're away from your loved ones and pissed, you call them.

A lot.

'Tina!!!'

'Hello, Neil! Merry Christmas!'

'Are you having a nice day? How is Ben?'

'We are having a lovely day at home. I'll take Ben up to Nan Hayes tomorrow. Have you had a drink, Neil?' She could always tell.

About an hour later, I decided I wanted to talk to her again.

'Tina!!!'

'Hello, Neil!'

'I wish I was at home, eating turkey!'

'Me too, Neil!'

'Tina?'

'Yes?'

'I love you!'

'I love you too. Wish you were here!'

A bit later, 'Tina!!!'

'Neil!'

And so it went on.

At some point I sang *Blue Moon* in what I imagined was a crooning voice, reaching across the miles to my wonderful wife. It was a magical moment, romantic, as befitted our first Christmas married, our first Christmas as a family.

'I really love you, Tina!' This could have been romantic if it had not been slurred, punctuated by a burp, and the tenth time I had said it.

Meanwhile, on the other end of the line, Tina was trying to be patient with me. She managed it better than the signals operator, who had to be threatened with a good filling in to patch me through. My poor wife was taking care of a seven-week-old baby, who still woke up throughout the night; and, if he didn't keep her awake, worrying about her dad would. My drinking didn't worry her, as that was normal army fare – but disturbing her day? Repeatedly? When she was trying to catch up on sleep?

If I had been sober, what would I have said?

Christmas done, we returned to routine. We moved from shop to school to wherever we could find. The nights dragged themselves to the dawn, when we stood blinking in the winter sunlight.

Coralici was an outpost taken over from the UN. We rolled up, this time to be greeted by the Pakibatt – the Pakistani Battalion. Their numbers were depleted, as they had been taken off for their split anuses to have time to heal. This nasty ailment was probably due to acute constipation, but Bobby the Truth told us it was due to them 'doing' each other. We knew that was a lie, but it suited our sense of fun to perpetuate the rumour.

The whole of A Company settled in Coralici, lodged in portacabins. The snow was at least knee-deep and covered a sheet of ice, which gave our patrols an added bit of excitement.

Once again, we set out to make the NATO presence felt. My Granddad Obbard had told me of the children in the war, always on the lookout for sweets. If some of them were lucky enough to have sweets, some of the soldiers would take them away, just because. I can remember the sadness on Granddad

Obbard's face when he told me this. I feel the same way when I recall how squaddies covered hexy blocks with jam and fed them to the children in Bosnia.

Sick humour, loss of empathy, cruel.

We played football with the locals, watching their scrawny legs running around, manipulating the ball with the speed, skill and agility I could only wonder at, all whilst wearing wellies, duffle coats and woolly hats.

Around now, far enough away from Christmas and still too far from going home again, some of us began to get really homesick. We had a certain amount of leave per platoon and were allowed to apply for specific dates. I had come in late, so there was no chance of any R&R for the foreseeable.

But Gilly was going home and we all knew about it!

'This time next week, I'll be having a lie-in!'

'Only three days and I'll be down the pub!'

'Only two days until a good old roast dinner, with Yorkshire puddings and lashings of gravy!'

'This time tomorrow and I'll be on the plane!'

'This time tomorrow and I'll be at home!'

This droning on, this rubbing in, this reminder to us all of the width of the chasm between us and normal life, it really was too much. The situation would need to be addressed.

Gilly packed his bags, all ready for his return home the next day. He may even have gone to bed early, his last words to us being, 'Make sure you wake me up!'

No one asked why. I don't think a single person in the entire region had not heard that Gilly was going home the next day.

Someone set their alarm for five minutes before Gilly was due to get up. We tiptoed to his bed, somehow managed to tie his wrists to the bedframe with plasticuffs and unpacked all his stuff.

Then we waited.

Gilly's eyes flickered open and a second's confusion passed into a jubilant realisation that today was his day to go home and be human again, before he clocked his empty suitcase, his stuff thrown on the floor and his bound wrists.

'Nooooo! You have got to be kidding me! Get these off!' He shook his wrists, twisting his body round, trying to pull himself free.

We left him like that, carrying on with our business, throwing questions at him as we prepared ourselves for the day ahead.

'What time's your flight?'

'What will you be doing this time tomorrow?'

'Don't you mean, what should you have been doing this time tomorrow?'

We laughed and, if it had been anyone else, Gilly would have laughed too.

We left it until five minutes before he was meant to leave and untied him. He shot out of bed, swearing, and shoved his belongings into his case again. He dressed and ran out without washing or brushing his teeth.

His family would love him!

With Gilly gone, we got back to the job in hand.

Another day. More patrols. More bodies. More tension to create. More unwanted memories. This was how it would be. All this crap, with the odd practical joke to remind us we could laugh.

A few days later, on New Year's Eve, we had a party. We brushed up a bit, washed the smell of death off our hands and headed off to the NAAFI, two or three portacabins all joined together, a few tiny champagne bottles. There were even a few squaddies milling about outside as we arrived, chatting and swigging those little bottles.

Let's skip to the next morning, when the arrival of 1996 was heralded in by a sore head and an even sorer backside.

I tried to open my eyes, but the light sent stabbing pains through my skull. I raised my hand to my face. My arm hurt. What on earth had happened? A sound came at me in waves, unrecognisable.

'What was that?' My voice was thick with sleep and alcohol.

'I said, "F**king hell!" You were out of order last night!'

It was Wardy.

'Why does my arse hurt?'

On another occasion, this may have yielded a joke.

Not today.

'You kept falling on it, you dick! It proper kicked off last night!'

That made sense. It had been very icy. I thought I remembered my legs whipping out from under me. I tried to laugh, but even that small shake of my body caused me pain. Everywhere.

'Who started it?'

'You, you idiot!'

Really?

As my brain started the cumbersome task of clearing, a few images came to me: everyone pissed, falling over, fists flying, towards me and away from me.

My brain was encouraging me to sit up when the decision was made for me.

'Get up, you bunch of tossers!'

It was Daff, named after Colonel Gaddafi. A full screw, or corporal. We found out later that Richie Benson was too drunk to deal with us.

'All of you out on parade! NOW!'

We scrambled out onto the parade ground, grabbing jackets and trousers on the way. Hopping along, trying to get our legs into the holes, button up the jackets, before we hit the cold. Then we stood, trembling, freezing, our minds suddenly more acute.

Pete Benson, Richie's brother, the company sergeant, joined Daff and we received a merry rollocking.

'If you were involved, stay behind! Otherwise, go!'

I thought I had better stay. To be fair, starting the mother of all fight fests sounded just like me. Three others stayed; every other squaddie waltzed back in like butter wouldn't melt!

I watched Pete yelling. I barely heard his words. I just thought about releasing tension and how a good drink and a good brawl last night had done just the trick. The party, the brawl, the aftermath…all these merged into the visual mosaic that was Bosnia.

One memory swam among the rest, its facts blurred, leaving me with images untethered to a time or a place. We were called to the river on a clear-up operation, rescuing heads and bodies from the swirling, bitter waters, where they were caught up in branches, grabbed by shallow banks or simply swept along, daring us to catch them.

We gathered in what we could and what was remaining after the fish had feasted on them, after the currents, the rocks, the tree roots, the plant life had knocked flesh away and pared the body down to its minimum: skulls like vessels, whose contents had poured through bullet holes or allowed in watery thieves. When we lifted them out, the water poured through eye sockets and the jaws hung slack to reveal the roof of a mouth or part of the tongue.

We wondered about the bodies, wondered if we had matched them up to their heads or if it even mattered. The skin was beaten and thinned, almost, but not quite, dissolved in the river, already catching the rhythm of the ripples. Fingers were missing and close scrutiny may have told us whether this was due to an act of torture or just trying to survive.

For variety, we also dealt with those souls who had been allowed to remain on land. These bones were dried, the skin leathery, the blood no longer fluid but clinging to the skin like mud, settling around rotting flesh.

These images are like photographs in my brain, tucked away most of the time, just out of sight, until they burst forth screaming 'Look at me!' when I least expect it.

The next stop on the battalion's tour of modern hell was Banjaluka. This time we were housed in a metal factory, which formed our HQ. Luckily for us, A Company had arrived first and had already cleared out the bodies by the time we turned up.

We set our tents up inside, organising our mattresses to suit. Jock rigged up the lighting and tapped into the factory power supply. A proper cowboy job, but it worked for us – we were two sections in this place, giving out the usual banter, unaware that invisible shards of metal were sliding down our throats as we talked. The secret was only revealed a few weeks later when some of us coughed up blood.

The patrolling started again. We never stopped finding bodies. It was like the earth was spewing up the contents of graves for us to rebury. Men, women, children, babies, mostly decapitated, replaced those we had cleared away the day before.

It showed a special kind of hatred to sever someone's head to prevent their soul from resting, and this was what troubled me the most. I had started out matching the faces to the bodies as best I could, but the task was too hopeless, too overwhelming, so I stopped.

It affected us all, even big guys, tough guys, even no-nonsense 'like it or lump it' guys like Rocky.

Rockie lumbered around, shifting piles of lifeless families with the ease of someone who works out and boxes regularly. As with most of us, he appeared to me to have shaken off the sights he had beheld, consigned them to the pits, buried them with the bodies.

I was wrong.

He was haunted by them.

One night, Rocky's screams pierced our fitful sleep. We leapt out of bed, brains preparing for battle, the hair on the back of our necks electric.

Rocky was flat on his back, his head straining upwards, his hands pushing the air near his chest and stomach. He was being pinned to his bed by the ghost of a man, maybe a man he had buried that day, pinned down and suffocated as he gasped and screamed, desperately trying to remove the corpse from his chest.

'Get him off me! Get him off me!'

We stared, questioning our eyesight, our mentality. I stepped closer to him, confused, just as the ghost left, and Reggie could move well enough to sit up. He burst into tears.

Some of us turned over and went back to sleep. I am sure I heard one man laugh. He wouldn't be laughing when they came for *him*.

At another camp, Jock rigged up the lights we had stolen

from the engineers and somehow tapped into the power supply of a nearby factory. The extra light lifted our spirits, kept the darkness and the demons at bay. We lolled around on our beds for a while, our heads full of bitter memories and our conversation superficial and simple. Jokes and banter gave us all the impression we were the only one suffering, the only one pretending to be trivial.

Fatigue kicked in and I settled down, hoping to slip into a deep sleep straightaway. I sensed the other guys giving in to their exhaustion and, at some point, we all fell asleep.

My dreams were disturbed by convulsive crying, desperate sobs which shook the whole tent. We all sat up and looked over at Smithy, whose face was awash with tears, whose body was being rocked by his utter, utter distress.

And whose mouth was closed around the barrel of his gun.

Someone shouted, 'What you doing?'

Smithy's answer was to pull the trigger.

The noise was unbelievable, a thunderclap to accompany the splintering of teeth and bone, the slicing of flesh and muscle. Smithy had turned at the last moment, survived, destroyed his face, sent bits of himself all over the roof and walls of the tent.

Others spoke to him, reassured him that everything would be okay.

Would it?

I left them all to it. And found another tent to sleep in. I wasn't a medic. I wasn't his friend. I never saw him again. His lasting legacy was a few jokes about him being able to smoke without having to open his mouth.

I have a recollection of another death around this time, a game of Russian Roulette, dressed up and presented as suicide. The army thought families preferred their loved ones to die in mental agony, rather than see them as idiots.

We moved on to yet another grim place, where a form of boredom started to settle on us. We were all building up a hard shell, men as machines, dealing with the bodies, the threat, the relentless discomfort, by seemingly repelling them with silence or humour. But this hard exterior imprisoned our angst, allowing it to rumble and fester inside us, with little hope of escape, unless you counted suicide.

One morning, when I was contemplating very little, in case it was difficult, Jock (a Platoon Warrior Sergeant) rolled round the corner in his vehicle. 'Anyone fancy a trip out? A wagon has broken down in some god-forsaken place. They've radioed for assistance.'

I jumped up and clambered on board, along with another four or five men who no doubt felt the same as me. Better to be doing something than nothing; it kept the thoughts at bay.

'You can be in charge, Obby!'

Fair enough. Would make a change.

We were invited into a pub at one of the first stop-offs. We tried in vain to communicate in pidgin Bosnian that we had to move on, but the locals insisted.

Inside was a veritable melting pot of nationalities and degrees of testosterone. We spotted mercenaries, paid for mainly by the Muslims, but Bosnians and Serbs may also have hired them; also the Mujahideen, all forming quite the social brotherhood.

Back at home, we might have heard conversations about politics or football, but not here.

'I have killed twenty!'

'Ah, but does that include any women or kids?'

'Does it matter?'

'I don't count women or children!'

'I have killed thirty-six!'

'I never kill women or children and have seen off over forty!'

After a while, some of them took their machismo outside and had a shooting competition, using their pistols to obliterate empty glass bottles lined up on a wall. Curtains twitched in nearby houses, but the civilians kept away. The only locals that made appearances were the interpreters and, if they were female, this had a whole new effect on the men.

One day, it was down to me and Whitey to dispose of the frozen shit and the other rubbish generated by camp. We gathered the bags, commented on the joy of such a job, and took them away from camp, flinging them on top of the rubbish that had been collecting there for a few days. The new additions sank into the mountain of filth, unsettling the stink and making our experience even more unpalatable.

While I stood around, cursing the level of hygiene and comfort my life had sunk to, Whitey fetched a huge tub of kerosene, which might have provided the battalion with about six months of heat. That, however, was not its destiny. Instead, we took it in turns to pour the kerosene over the mountain of shit, unwanted containers and rotting food, passing the tub back when our muscles screamed with the weight and exertion of lifting and pouring whilst bracing our legs as we tried to balance on unsteady, shifting bags. Brownie had joined us by now, as he had a bag to add to ours, and, although he did not help us at all, he was very encouraging!

Among the rubbish, I found a deflated football, so we naturally dowsed it in kerosene too, knocking it away from the pile for future employment.

Once the whole tub of kerosene was gone, being soaked into putrefying waste or left to form tiny rivulets over impermeable plastic, we settled the tub on the top of the pile and jogged over to the football.

It was my idea to light the match to the football and then kick it over onto the pile, igniting the bags in one smooth move. Unfortunately for Brownie, I had not waited until he had deposited his bag and moved away, and he was therefore right next to the blast when it went off, engulfing him in the swirl of detritus and leaving him covered in human excrement.

Anyone passing would have been unable to tell who it was, but for the unmistakable northeastern accent which railed at me, bemoaning my actions. If I had not been laughing so hard, I might have taken some notice, but I still wouldn't have cared.

Bizarrely, a guy called Arnie opened a bar and set up a trade in Hekwap – a truly awful beer, which sported a white label with a picture of the Virgin Mary and Baby on it. Despite its incongruous image, horrendous flavour and inflated prices, it gave us something to suppress the day's memories and enable us to participate in functioning conversations about the banal.

We had precisely four toilets, four phones and four showers. It was easy to find them – just follow the queues. Naturally there were no queues for the officers and NCOs, who had more than enough loos. I dare say they didn't have the threat of rats either. Richie and Jock worked on our behalf, thinking maybe a decent loo with the luxury of cleanliness and no one knocking on the door would be a nice treat after a long day locating mines and occasionally shifting corpses.

Days went by, where we patrolled and returned to camp. All very tedious, but for the threat of mines and the face-to-face encounters with death and the depravity of the human race. Sometimes the patrols were replaced by guard duty.

Back in the UK, Edward got his diagnosis of cancer. He was told that he was fit for a smoker (he was in his early 50s and could run 1.5 miles in less than ten minutes). It was confirmed that he had no cancer on the lungs, just in the tube leading into his lungs. His operation would be in February and Tina's plans were to stay in Neenton for that time. I would meet her there when I had my R&R in February.

Of course, thoughts of Tina and Ben, of Edward and the rest of my family floated into my consciousness every day, but I chased them away, so I could concentrate on my job in Bosnia and not make it worse by filling myself with the pain of missing them. I always needed to be alert when on duty. Sometimes a shot came in from the hillside when I was on gate duty. I wouldn't retaliate, just move round the Warrior for protection. No point in shooting blindly. Intelligence said it was probably a sniper.

Occasionally the intelligence guys would wake me up in the night with details of a threatening position.

'Acquire the target and hit it.'

I did exactly as I was told. Crawling back into my bed, I would fall asleep immediately.

Chapter 7

Early 1996. The rumble of our APC engine faded into the silence of Arapusa. We jumped down, looked around, hoping for some comfort and acutely aware that that would come at a price. The hills watched over us, probably shielding Serbian positions and the demilitarized zone. We breathed in the silent air and steeled ourselves for what was to come: our mission, dictated by a group of men on another continent.

Arapusa nestled at the foot of those guarded hills. It was a village that ought to have been beautiful, but the buildings looked like they had been flung together or blown apart, then garnished with the carcasses of pigs. Their rotting smell was stunted by the winter air, sucked up by the remnants of a snowstorm, which had failed to cover them or sweep them away.

Somewhere, in another world, people were abandoning New Year's resolutions, all warm at home, too much food in their stomachs, giddy with alcohol. Tina was holding my son for me. Here in this icy place, where my shaking hands were relied on to work wires and plastics, to fight the threat of death – and I had to control them well enough to protect us all – that world seemed like a dream that belonged to someone else. The last time I saw snow like this, I was leaning with Tina against a window, watching snowploughs in the valley below. I pushed that thought away quickly.

A few of us made a claim to a big house with a balcony. It didn't have any furniture but gave us enough space for some kind of privacy. Plus none of us had ever owned a balcony! The others were happier to stay in the village, deciding on the best house to call a temporary home, looting one house to furnish another, checking for rare delights, but we soon made for the hills glowering over us. Despite the good intentions and the signatures on the Peace Treaty, we needed to know who could watch us; we needed to unearth the secrets of the area, face the newly befriended enemy.

As we made our way up the road that snaked out of the village, the sound of our boots punctuated the silence, displacing mud and slush, compacting snow which mirrored the shapes of our worn soles, occasional puddles fighting back. It really was bleak.

Eventually, our feet and hands complaining painfully of the cold, we came upon a trench drenched in mud and an enclosure behind it, housing 4-5 Serbs. Wary smiles all round and greetings in uncommon tongues. We had no interpreter with us this time, but it was, someone important had said, important to build some kind of rapport after the horrors of ethnic cleansing. We tried our best, despite everything, despite what we knew or guessed at, to be friendly.

They waved us in and indicated seats that were meant to preside in dining rooms used for best, their backs and legs far too ornate and majestic for this trench in these hills. No two chairs matched and I wondered if they had been polite enough to take only one chair per house.

I accepted the invitation to sit on one of the wooden chairs and took in the sight of the men. Their uniforms were barely that – just a makeshift mishmash of casual and camouflage, like they had been on their way to a bar or the cinema when someone had made them wage a war. They didn't look well. Malnourishment had taken its toll on them. One man in particular must have only been in his 30s or 40s but he looked well over 50.

One of the others offered us a glass, oddly clean. It was coffee, which I took without question. We had been told never to refuse Silovitch, as that would offend. It was probably not the same with coffee, but it was never a good thing to offend soldiers in a war-ravaged area, so I nodded my thanks and threw my head back so that the sharp, warm fluid hit the back of my throat and instilled a drop of warmth in me.

'*Sehr gut!*' I tried, and was surprised when the faces smiled more broadly and replied in the same language.

We started what could loosely be called a conversation, disjointed items of vocabulary supported by body language. It was all very friendly, if you discounted the weapons. As we tried out phrases we thought we had forgotten, the Serbs managed to communicate their hatred of all Muslims, due to their tendency to move in and undercut the local workforce.

I had some sympathy for the Muslims – who doesn't want a better life for their family? – but held back from sharing that. After all, these guys had guns and we were on their turf, smiles and coffee or not! It would have been foolhardy to point out that they had worked in Germany, been 'job stealers' themselves, so we just told them the same thing was happening in the UK, outsiders coming in and taking our jobs, and we bonded more over our shared common enemy: the threat of the immigrant.

The old-looking guy was leaning forward on his carved dining seat, studying us intently, searching for the right words. He had been shocked that we suffered from the same problems. Why did we, in the UK, put up with it? Why didn't we start a civil war? Why didn't we do as they had done and rise up and expel these outsiders?

'Expel'??

What could I say? What could I say to that, even when fluent and using a common tongue? I just looked at him and in my very best pidgin German uttered a sentence to end the conversation: 'John Major says we are not allowed!'

He accepted this proclamation with a sage nod of the head, sitting back in his chair, his respectful acceptance of this statement awarding John Major far more kudos and power than he really deserved.

A short while later, another Serb put his head into the trench and, with barely a glance in our direction, barked something at his men. He must have told them to draw a line under our little get-together, because it came to an end and a short while later, we were making our way back down the hill, bearing the gifts of a belly warmed with caffeine and a couple of chairs to make our stay in Arapusa more comfortable.

Despite the smiles and the housewarming gifts, we were under no illusion about our relationship. Peace treaty or no peace treaty, if they shot at us we would aim to kill.

I would have no problem with that.

Back in the village, we helped clear out four or five houses for the attached personnel: anti-tank units, Support and Fire, Heavy Mortars (at 84mm, bigger than anything my platoon dealt with), not to mention the cooks who needed somewhere to set up their kitchen and boil our vegetables until they were mush and devoid of any vitamins. It was still better than compo rations. Just. We left them disguising stale bread as delicious doughnuts, ignoring the shelves of food we had found in the houses, the corn on the cob still bright from the sunshine.

My mouth watered but none of us could take a chance. You can't see poison and you cannot underestimate the lengths people will go to to cause harm once their spirits have learnt to hate.

The scene playing out in the centre of Arapusa was not unlike other places we had been. Our understaffed units had found their rhythm; any bitterness about warring politicians sending us off unmanned had long since dried up. We arrived in these places like travellers in really hard vehicles, dragging pipes out, reassembling wood burners, firing up generators looted from Kislejak or 'The Mud Factory'.

We didn't care what we burnt to keep warm. We didn't care what we did in buildings that families had called home. We didn't even care if we ever found someone living in one of them. We just used threats or the butt of our rifles to move them out, yelling at them to just go, whether they spoke English or not. They would get the message. It never occurred to us to let them be and move into another house. If they died of hyperthermia, it was tough. I suppose a corner of me may have thought it a bit of a shame, but in the end, I chose myself over them.

This village, however, was like a ghost town. We worked our

way through it, working outwards from the main crossroads, where we had set up the camp. We carefully moved away from the camp, where we at least felt a little normal. Soon the silence wrapped itself around us again, so, between the mines and the booby traps, between half-built houses and dead animals, we filled the air with short, barked conversations. We were angry; or, if fear or disgust permeated the cold, we dressed it in dark humour and rejected it.

We explored houses, once homes, room by room. Found drawers pulled from chests, toys waiting for children, photo frames askew. Each smiling face, captured in a happier time, that connection between the photographer and their family, those birthdays, celebrations, records of relationships, proof of love and need and pride, each face provoked in me unbearable questions. Where they alive or dead? Had they killed? Been killed? Had they been raped?

After a while I tried not to look at the photos.

The school cellar was packed with tables and chairs piled up, the classrooms empty. We wondered briefly why, but there were simply too many questions for answers and we trudged on, replacing the stone-cold silence of Arapusa with bawdy comments and laughing at the expense of the people who had left, because that was what kept us sane.

I thought we would manage another day of equilibrium, but one of us, Seb, allowed humanity in. In someone's bedroom, he suddenly yelled into the still air, his anger, frustration and fear ripping radiators off walls and metal shutters off windows, hurling them to the ground below.

The rest of us yelled back at him, anger and bafflement mixed with concern, mainly for our own lives. 'Seb! Mate! Stop! Watch out for mines!'

But we avoided death for another day and Seb either found his sense or ran out of radiators and shutters and calmed down in time for the worst to come. We had worked our way up to the other end of the village, where we found the vestiges of an illegal checkpoint. From here, there was a clear track that invited us, ground pulverized by hundreds of feet before ours.

As we moved along this path, we saw that it led down to the river, the perfect place for a picnic in the summer or a quiet place to fish.

Once. Perhaps. Before.

At the end, where the edge of the land melted into the water, we found piles of empty suitcases, then piles of clothes, probably once taken from chests of drawers in warm bedrooms. And there was blood and the slivers of bone and brain, which clung to the land when the rest of the person was hurled into the river, to be carried away forever.

***

On the way back to our temporary home, the icy silence of this place took hold of my gut. I wanted to hear a child excited to find a lost toy or a baby cry or a wife call out to a returning husband. I had heard that no birdsong can permeate the air of Auschwitz because of the memory of evil that exists there, wreaked by men on each other, and, as I trudged through the snow, the ice, the mud, I wondered if Arapusa would ever recover.

Would I ever recover?

My thoughts were disturbed by some unrestrained laughter from one of the houses we had commandeered. I looked at the others and, without speaking a word, we decided to go and see what was so funny. Maybe this was just what we needed, a good laugh to brush away the shit we had endured that day.

As we entered, I glimpsed the edges of the 'Pig Board' already put up on the wall of someone's kitchen. I could feel myself start to grin even before I could see it all properly. What now?

Whenever we went on leave, we would naturally try and sleep with women. Although that is fairly standard for a group of young, fit men who have had to restrain themselves for weeks or even months, my battalion had a special competition going: to find the man who could sleep with the ugliest woman and bring a photo back to prove it.

So, returning back to the bosom of my comrades after a grueling day raking through the belongings of ghosts, the 'Pig Board' would surely help me back to normal. What would it be this time? Obese? Deformed? Pitted skin? I couldn't wait. It never failed to make me laugh.

The crowd fell to one side to let us see. Whatever the new picture was, it had grown men doubled over, crying with laughter. Someone was slapping the shoulder of the picture's owner. This must be good!

It took me a few seconds to register what I was looking at.

It was a photo of a woman, pale, ancient, whose mouth had fallen open in the moment of her death.

'What the…?!' I yelled. This was not on. This was simply unacceptable. I felt sick.

One or two of my lot groaned and lashed out, 'That is too far, mate!'

'Take it down! That's someone's granny!'

The laughter dried up for shame or turned to recrimination. We had stopped the fun, reminded them that compassion existed in the world and that giving up on that made us as bad as the people who had created this mess in the first place.

There was a yell from outside. By now I was able to tell immediately whether to be on guard or not. This yell was as near to joy as you could get in this sort of situation.

The radio was up and running.

I went outside, glad to leave the 'Pig Board' and the idiots who had gone too far. Luckily they took down the picture of the old lady, and who knows if this was guilt or pressure from the rest of us? After all, if any of us held the moral high ground, it must have been bad!

I wasn't the first to get to the radio; already a queue had formed. Someone had erected a huge mast and it waved about high up in the air, no doubt watched with suspicion by my new Serbian acquaintance in his trench.

The wait felt endless as we watched each other move closer to the radio. That lump of plastic that was our gateway to our other life, the one that ran parallel to this one.

Once or twice the signal failed and left disappointed squaddies repeating themselves into the mouthpiece or bashing the radio in frustration. Others took too long and we relieved our boredom and tempered our impatience by listening in to their conversations.

When it was finally my turn, the clicks and the whirs and the sound of air as my connection was bounced from radio to ship to satellite to the place I called home felt endless. Every second, I was expecting to be cut off.

The ring tone. How many times did it ring before Tina answered? If I got to five, I knew she was out. Disappointment for me, joy for the queue behind me.

'Hello?'

'Tina! It's me! Can you hear me alright?'

The buzz of hearing her voice, of our brief exchange of words, was never quite the same as normal. We tried to fit so much into a few moments, questions flying, answers steeped in concern for the other's feelings. The baby was doing well, Tina was tired but coping, we missed each other.

When Tina asked me how I was, I said I was fine. I would not go into detail, as there was a queue behind me and no way of knowing whether the signal would fail and how long we would have until the next call.

I could have told her about coffee with people who murder and rape because they don't like being 'undercut'. I could have told her about trips to the riverside and photographs of people whose lives had been destroyed. I could have told her that we were turning into people who laughed at dead old ladies.

But I didn't.

That could wait.

I finished the call reluctantly. The guys behind me had been waiting for some time and I was pushing my luck now. Plus, my gut was starting to complain.

Tina and I said goodbye the way you do when there is no way of knowing when the chance to talk would arise again. Romance and gushing sentiment was out of the question, so we settled for just repeating 'Goodbye and take care!' a few times. Within seconds I was heading back into the silence again, leaving some other guy to take up the radio and re-connect with civilisation.

I picked up my pace. Something was going on in my belly. It was complaining of some grievance by contracting painfully, swirling coffee and rations about threateningly.

The house with the balcony was just about in sight when I was overwhelmed with the urge to expel the contents of my stomach by, frankly, either means: I was not fussy.

I have no idea how I managed to keep it all together – or in – until I got into a bathroom, and the battle of vomit versus diarrhoea was on. I am sure that the sight of my face would have been most comical, had anyone seen it. One minute it radiated pure bliss, as my body noisily emitted some kind of watery stink from one end; the next minute it was shocked, as bile and sick launched itself out of my mouth. I managed to get most of it into the bucket by hurling myself around in tune with my bodily functions. This was not easy: it meant balancing on the edge of a bucket lined with a black plastic bag, which threatened to rip as I filled it. Running water and a flushable sewerage system would never be taken for granted again.

I was fully aware that the noises would be reverberating round the house and that my housemates would be having a laugh at my expense. As things calmed down a bit, one or two quips filtered through the door.

Ha bloody ha. They might not be quite so jovial if they had to use this bathroom before I could deal with my redecoration.

I wiped away the worst of it, twisted the top of the bag up to limit exposure to the smell, splashed a drop of water from my flask into my rancid mouth and then staggered out, leaving the full bag in the bucket for someone else to remove. I made my way back to my bed. There I threw myself down, letting the jibes and banter flow over me. I was too weak to bother with anything but lighting a cigarette. I drew on it and savoured the taste of the nicotine on my tongue.

My peace lasted precisely 25 seconds before my blasted gut

informed me in no uncertain terms that it had not finished. I stubbed out my fag as carefully as the emergency situation would allow and bolted back into the bathroom to a loud cheer from the guys.

This went on until someone suggested I go to the medic. I never did find out whether it was out of sympathy for me, or whether they were simply getting fed up with me hogging the bathroom. Either way, I somehow managed to drag myself the few feet up the road to Mick, or, to give him his official title: Mick the Mad Medic.

I never knew why he was called that. Whispers of him screwing another soldier's wife back at base may have had something to do with it, but I didn't really know. He was quite matter-of-fact when administering advice and medication, and you would never compare him favourably to, well, any other doctor on the face of the earth, but that alone did not deserve the title. Compassion didn't register with him. He handed out painkillers, if necessary, in a no-nonsense manner. When I turned up, he simply asked whether I had eaten anything dodgy, or maybe failed to wash my hands properly? Told me to wait it out and drink plenty of fluids.

I went back over the last few days and shook my head. I had come into contact with so much evil and death in that village, it could have been anything and everything.

Before my stomach could scrape up any last vestiges of a long-forgotten meal and present it, with a flourish, to the unfortunate medic, he told me there was nothing anyone else could do for me and that all I could do was rest for 24 hours and avoid anything except the odd sip of water passing my lips. 'You are going to feel like shit!' he informed me.

I made my way back to my bed, muttered to the others to give me some space (no one argued), checked there was a clear passage to the bathroom door and lay down with a groan.

I spent the rest of that day and most of the next wondering whether this would be the lowest point of my life: helpless, sick, away from my family, in a corner of the world where man's inhumanity left its mark wherever we looked. At odds with my mood, a crew had turned up to film us for a documentary. The rest of the battalion scrubbed up and played for the cameras. If I had been well, I might have seen it as a decent distraction and been just as excited as the others. As it was, with the state I was in, I couldn't have cared less. Also around this time, a guy called 'Kes' got his fifteen minutes of fame by blasting hell out of a Serb position. All this happened whilst I chain-smoked and concentrated on stopping my guts turning inside out.

At nights, we would stag on – slang for guard duty. It was also referred to as STOYB: Stag On You Bastard. Most soldiers would stand next to braziers for warmth, stamping their freezing feet in the snow. I wouldn't, preferring to stand away from the light, because Serbs would sometimes take a pot shot at us in haze of drink. This was unusual, as they knew the score, but we all know what drink can do to a man's brain. Any 'brothers in arms' mentality went by the board. If I was near enough, I would retaliate, but the Serb position here was too far away.

On another occasion, some of us decided to set fire to a car. This fulfilled two needs: to keep warm and entertain ourselves.

It was relatively easy. We chose the garage of a house some of us had been staying in. For this reason it had been kept fairly nice, so, as if that made it okay, we rolled the car out of a garage in the village and used some of the kerosene to ease ignition. Then one of us threw a cigarette into it and we enjoyed the whoosh of air being sucked into red-hot flames. We stood around, thoroughly enjoying the warmth, smoking and joking about.

Unfortunately this moment coincided with the return of the first surviving villagers, who happened to own the car and the drive it was burning on. The couple appeared out of nowhere. The poor woman took one look at the car and burst into tears. Her husband rolled his head back in disappointment but had had enough violence in his life and too much respect for the uniform to take us on. Their kids just looked frightened.

We didn't care one bit. We were mainly oblivious to the bigger picture and just coped from day to day. If we felt compassion or guilt, if what we witnessed shook our vision of the world, it was later, when we were going about our daily lives, when we least expected it and wanted it.

As I approached my R&R, in the February of 1996, I kept my outward excitement more low-key than Gilly, but I allowed myself to dwell more on thoughts of home. I couldn't wait to see Tina and Ben again.

Fourteen days' leave turned into ten once the journey was taken into consideration. Time seemed to slow right down on that journey home, but eventually I was on British soil and Tina and I were together again.

Tina's parents' home – my home – welcomed me. I stepped over the threshold and was immediately met by a huge ball of fur which flew through the air, spun itself round, tongue licking, tail wagging itself almost off. Khan!

Everything stopped for a few minutes, until Khan had settled. Even then, she followed me everywhere.

Edith held Ben, who was passed to Tina. I would not have known he was Ben, he had grown and changed so much! I held him, a little clumsily. Tina reassured him that it was okay, I was Daddy.

Then I saw Edward.

Edward had had his operation by now. They had broken bones in his back, his shoulder, opened him up, removed one lung, scraped out the tube and sealed it up only seven days ago. He had needed heavy doses of morphine to cope.

And here he was, in winter, with snow on the ground, in a basic council house – no double-glazing, no central heating – with only a prescription of 12-14 paracetamol a day!

I greeted him as I normally would, hiding my shock, trying to keep it all casual.

My main emotion on seeing this man I admired so much was anger. He was clearly in a lot of pain and I did not understand why he had been allowed to recuperate at home, with such inadequate pain relief.

I visited my parents, I did what was expected of me, I ate as much as I could, I drank some more, I held Ben, learnt his routine, enjoyed being a husband again, walked Khan. If Edward had not been so poorly, it would have been a perfect time.

The ten days passed too quickly before I had to cross that chasm again.

'See you next time, Edward! Look after yourself!'

'You too, Neil. Next time you're back, we'll walk the dogs together!'

And then he said, as I walked out, 'If anything happens to me, the army will get you home.'

This became a significant omen.

Back in Banjaluka, Major Wim had gone and been replaced by 'Robocop', a new officer named Major Green. Two Platoon had taken over some flats. In my absence, I had been allocated a room share with Brownie.

Cheers, guys!

In compensation for my roommate, I had a balcony. In another room were Stevie, Gilly, Mo and Johnno, four more in another of the flat's bedrooms. The main area of the flat was open-plan.

The banter and practical jokes didn't wane. When it was my turn to get wood for the wood burner, I took the slats from under Brownie's bed!

From the windows, we could see the school, with kids playing football on the field, so we joined them. We told ourselves it was in NATO's brief to interact with the community, but it felt good to be doing something normal. We could also see the local café and there we ordered ourselves espressos or Slivovitz.

There had been artillery damage to the outside of the flats, and this had not only caused a lot of dust but had also loosened some concrete slabs, on which we made small fires outside, for the rubbish.

There was always porn lying around. It always appeared, seemingly from nowhere, wherever we were.

Spearheading the porn industries drive for equality, Fiesta offered a page 'for the ladies', where the male form could be enjoyed in all its glory. Every now and then, Brownie awoke to find I had pinned this page on the wall above his bed.

'I'm not gay! Stop doing that, Neil!' But it was all in good humour.

Richie Benson was seen less and less, mainly because he was permanently pissed. Funnily enough, this was his normal state when we were in the field. We had a new Platoon Commander, not only young but fresh out of the factory.

One night he burst into our flat, yelling about a fire down at the police station.

'Get your body armour on! That place is full of bullets and shells. If it goes up...!'

Brownie jumped out of bed and started to haul on the protective vest.

'Come on Neil! Quick!'

I was mightily peed off at having been woken so rudely.

'F**k off! I am going back to sleep! He hasn't got a f**king clue! If a bullet hits me from five buildings away and through the walls of this flat, it is my time.'

So I went back to sleep, wondering if I would wake up again.

Chapter 8

As I was still alive the next day, I was able to embark upon a mini tour with Brownie, who was good at signals, Stevie, Mo, Gilly and a guy called Socks. He was really nice and – random fact – his wife ironed her own hair on an ironing board before hair straighteners became fashionable.

Our brief was to work our way around the local area, handing out NATO colouring books to children, with dot-to-dot pictures of grenades, shells and mines. You know... the stuff of fairy tales. All this was designed to minimise the maiming and deaths that these items would inevitably cause, if used as a toy.

Sadly, another one of our tasks was to distribute posters to help reunite missing relatives. How many of these missing loved ones had we shoveled onto the sides of roads or the banks of rivers? It would have been heart-breaking, if we had let it be.

Socks was in charge of the itinerary. We set off with our posters, colouring books, a female interpreter and the order not to accept invitations to drink, which was fine by us, as it would only slow us down. We studied maps showing up minefields and I made it my business to learn them. You never knew when this might come in handy.

We made our way round the planned route, doing our job. Children were happy to get their gifts, adults were pleasant enough, but there was often an underlying anguish caused by a void in their lives which might never be filled.

One night the interpreter set us up in a café/pub. We settled in for a big session and greeted the locals, who came in waves to thank us for our work and buy us drinks. I suppose it should have been humbling, but we didn't think like that at the time. Before long, the pub had run out of Slivovitz. This predicament simply had to be resolved!

A man who, we had learnt, was a member of the Serbian militia stood up, putting out his cigarette in an ashtray on his table as he did so, and said something in Serbian.

'He has some bottles back at his place,' explained the interpreter. 'He asks if anyone can go with him to get them?'

I volunteered and was soon being chauffeured back to his place on the back of his tractor. After a few minutes, I tapped him on the shoulder and intimated that I would like to have a go at driving it. He nodded, pulled over, and pointed to the buttons I would need.

We swapped places and I manoeuvred the vehicle just fine, following the direction of this man's hands as he indicated turnings. All this despite being a bit woolly with the alcohol! I even worked out that there were minefields either side of the road we were on. That kind of cleared the brain!

I was concentrating on keeping the tractor on the road, avoiding the piles of snow that had collected along the side, not wishing to wander inadvertently into fields whose crops would turn us into a mangled crush of metal and bone, when the barrel of a gun was thrust into the back of my head.

My mind raced. What did he want? Had I done something wrong?

I somehow continued to drive, feeling the gun fall away from my head and hit it again, according to the rhythm of the road. I asked him, in broken German, what was happening, and it took all of my concentration to work out his intentions.

I was being kidnapped.

There was only one thing for it.

I pushed my head back against the pistol. I had remembered that the trigger on some models could not strike the bullet properly if there was pressure on the barrel. Then, whilst my kidnapper's 'upper hand' was lowered and he was no doubt rethinking his strategy, I swept right, straight into a field.

He lowered the pistol, screaming, '*Meena! Meena!*' and this moment of panic gave me the chance to swing round and grab the gun. I didn't reassure him about the mines. It served my purpose to let him believe death was potentially imminent. In any case…he may have been right!

I put the pistol in my pocket, clasped my aggressor's arm, made sure he was looking at me and said, *'Ich bin dein Freund!'*

His eyes tried to focus, but the horror of what he had done, of what lay around him, buried in this field, played out in his mind.

'Ja! Ja!' was all he could manage.

I checked the pistol was out of his reach, patted his arm reassuringly and accelerated round in a huge U-turn, until we were 'safely' back on the road again. Bizarrely, we continued our journey to his place. There was, after all, a pub full of people relying on us…returning empty-handed might be more dangerous than my current situation!

The man did apologise. He spent the rest of the journey apologising, in fact. I worked out that it was all about money: five marks was all he received in wages a month. This was simply not enough. I nodded and showed that I understood, but I was on high alert. If he tried anything again, I would knock him out.

His place was an open-plan barn. Inside, he flicked a switch and the place was flooded with lights of every colour, dancing over the walls, looking for the crowds of people who used to join them before the war made music and fun a memory.

The Slivovitz was behind the bar. We dragged it out and piled a couple of boxes of the stuff onto the tractor before reverting the barn to darkness again. Maybe his business would be vibrant again soon.

As you can imagine, I let him drive back to the pub.

The Slivovitz was well received, injecting some more party atmosphere. My attacker and I mingled as if nothing had happened, but the whole incident infused the evening with menace and uncertainty. I told Socks what had happened and we decided to hold back on the drink so we would be able to keep an eye on things and act if necessary.

I went over to the guy who had just had a gun against my

head. I managed to communicate, through body language, German and Serbian, that we were one and the same, brothers-in-arms, that we could offer British friendship. I assured him that I would inform the chain of command back at base and try to get aid agencies to support him.

The evening was pleasant enough, but I was glad when we left.

We went back to the house of one of the locals, a farmhouse, where there was more Slivovitz. They had three rooms. The family slept in one of these rooms, Socks got the one with the kitchen and settee all to himself, as he was our commander, and the rest of us were gifted one room and a huge bed, with a picture of one of the ugliest women I had ever seen on the wall.

I muttered, 'That's you, Mo!' as I flung myself onto the bed. I was exhausted. Near-death experiences and copious amounts of Slivovitz have that effect.

Despite holding back from drinking the night before, my head still felt as if it was being hit repeatedly by a hammer the next morning. We were all starting to stir, making various pitiful noises as our hangovers kicked in, when the owner of the house opened the door. 'Breakfast?'

Gilly didn't hesitate. 'Yes, please!'

'No, thank you!' I said. The others agreed. Our host nodded and left.

'Why on earth did you lot turn down breakfast?' Gilly was astounded.

Two minutes later, he understood why, when his breakfast arrived.

More Slivovitz! And he had to drink it!

When we had stopped grinning at poor Gilly, we all went outside to wash at the pumps in the yard. We splashed our faces and refilled our water bottles. We cooked our boil-in-the-bag breakfasts on a hexy. And then we set off to retrieve the Warrior and the interpreter. When the vehicle arrived, I asked Cary, the APC Commander, for a few ration packs to offer our host family. Payment made and gratefully received, I asked if I could use the toilet before we left. I needed a shit, so the usual wall or bush would not do.

Oh man!!!

The toilet was basically a shack. Inside was a plank with a hole in it and a pile of sawdust for wiping your arse. The stench was overwhelming! I was about to do what I had to do and get out, using only shallow breaths, when a faint noise I had noticed on entry became suddenly very loud.

I looked through the hole in the plank and saw the cause of the racket.

Pigs! They kept a pig pen underneath! They were walking around snuffling, disturbing flies on days' worth of shit. It really was the most disgusting toilet I had ever seen…and that was quite the claim!

Chapter 9

It was a relief to be going back to Banja Luka after all this, but my sentiments were short-lived, as the news filtered through to me that Edward had died. Apparently the cancer had spread to the tube to his other lung but the treatment hadn't come quickly enough.

Tina was naturally devastated and all I could think about was getting back to her. I spoke to the Adjutant, the Commanding Officer's right-hand man.

'No, Neil. You can't go home. You're not really entitled as he was only your father-in-law.'

On hearing this, I simply walked away from him, muttering, 'Whatever!' and went to see Cary and Youngy (Corporal Young). I told them the Adjutant had refused permission for leave. I explained about Tina, that we had a baby only a few months old. They promised to sort things out for me. Meanwhile, back in the UK, Edward's family were asking the LI for help and the right people were reached.

I was allowed a week's leave, excluding travel time, five days, which I saved for the funeral.

Tina was driven by her Uncle Michael to meet me off the plane. She was devastated. I hugged her tightly, aware that I was filthy and must have stunk, for lack of decent showers and washing facilities. She cried all the way home, telling me what had happened, as I held her in the back of the car.

A few days earlier she had left the UK and driven back to Paderborn with Ben. She wanted to prepare the flat for my return from Bosnia and get back into a routine at our home. The journey had been long: UK, ferry, Belgium, Holland, Germany. All this with a four-month-old baby! She had almost run out of diesel and had had to reroute to avoid the motorway and get to a Shell garage, as a breakdown of any kind on the autobahns invoked a hefty fine.

She arrived in our flat at around 2am and had a few hours of rest and time to get some food from the supermarket before the phone call from the Families' Officer. Tina learnt that Edward's health had plummeted suddenly and he was about to die. She had to get to him.

The compassionate care in the British Army is amazing and this was proven that day. Tina was told to pack a bag and be ready to go in 15 minutes.

By the time the call had ended, the car was waiting for her. She had dressed and checked the bag she had not yet unpacked, then she and Ben were whisked to Hannover airport, where a flight had been delayed for them to board. They were driven to the foot of the plane's stairs and escorted on board. The other passengers stared. Who was this person?

On arrival in Heathrow, the passengers were asked to wait until Mrs Obbard had disembarked. Tina collected her things, picked up Ben and descended the stairs, climbing into the back of the car that was to speed her to her father's bedside.

The driver parked up at the hospital and helped Tina out. She started to thank him, but he interrupted her. 'My job is not to leave you!' So he came into the ICU with her.

There, Tina was told that babies and bags were not allowed. The driver explained the whole situation and she was allowed to leave the bags at reception and take Ben inside, as long as he didn't go onto Edward's room. Tina's sister Anne was informed of Tina's arrival, much to her surprise! Once Sally and her husband arrived, the driver left. Job done.

Tina saw her dad, but he never came round or spoke again. She made sure Ben was looked after, but spent Edward's last days reading to him about mundane things, like the changing style of number plates. It didn't matter; she just didn't want him to be alone, wanted him to know she was there.

He died on Thursday, 7th March 1996, ripping the heart out of the family.

'The last thing he said to me, Neil, before I left for Germany, was "Our Tine, the army will look after you!"'

The inquest implied he had died due to smoking, suggested a heart attack, and confirmed it was pneumonia, but suspicions built up inside us about paracetamol poisoning, health service failings.... The anger bubbled inside me. Edward's death, I was convinced, could have been avoided. I felt his loss acutely, felt Tina's desperation. I felt helpless, wanted to fight, but Edith wanted to let him go peacefully, to accept what had happened and not drag out the anguish to unreliable conclusions.

The funeral was at Neenton Church. Tina had found some civilian clothes for me to wear whilst on leave – black jeans – in a charity shop and I scrubbed myself up. Mark, Edward's brother, was the Quartermaster for 5LI. He issued me with no. 2s, all tailored to my size, for the funeral, so I could be at my best for Tina's dad. I even put aside my contempt for the church to honour Edward and to prop up my distraught wife as she said goodbye to her father.

They stopped writing down the names of the congregation at 500. The church was bursting with people who loved Edward. So was the graveyard; we had to put speakers up outside so everyone could hear the service. Coachloads came and filled the fields, the pub car park.

It was a lovely, casual service. Afterwards we drank to Edward at the Pheasant Pub, opposite the church, all of us devastated by our loss, no one quite believing he was gone forever. He was known for being a fantastic family man, an amazing soldier, an all-round great guy, and we will always miss him. For Tina, he was just the best dad; for me, a kindred spirit.

I spent the rest of my leave learning to feed Ben, now that he was no longer being breast-fed. He was a robust child, his health contrasting with my own gaunt and tired expression. It did me good to be in the role of father and carer again, just for a few days, before my final stint in Bosnia.

For the few weeks between my compassionate leave and leaving Bosnia for good, I spent my time milling around on patrols. It was mainly uneventful.

In the spring of 1996, I left Bosnia and returned to Tina. I had a month's post-op leave, which I spent visiting my parents, my Nan O and Granddad Obbard, and my uncle in South Germany. Tina and I rebuilt our routine and life, adjusting to our loss and enjoying Ben's development, his laughter filling spaces where sadness might otherwise find a place.

In spite of all this, part of my routine was drink and part of my routine was fits of rage, where I drove my fist into walls. When I was drunk or my knuckles were bleeding, the feelings didn't come, the visions didn't come.

I didn't feel like a worthless child, or a man lost in a sea of corpses.

Chapter 10

I was recommended for the NCO Cardre Course, designed to enhance leadership skills. This meant six weeks in Sennelager Camp, 300 metres from my flat. I only bridged that gap a few times, sneaking out of the back gate when I could get away with it.

There were over 70 of us, including, thankfully, Wardy. We were engaged in a series of courses such as PT, pedagogy, supervision, and the qualities of an instructor, to name but a few. All of these aimed to promote our strategic thinking at least one or two levels through CMADE: our confidence, manner, attitude, diligence and enthusiasm.

I entered into all the courses with a determination to do well, but it didn't quite work out like that. At some point, probably when running, I had damaged my knee and it had swollen up out of all proportion, the pain almost unbearable. Mick the Mad Medic had given me painkillers but the discomfort took hold and caused my concentration to lapse.

Richie, who was one of the instructors, had a word. 'Neil! Liven up, mate! You need to push yourself a bit more…you can do better than this!'

I had done two weeks of the course and didn't want to jack it in or let myself down, so I dredged up all my stamina and learnt how to whip up some more.

The summer heat mixed with the strength of the drugs made life almost impossible. I was almost too tired to keep popping the pills, and the stomach upset they caused led to greater dehydration issues.

Out on exercise, after a day-long route march, I was due to stag on. We had already created shell scrapes and dug holes up to our waists and the length of a man and his kit. We had positioned our bashas next to these holes and cleared a track between them, forming a triangle, with the HQ in the centre and stag on positions set at the three corners. Along the tracks was 'comms cord', basically a length of green string to guide us in the dark.

Arriving for my first stag on, my partner took one look at me and told me to get my head down; he would cover for me. We did two hours stag on, overlapping so that one of us was always fresh. When my first partner was relieved and I still had another hour to go, his replacement woke me up.

'Where am I?'

I'd wandered off down a track and was found an hour later, flat on my face in the middle of it. I had fallen asleep whilst walking, and was so out of it that the fall to the ground hadn't woken me.

The next person to stag on was late, probably complaining his sleeping bag zip was bust or he needed a couple of minutes more sleep or some other attempt to cling onto a few more minutes' rest. I had been on stag on, in body at least. Now I collapsed into my shell scrape and knew nothing else until the next day.

The course continued and, remarkably, so did I. I was either doped up or in agony, but I did everything that was asked of me, even repeatedly circling the 'Ring of Death', a tedious route used as a punishment for someone's cock-up or just on an instructor's whim. All part of the tests.

Wardy left to transfer his badge, move to another regiment, as he 'couldn't be arsed'. The course passed, I had a month's leave and my knee had the chance to get better.

Chapter 11

Newly commissioned, I transferred to B Company and made a start on my Northern Ireland training. We had known NI was on the cards after Bosnia.

The Light Infantry had supposedly done more tours than anyone else in the history of Northern Ireland and had actually been the first regiment in, so it felt natural to be going. In training we learnt all about the turbulent history of this corner of the world and undertook exercises in preparation for 'worst case scenarios' when out there.

Could it be any more traumatic than Bosnia?

On Sennelager camp stood 'Tin City', a town built to practise urban warfare, essentially just for NI. Most of the houses were just facades, but some were fully furnished houses. As NCO, I had to practise leading a team, learning things like the Rules of Engagement. Lives would depend on my decisions and I didn't take that lightly. On these exercises, other units took on the role of citizens, but there were also dummies connected up to microphones.

The IRA's habit of sending proxy bombs to the barracks also had to be addressed. They might take a man's family hostage until he drove into the barracks bound into a vehicle rigged with a bomb. Upon arrival, he would be offered something with which to extract himself from the vehicle and shown a clearing to drive into, where detonation would cause minimum damage to everyone else.

Bomb-making was another of the IRA's crafts. Fertiliser above 27% nitrate was illegal over there, but IEDs, or Improvised Explosive Devices, could still be easily manufactured and placed on our cars or used in mortars, due to the ease with which sugar, fuel oil and other ingredients could be purchased.

We would be patrolling around Belfast and would need to be sensitive to even subtle changes which might mean an incident was about to occur. These were called Combat Indicators and included the absence of children playing in the street, a bin out when it was not bin collection day, a window open on a cold day.... I was selected for Search Training, which was a privilege and extremely interesting. The Royal Engineers trained us to search all urban locations. We compared blueprints to the real buildings, checking for discrepancies in the measurements, which might mean a false wall had been added. Fibre-optics were an advanced tool for this time, but we used them to examine cars, drilling a hole and exploring its insides.

Most fun of all was the riot training.

To make it realistic, the riots came from nowhere. Wham! I suppose my impromptu fights in nightclubs must have helped to an extent, but here, even in training, they used real rubber bullets, real petrol bombs. At any point we could have been badly injured, and this tends to concentrate the mind!

In the blink of an eye a small army of men appeared with trolley loads of missiles, such as bricks, firebombs and petrol bombs, which they proceeded to launch at us. One of each team was trained to use the baton gun, responsible for propelling huge, solid rubber bullets into some poor soul.

And we had to react, protecting ourselves and working strategically to end the situation in our favour and gain intelligence to prevent further attacks.

The commander analysed the make-up of the attackers and pinpointed the ringleader, unless he had been informed of this by intelligence. A 'snatch squad' of four to six men stood ready to run out and grab this person the next time the attackers withdrew under our fire. The snatched enemy would then be handed over to the RUC for questioning.

Our uniform for such events was like something out of a Robocop film, accessorized by leather gloves, shin and elbow pads, forearm guards and our rifle and webbing on our back. We also had a shield, either 3ft or 6ft, and 2ft of blue piping.

Heavy stuff! I pitied the poor guys who were charged with carrying the fire extinguishers in amongst us.

The exercises were set up to feel real and so we acted for real, which meant leathering the attackers, hammering their hands with the pipes when they pulled down our shields. I didn't care that I was hurting my comrades. It was 'them or us' and they made it their mission to really hurt us.

Procedures in Northern Ireland had to be strictly adhered to. Our relationship to the police under the Northern Ireland Emergency Powers Act was set out in training and it was in our best interests to understand our limitations and the balance of responsibility.

We were issued with 'Gold Cards', which gave our unit's details as well as how to claim if any damage was caused by us in the course of duty. Person checks were covered. We should ask for the name and date of birth of anyone found in the area of a specific incident, and detain them if they refused to give this information. We would also have the right to run plate checks on cars.

In Belfast we would function out of RUC stations and also army barracks as part of our patrol. The immediate vicinity of these bases would be highly dangerous and we would need to be clear of the first couple of hundred metres or so as quickly as possible, which meant pelting out or back in. Our lives could quite literally depend on it.

If an incident occurred, there was a strategy in place to deal with it.

As we moved around, we worked in multiple teams. I was the team leader on one of three teams. Above us was the multiple team commander, who usually worked within the middle time of the three.

Let's say a sniper shoots from a window.

We locate the source and move into position to seal the block the sniper is in. My team fans round to one side, the furthest team to the other, and we meet around the back whilst the middle team seals the front.

Bingo! We have created a 'Tarmac Island', allowing the

RUC to enter the block and locate the sniper, who has been unable to escape.

Often we worked alone, but ghosting teams, teams that shadowed our movements, were not uncommon. They followed behind us. Once sealed, we sent for the SOCOS (scenes of crimes officers), the RMP (Royal Military Police) and the dogs (four-legged creatures, good at sniffing out criminals).

On entering the house or its neighbour, if the sniper had moved into there, the first job was to turn off the washing machine, just in case any evidence was being washed away. The RUC then removed the washing machine for analysis before bagging and tagging the suspect in white suits, ensuring all trace evidence was protected. Once the evidence was secure, out came the plasticuffs and our suspected sniper was unable to move his hands at all.

As a sniper, I was especially interested in learning to work and liaise with COP – Close Observation Platoon. These could observe a house from that house's own garden without detection (Oldy used to sit and play cards in a hide!) and their appearance out of nowhere was always a distinct possibility in the field.

The whole unit moved to Northern Ireland in Christmas leave 1996. A team of professional movers swept into our flat in Paderborn, packed everything away, labeled boxes and went. It all reappeared in 59 St David's Close, a two-bedroomed house in the married quarters opposite the motor transport park and just up the road from the swimming pool.

I am not pretending that things were really bad in Belfast at this time, but we still needed to be vigilant. Car bombs were not yet consigned to history, so Tina and I got into the habit of checking under our car for telltale signs someone was trying to murder us.

My first role upon arrival was to take over from the Royal Anglicans, basing ourselves temporarily in the MPH-Musgrave Park Hospital, and patrolling for them whilst they had a break. We were the permanent resident battalion and relieving more temporary battalions was part of our role.

The Commanding Officer told us to go out as much as possible to get to know the area of responsibility: Belfast. This would make the coming months easier when we embarked upon our four-month rota, one month each to be spent on Ops Company, Shadow Company, Guard Duty and R&R/Training.

Early on in my first month there, I was out and about in Belfast, still functioning from the hospital, when I saw a firing pack, or what looked like it. I drew it, noted where I had found it and handed over the information to the Intelligence Officers. Nothing appeared to happen, or at least I was not kept in the loop if it did. Shortly afterwards, however, there was a mortar attack against one of our patrols and I couldn't help wondering if that firing pack was at the heart of the incident. The whole thing had misfired, breaking up without causing any real damage, which always raised questions about sabotage. There were so many variables, you couldn't trust your own instincts. The more time I spent there, the more suggestions of agents and double agents came my way. There was even talk of soldiers selling to the IRA, usually for money, not out of political conviction.

Of course, this kind of thing should be taken with a pinch of salt. Maybe we had all watched too many thrillers in our youth. Back in the real world, Labour won the election and the Peace Process started to take real hold, led by Mo Mowlam.

Chapter 12

We slipped into a cycle of month-long guard duties at the barracks, which may have served to protect us, but they also exhausted us. Now a Lance Corporal, my cross was lighter in some areas and heavier in others. I had more responsibility in general and, as 2i/c, I was responsible for signing for the equipment such as torches, batteries and anything needed for ECM, Electronic Counter Measures. The latter served to block the frequency of RCIEDS – Remote Control Improvised Explosive Devices. The 'White Sifter' could block frequencies in a wide area, regardless of whether they were bombs or Republican televisions.

Despite our appreciation of the Republicans' fight, some of them were trying to kill us, and, if all we could do was block a few TVs from time to time, we did.

Thus we won hearts and minds.

Guard duty took place in 'sangars', fortified positions housing one or two men. They were situated all around the edge of the barracks. Their role was to keep the camp safe. Two on duty together meant one could provide cover for the other when there was a drive-by shooting, radioing information about the vehicle and so on. There was also a sangar across the road in the married quarters, always popular with single men, who took it in turns to do their actual job, whilst one of them was serviced by some local girls inside the sangar – the so-called 'Sangar Bangers'.

'Neil? About that rota…'

I told them I would do what I could to get them laid. I suppose it helped pass the time! 24 hours on duty gave you a lot of time for tedium, and who was I to stand in the way of a few comforts? After all, we spent 24 hours on, 24 or 48 hours off, and 'off' would mean still on duty, just not on guard!

My personal guard duty was relieved only by a few hours on a plastic mattress, surrounded by eleven men on eleven other plastic mattresses. All of us slept in the guardroom, fully clothed, our rifles disassembled by our sides, set out ready for a quick assembly, bullets ready to load. We were ready, if we needed to be.

We couldn't really complain. Our tour was quiet compared to those of many of our former comrades. We were trained to deal with any eventuality, including mortar attacks on the camp and relatives of hostages rolling into camp wired to a bomb. We were trained to a level made possible only by others' mistakes, others' deaths. We were lucky enough not to face as much as our predecessors.

One thing everyone on tour in Northern Ireland witnessed was the marching season. This is when parades or walks take place to commemorate historic battles and re-establish the sense of self-worth the communities in Northern Ireland have. The Orange marches are the most widespread. Some of these 'walks' are contentious, stirring up sentiments of animosity and distrust, everyone watching for that toe over the line, that sign that ground has been won by them at your own cost.

Belfast was already sectioned, reminiscent of Palestine. Walls had risen up to divide the city; the Royal Ulster Constabulary had thrown up cordons to control the movement of the population, to create diversions and detours, to prevent those disturbed by the walks from interfering with them, like a match to dried wood.

In the marching season, every company was on one-hour NTM: Notice to Move. In other words, we had to be ready to act, fully armed, within that set time. All three companies, the support company and HQ were on standby. If we were not directly on duty, we had to be within one hour of it.

We were prisoners to the cause.

Sometimes I spent all night geared up, waiting with a Saxon, a mechanized troop carrier whose sides opened out to protect us whilst creating a threatening image to our threats. Heading into a riot or crowds of Republicans, armoured up with shields, we walked behind the Saxon's wings or at the side of the Saxon, on the tip of the wings. It all depended on the width of the streets.

We were on constant high alert but were not allowed to bang our shields, as this riled the crowd. Instead, we walked steadily, hearts thumping, brains racing, often towards a riot which would claim our time for up to 24 hours.

I had nothing against the Republicans apart from their desire to take me down, and I was the Loyalists' friend only because they *didn't* want to take me down. To have all this aggro based on religion seemed a waste of energy and lives to me, but here I was, a pawn in the war.

Riots were a day's work for us and the RUC. Don't get me wrong, it was definitely a bad day, but we just got on with it.

Typically, we headed towards the sea of angry faces, flicking glances up at windows, down alleys, waiting for that first engagement. The protective gear was heavy and uncomfortable. Combat 95s, they were called, or '1995s' after the year we would have received them, had someone somewhere been able to fulfil the order. It was mildly fireproof, so we were advised to wear our Temperate Combats, which were an older version, or at least wear long johns underneath, for a spot of extra protection. The layers might have been welcome in that Bosnian winter, but, along with the shield I had to carry and my visor, they made me sweat.

The sky would turn black, like some kind of apocalyptic weather system. There was a second when we were suspended between not knowing and knowing, before we braced ourselves for the rain.

It rained missiles. Darts, scissors wired open, bricks, stones, slabs, dirty hypodermic needles, anything that could be lifted and thrown to cause maximum damage. Most of these improvised weapons could cause as much harm as a bullet.

Then came the firebombs. These crashed onto our shields or the ground between us most of the time. They flared up, burning the petrol as well as the sugar inside them, creating another hazard for us as we needed to get past the flames and extinguish the homemade Napalm on our shields or even our boots. Luckily our best friends in these line-ups were those men with the fire extinguishers, always on hand to handle the flames. If any of us was burnt or seriously injured by a missile, we withdrew for treatment. Otherwise we got on with it.

We spent hours like this. Attack, defence, avoiding injury, dealing with injuries, watching each other's backs. Every time I was determined I would make it through, and that one thought, that one basic aim, became my mantra. I needed to survive for Tina and Ben.

Occasionally a rioter would break their line and spray bullets from an AK47 before being sucked back into his crowd again. Unlike today's terrorists, they didn't want to get caught.

As with any workday, we needed a break, needed to revitalise ourselves. The RUC had eight-hour shifts and it was not unheard of for them to actually hand over their shifts in the riots, whereas we went on for over 24 hours if necessary. I have huge admiration for the RUC as they were enormously professional.

When there was a lull in proceedings, we pulled back for a few minutes to grab a Haver Bag from a box. Its contents varied little and they were usually crushed, wet or melted, their packaging broken and mainly the cheapest brand on the market: pasties, crisps, KitKats or Penguins. Worst of all was the drink: 250ml of 'Vitazade', which came in unnatural colours and worse flavours. Bright blue bubble gum? We got calories but no nutritional value whatsoever!

Haver soon became Horror in our vocabulary.

Norgie flasks were available, spewing out hot tea. Even in a riot you need a few minutes for tea and a fag.

At the end of the fun day out, we might get wraps, or be encouraged to go back to the cookhouse for an Egg Banjo and another mug of tea. This is where we stocked up ahead of a call-out and replenished afterwards.

There was added excitement to camp life when the King's

Regiment did a short tour with us. We were residents, permanent, but up until the Peace Process started in earnest, others did a more temporary stint around the marching season. On the occasion of our first season, it was the 'Kingos' who turned up. They stayed in the 'Bubble Gym' – a sort of polythene aircraft hangar.

'Watch your stuff!' Ash, B Company Sergeant Major, told us. 'Hide f**king everything! The bloody scousers!'

There was a kind of fun you get in regiments of the army that the Kingos were particularly fond of and especially good at. You steal stuff from other regiments as some kind of trophy and wear/carry it like a badge of honour. They even went out of their way to sleep with the wives of men in other regiments, who were on tour, carefully placing their calling card in the husband's mess dress uniform pocket before leaving the quarters. 'Your wife has been serviced by a member of the "insert as applicable" Regiment'. This happened whenever regiments served together.

It was full-on banter with them and we tried to give as good as we got.

Until some of them were hit by a drive-by shooting and the mood changed.

You could move around Belfast and feel the atmosphere alter as quickly as the street names. Anywhere blatantly Republican was avoided, unless there was trouble: the so-called no-go areas. Obviously we felt safer and more welcome in the Loyalist areas, but both had terrorist elements, there was no doubt of that. Whether anyone in the British Army turned a blind eye where the Loyalists are concerned, I don't know. I was glad to see the Peace Process start to unfurl, for the sake of the people living there as much as for myself. One step in this delicate programme was the abolition of the six-month tour. This meant more duties for us, tasked by HQNI Lisburn, and I saw even less of Tina and Ben. A constant concern was their safety; a constant nightmare was Tina being blown up in my car. We had to check it every time we used it, dropping our keys so it didn't look obvious. Ben had started to check under it, announcing, 'No bombs, Mummy! All okay today!'

Northern Ireland is a beautiful place. I barely saw Tina and Ben – my 80-90 hour weeks saw to that – but when we could, we unwound on the Giant's Causeway or Crawfordsburn County Park, Bushmill's Distillery, Port Rushmore, Port Stewart…. All such fantastic places, but it is hard to appreciate all this when you are under threat from people who see you as the occupier.

I even visited White Park Bay. It was just like in the photos of the Empire Youth Manual.

It had not changed.

But I had.

A lot.

I did not discuss my memories with Tina. When they rose up and swirled around my head, I pushed them back down inside me with the others. They settled in.

This was a mistake.

During the years in NI, I visited a few of the RUC stations, often using them as a base. One of these was New Barnsley Police Station, which held the record for the most attacked police station in the world. It was basically a couple of portacabins behind a huge corrugated iron fence.

I wandered out of the station to start a patrol with probably around eleven others, taking time to admire the mural on the wall opposite. Both Republicans and Loyalists had nurtured the most incredible artists and this particular mural was one of the most impressive. However, as we paused to look, a woman started banging a dustbin lid on the pavement, warning who-knows-who that there were soldiers about.

'Front up!' yelled the Platoon Commander.

I had allowed myself a few minutes on artwork, in awe of the talent displayed in front of me. I hadn't seen the small group, men and children and all between, marching straight towards us, grim-faced. But I did see the swarms of them pouring into the main thoroughfare from side roads, up to fifty or so at a time.

I stopped counting at about three hundred.

By now we had grouped more closely together, moving backwards, away from our aggressors, without taking our eyes off them. However tempting it was to fight back, we had been instructed only to fight if we were in danger of death.

Then came the missiles, mainly stones this time, but our patrol uniform was very different to our riot gear and the soft berets designed to make our presence appear less militant gave us little protection. The stones fell between us as we reached the haven that was New Barnsley Police Station, and we sheltered outside, near the fence, under a corrugated overhang.

We had a few minutes drinking tea and smoking fags until the noise of stones on the iron shelter faded; then we went out again and recommenced our patrol through emptier streets.

Another time, I was the commander of a small group of about four, leaving Fort Whiterock onto the Kennedy Road. We were passing a pub when its doors opened, allowing the sound of laughter and heated debate and calls for more beer to float into the midnight air.

Unfortunately for us, the men leaving the pub were sufficiently tanked up to start something.

'Soldiers!' they yelled, their battle cry alerting everyone in the pub behind them.

British soldiers as entertainment at the end of an evening? Great!

We slipped quickly into a nearby alley before a load of alcohol-fuelled Republicans could scramble and get to us. But it was a dead end, unless you counted the 12-foot wall, topped with Ulster railings, whose spikes and barbs had been designed to shred your flesh.

'Front up!' I cried, and we looked to the mouth of the alley, which was filling with angry men made braver by beer. We cocked our rifles and stepped back, ready.

We reached a stand-off. They had numbers, we had firepower. I stepped forward.

'Look, guys, we all want to go home tonight, don't we? You can get us, for sure, but before then, we can easily manage to get 25-30 of you...which 25 or 30?'

I paused long enough to hear the nervous breathing of my team, their bodies taut, rifles ready to choose the men they would kill in order to survive. The crowd swayed threateningly, blocking our way to freedom. Some of them still held their glasses or bottles; otherwise their weapons would have to be boots or fists. One man held out his arms, as if restraining them. I didn't recognise him as a known player. Nevertheless, with so many, this would not end well.

I looked at the man whose body language labeled him the ringleader, pointed to the opposite direction to the pub and said, 'Why don't we go that way and you go the other. That way we all get to go home, don't we?'

I hoped this would work, that my words and logic would permeate his drunken state. This could go either way.

He raised his hands.

He was going to point at us, order a charge…! I gripped my rifle harder.

But it was alright. His voice rose. His entourage joined in.

He was simply conducting a Republican song. They ambled away, singing heartily, as if they had single-handedly beaten the whole British Army. I signaled my team to leave and I followed, covering their backs. We ran off, sustaining no greater injury than sore feet.

This was just one of many close calls which chipped away at me.

Some terrorists did not limit their criminal activities to fighting the cause. They formed crime syndicates, demanding protection money from drug dealers or demanding sole distribution rights, exacting punishments on the community for indiscretions such as joyriding or even just 'mouthing off' to a certain family. The sentence included knee-capping, delivered with a .22 caliber. Republicans turned children into spies, sending them out to play, to count soldiers and monitor equipment, find patterns in patrols. This was 'dicking'.

One of our jobs was to accompany the RUC on patrol in Snatch Land Rovers, designed especially for NI but also used in Iraq later. This came under MACP – Military Aid to the Civil

Power. We didn't mind this. These guys were proper heroes, and they would have to live here long after we had gone.

Chasing joyriders was one fun activity, if they hadn't already been caught by the 'community police'. If we caught them we would smash into them, a wonderful example of the RUC and British Army working together.

With all this summary justice going on, it does make you wonder why anyone would go joyriding!

Our vehicle patrol became fun in a different way in the Orange Suffolks. These were two Loyalist streets in the middle of a Republican area, hugely dangerous, protected by an RUC station nearby. Here, we found that shining our vehicle spotlights up at the windows at night yielded results as we were treated to a proper morale boost in the form of naked women.

When out on patrol like this, we relied heavily on our driver. One particular night our driver was a heavy smoker and useless to boot. He simply couldn't do his job. He wasn't reacting quickly enough, couldn't work out directions. This was unacceptable in a Republican area.

So I punched him and told him to sort his life out.

I did report my actions, more to get him dealt with than to absolve my own wrongdoings. I didn't actually see anything wrong in my own behaviour, I just respected the army's need to know in certain cases. Like when I found someone asleep in a sangar and pushed them down the stairs. Okay, I threw them down a ladder, but I did report it and, on that occasion, admitted I had been a 'bit rough'.

These things happened.

My code extended to protecting others if they had not done anything which endangered others or caused harm. James Stanley, for instance.

James used to go out on the pull, telling everyone he was a chef, as this was far less contentious than being a soldier in the British Army and less likely to get you killed.

One night James came in late. He had been dropped off outside the barracks by the RUC. He was visibly shaken.

'I might get done!'

'Why?' My mind was racing. What on earth had happened?
'I pulled a girl, went back to hers...'

So far so good, I thought.

'I woke up and realised I was in a Republican area. F**king flags everywhere! You have never seen anyone get dressed as quickly or as quietly as me! I got out, flagged down an RUC vehicle and here I am!'

He didn't know if it had been a potential 'honey trap' or an unlucky coincidence. Had he escaped an attack on his life just in time? Had the woman even known he was British Army?

The next day the Guard Commander asked James why he had been dropped off by the RUC and promptly bubbled him to the OC, which I would never have done.

The autumn of 1997 offered me and Tina a break from Belfast. Tina went to her mum's and took time out to visit Granddad Hayes, who was so ill he needed to go into a home. I undertook three months of Corporal training on the Brecon Beacons, whilst still having to do guard duty in the evenings and at the weekends. The course was basically a battle camp where we were trained in Skills at Arms and tactics. The idea was to be able to teach all the skills, elevating ourselves to full instructor status.

I soon knew all there was to know about a range of weapons, including, crucially, the H&S issues: GPMG, 94, SA80 and Browning 9mm. I sat through every lesson, analysing the pedagogy, seating formations, structure etc. Homework was to prepare three or four lessons, one of which would have to be performed the next day. As we didn't know which, we hedged our bets and hoped for the best.

As usual, teamwork played a great part. When we had to display knowledge by repeating paragraphs word for word, we mouthed it to one another when our memory failed us. However, the sight of my team's jaws and tongues twisting comically as they tried to communicate some word or phrase tickled me! I nearly always missed something out.

The SASC critiqued our lessons. We did call them the Shit and Shovel Corp, but their real name was the Small Arms School Corps. They knew their shit, were good people.

The course was excellent. I learnt how to teach people in the field, run a range with all its safety precautions, oversee safe firing by checking there was no overlap in the permitted 570-mils range, deal with safety staff in the butts (where the targets are), pulley systems, grenade ranges. We covered everything as a body (soldier), instructor and safety staff.

For the second part of the course, Tactics, we were in the field virtually every day, with the odd day of theory on, for example, the orders process.

We practised section attacks and being in command of these and of the fire team. We were assessed permanently, taking on the role of 2i/c, section commander, platoon sergeant, platoon commander and so on. We had every perspective, so that we could take the place of up to two ranks higher in battle, if necessary. This is something the British Army is good at.

The course, which attracted all kinds of soldier, including SAS, was physically and mentally demanding. It offered no respite whatsoever. The Brecon Beacons in winter made the NAVEX (navigation at night) section particularly challenging. Sennybridge seemed to have its own weather system, a whole level worse than the usual fog and rain for this area, and, we understood, potentially murderous.

I passed.

Not bad for a scrawny lad from Bridgnorth.

When back in Northern Ireland, I spent quite a lot of time based at Girdwood Barracks, a mortar-hardened accommodation just off the Crumlin Road. Fifteen of us often slept in a tiny room in bunk beds. It was so cramped we had to sleep with our kits and with our heads turned sideways. It stank for lack of windows. From here we were patrolling the Clonards, row upon row of boarded-up houses, when a bomb went off and moved the earth so much that houses shook in their foundations.

I ran to kneel behind a wall, rifle ready, awaiting the gunman that usually followed such an attack. As I waited, poised, a billowing shadow fell across me.

'You need to leave.'

I looked up. It was a Catholic priest. I had found myself in a church's car park.

'I think there's a gunman around. I'm only here until it's all clear.' I repositioned myself to see through the sights.

'Son, this is holy ground!'

I could not believe my ears! He was actually turfing me off church property, risking my life! The hypocrisy!

I had an idea.

I crossed myself, touching my shoulders, forehead and chest quickly.

The priest's voice softened. 'Are you a Catholic?'

I nodded.

He let me stay.

Bloody hypocrite. Bloody church.

I didn't think it was a load of 'pup' any more. It was a load of f**king bollocks.

On the periphery of all this, the Peace Process was taking a firmer hold. And people were starting to relax a little, allowing complacency to forge errors.

The Peace Process had to work. For everyone, whatever side you were on, even for those of us caught in the crossfire. I was impatient to be finished in Belfast and keen to see peace prevail. When ministers came to Girdwood, I spoke honestly and openly to them, glad to see something real happening.

Tina and I were then invited up to Hillsborough Castle to share our views more formally. Some more soldiers of various ranks were also invited to the formal meal. Tina and I looked forward to it. Mo Mowlam was going to be there, with an entourage of several politicians. It was a night out, the chance for Tina to dress up and for us to air our strong and honest opinions on the Northern Ireland problem. I would not be barring any holds.

Hillsborough Castle is the official Residence of Her Majesty the Queen in Northern Ireland: a long, low Georgian building, with a portico as the main entrance and stunning gardens. We enjoyed a meal of several courses in an elegant dining room.

When I was approached by the great Mo Mowlam, it

was clear she was a no-nonsense woman. She suffered from cancer, and treatment, I suppose, had left her in need of a wig. I had heard that she often removed this as a sign of her transparency and honesty. She was direct and I really felt that she listened.

'If you can bring peace, fantastic!' I said. 'Personally I don't think you will get a single weapon off the IRA, and they ALL need handing in, from both sides.'

She asked me what the solution would be, in my opinion.

'Education,' I answered, without hesitation. 'The indoctrination that takes place from an early age needs to stop. That is the only way forward!'

The politicians really listened and I think we surprised them with some of our accounts of life there, such as the painted walkway in the Ardoyne, an area of Belfast, followed by anyone wishing to avoid being seen by look-outs on the towers of the local RUC station, Old Park.

'Are they really still there?' one politician asked me.

I nodded.

I had a sense that Mo Mowlam meant business, that she really wanted a lasting change and that our thoughts were being taken on board. I did learn that the eventual weapons amnesty had yielded little fruit: just a few guns from the Loyalists. Nevertheless, the Good Friday Agreement was signed on 10th April 1998 and I was proud to have been a small part in that process, even if I had not seen Ben develop and rarely saw Tina.

There was the odd bit of unpleasantness from people who had taken against me, whether I deserved it or not. Harry Johnson, the new Company Serjeant Major, was one who didn't like me.

When KAPE tours were on, where we set up stalls at fairs to 'Keep the Army in the Public Eye', Tina would sew ghillie suits.

Around this time, I had a frozen shoulder. Harry Johnson confined me to camp, following, to the letter, battalion policy. However, I was still working on camp, doing more than I would be at the fair itself. Also, greater issues were at stake.

'If I'm confined to camp, I can't get my kid's Christmas present!'

Harry informed me and the OC that it 'wasn't his f**king problem', so Tina spoke to the CO, who called Harry in and informed him it wasn't his place to confine anyone to barracks! The MO (medical officer) wrote on my sick chit 'not to be confined to barracks', which mightily peed Harry off.

'Your wife should keep her nose out of things! I don't tell her what to do!'

He was very cross indeed, so cross he was puce.

'Well,' I replied (I was ready for this one), 'I think you'll find you ARE telling her what to do! You're making a decision that affects where I go and that affects her!'

I had the last word, as usual.

Another event that both highlighted my steadfast adherence to guidelines and caused me some regret was connected to Divis Key Point.

Divis Key Point was a communications station on top of Mount Divis, a mountain overlooking Belfast. It was of such strategic importance that it had to be defended to the death. Charges had been set which, in the event of an attack, would have to be blown.

I was patrolling around it when I noticed that one of the sheds up there had been broken into. Immediately I radioed B Company HQ at Girdwood Barracks. 'There is a break-in in one of the communications sheds on Divis KP, sir!'

There was a sigh on the end of the line.

'Corporal Obbard, I am in the middle of a mortar drill!'

'But sir! I know you're in the middle of a mortar drill, but this situation is occurring now!'

'Corporal Obbard, I said I am in the middle of a mortar drill!!'

'No problem, sir! I will log the incident now!'

I did just that, as per British Army protocol.

Later, when questioned, I said I had logged the incident and that it should have been logged at the other end of the line too.

'But there was a break-in!'

'I know, sir!'

'Why didn't you tell me immediately?'

'I did, sir, but, if you remember, you were in the middle of a mortar drill. I did log it and it should have also been logged at your end. There were four of us, sir, so plenty of witnesses!'

I returned to the log book a couple of days later. I wanted to re-read my entry to check its clarity for a third party.

The log book entry had disappeared. Someone had removed it.

Grassing up and lies are bad enough, but this level of fraud by an officer undermined all my beliefs in the army. I felt I had integrity, toed the line on issues of security and protocol, and I had been undermined and would look like a liar if anyone investigated the incident.

Returning to Belfast as Local Corporal (until it was authorised by the powers that be, we had to fulfill our new rank unpaid), I was also Guard Commander. At that time there were only two section commanders or two full corporals in the company. The redeployment of so many troops elsewhere meant I was full-on: day on guard, day off guard (but still working from 8-5), with the odd evening or afternoon free.

One of my first roles as Corporal was searching cars as they entered the barracks. We chose random cars, usually letting one or two pass between those targeted for a thorough check. On my first day we had a great many contractors arriving for various jobs.

At some point, a couple of hours in, the RSM called me. 'Corporal Obbard?'

'Yes, sir?'

'The CO has just taken three quarters of an hour getting into camp. Why?'

'I am searching cars, sir.'

'Use your discretion, Corporal.'

'I am, sir. There are lots of contractors in today. I am in charge of the safety of the camp, sir! I am doing exactly what I should be doing!'

'Don't get smart with me, Corporal!'

'Okay, sir, but it's on you if the camp blows up!'

My role in this little dialogue was, apparently, unacceptable and I was awarded five extra duties.

I never did them. Not out of some sense of indignation or subversion, but because I didn't have enough hours in the day to do my usual duties, let alone five extra!

Around this time, we had a do in the Corporals' Mess and one of the NCOs took a dislike to something a waiter had done or not done and properly battered him. Not a quick punch, or a sharp kick – a proper battering.

Nothing was done to punish him. In fact, lies spilled out of people's mouths to protect him. This was way above friends helping cover up a slight indiscretion.

Was this the British Army? Was this my 'family'?

Around this time, the 1998 marching season, Granddad Hayes died, but the new Platoon Commander was a total tube and wouldn't let me have 48 hours to go home for the funeral precisely because it *was* the marching season.

It upset me that I couldn't say a proper goodbye to my granddad. I thought about his strong arms and the way he'd fed the fire at home when I was growing up.

I might have forgiven the Platoon Commander. After all, it was a busy time. What did make my faith in my superiors waver was his denial I had ever asked. That kind of lie did not sit well with me. The army was my family and this betrayal took something from that.

As my tour of Northern Ireland drew to a close, one of the Platoon Sergeants was posted out and I became Local Platoon Sergeant. I enjoyed going out and about on patrols in this role, as a multiple commander: instead of one team I had anything from two to five teams. I was in charge of the platoon during the riots and marching season, where each day was a battle to ensure all my men got home safely. I also undertook a range of different roles in barracks.

I had to introduce a new Platoon Commander, Mike Morris. He seemed a nice guy, but, until we had worked Sandhurst out of him, he would not do! The OC made sure I was aware what was needed. He was in charge on paper, but we had to nudge him to fit.

Mike had Sandhurst ideas on how the men should spend their downtime. We knew the men and how they would react and how they needed to spend their downtime, and, after a few discussions, so did Mike.

Mike liked me as I had steered him in the right direction, despite appearing brash and arrogant. He turned a blind eye to piss-ups in blocks, despite Harry Johnson saying they were not allowed.

Harry puffed himself up and came up to put a stop to our fun.

'But Mike said we could have it!'

Mike made out he didn't know Harry had said no to it and our booze-up was allowed to go ahead. This was just as well, as we were saying goodbye to a valued colleague. He needed a good send-off and steam, in general, needed to be let off. The OC bollocked Mike later but he took it in his stride.

I like to think I helped Mike be a better leader. I told him once something that had helped me: Mistakes in managing people always happen – accept it and move on. 'A mistake is evidence you have tried' was another saying I shared with him. I can't take credit for that one; I had once read it printed on a sachet of sugar!

I wasn't present at Omagh for the bombing in August 1998. I may not have questioned where our men would have stood and whether a different position would have saved lives. I didn't have those images seared on my memory, didn't have to clear up those particular bodies.

I just heard the dialogues in my earpiece, carried to me on radio waves, heard the updates, counted the casualties, ticked off the deaths, heard the strain and emotion in voices, knew that this day would never be forgotten.

Another act of violence against humanity, the effects of which radiate far more widely than imagined.

The words replayed in my head long after I had turned my radio off.

Northern Ireland was in a better state when I left, but my experiences there had chipped away at me more than I'd realised. It was time for a change.

Just around Christmas, Tina and I had decided to have another baby. Tina had fallen pregnant with Ben at once, but that was unusual. It couldn't happen twice so quickly, could it?

It could.

So, happy that we were bringing another child into our lives, Tina and I looked forward to our fresh start.

Unfortunately for me, Harry Johnson and fate had two unpleasant gifts for me.

Tina and I were looking forward to a short break, a long weekend in the Isle of Wight, squashed between Belfast and Bulford. It would mean leaving early on the Friday and all I had to do was ask Harry.

'No f**king way!'

I tried to reason with him on more than one occasion during the final week, but he was having none of it.

On the final day, after the Friday Fitness Parade in early spring 1999, I received a message from the Family Officer. He needed to see me.

Tina was in his office when I got there. My heart sank. What had happened?

'Nan Hayes died last night, Neil.'

My mind screamed 'F**k!' but outwardly I was calm. My grief was folded up with the rest of my emotions. I did not cry.

I phoned my mum to check on her. She sounded all right, considering. She even persuaded me to continue with our holiday plans.

'Are you sure, Mum?'

'Yes, Neil, I'm fine. You go!'

My next port of call was Harry Johnson.

'I need to leave…now.'

'You are going f**king nowhere! You will f**king stay here, even if you miss that f**king ferry!'

'My Nan died. I'm going!'

'I can check, you know!'

'Knock yourself out!'

I would miss my Nan, and I am sure she would have appreciated sharing that last word with me!

In March 1999, Tina and I moved to Bulford in Wiltshire. Ben was three and a half and our second child was on its way. Tina had been over, as part of the Wives' Club, to suss out the new accommodation and present to the other wives what they needed to know for a smooth transition.

In the early hours of one morning, Tina woke me up.

She was bleeding.

We phoned the midwife, who told us to go straight to Salisbury Hospital. I carried Ben to a neighbour's and off we went, Tina visibly upset.

We were told Tina had miscarried and she would need a small procedure to clear out her womb later that day.

Tina cried. I held her, would have done anything to put things right for her.

'Try and get some sleep, Tina…come on!' I encouraged her to settle down against the pillows and held her hand until she was dozing. I stayed with her until she had settled, then went home to take care of Ben.

Later that day, Tina was asked if she would mind a trainee midwife participating in a scan. Tina said no, she didn't mind at all, and they began to run the ultrasound sensor over the gel on Tina's belly.

Tina glanced at the screen, bracing herself to see our baby resting silently there.

'What is that? I can see something flutter!' The student sounded cautious.

The midwife took over, checking, measuring, watching, until finally: 'Mrs Obbard…you were carrying twins and one of them is still fighting fit!'

Obviously we were both delighted and forever in that student's debt. We returned to our lives in Bulford, relief and sadness mixed together, and awaited the arrival of our second child.

As I was only going to be stationed there for a few months before I went to ATR Winchester again, we barely unpacked and I also suggested I didn't go with the company onto the field. There was no point in the men getting used to me.

So, as the battalion had a mechanized role, I became the fleet manager. It was a welcome respite after the patrols of Northern Ireland.

I still did the fitness training with the others. My new CO was ex-SAS and we were therefore the first battalion to do the new CFT – Combat Fitness Test – undertaken with all attached personnel. It involved a 12-mile run with 44 kilos of kit in three hours. Night runs were not uncommon either.

In my downtime, I had nothing to do but fitness training. I swam, representing the regiment in galas and winning with my signature butterfly stroke. I played five-a-side football, bench-pressed 100-150 kilos and squatted 200 kilos.

Friday mornings, soldiers of all ranks participated in 'thinking runs' on Salisbury Plain, setting off at different times, staggering the race. There were stands which we had to approach in order to fulfil a task, such as repeating a fire order to an instructor on their demand, before falling in and continuing the run.

One night I was on Corporal's Duty, known as COS (officially Company Orderly Sergeant), when I heard an almighty racket from downstairs. I ran down, located the noise in one of the changing rooms and burst in.

Three guys I knew well from Northern Ireland and liked, Davey, Tom and Harvey, were jumping on top of a wooden locker, which was on its side...

...with a man underneath it, crying out in pain.

I yelled out, ran over and pushed the locker off him. I helped him to sit up. His face was smashed in, blood everywhere, swelling, the first signs of bruising.

'What the f**k?!' I asked, incredulous, eloquence evading me.

'He's a f**king knob!'

I looked more closely at the victim. It was the company

clerk. Yes...indeed he was a knob. Never sorted anything out.

'I know he's a knob! But...*this*?' I opened my hands, indicating the clerk/knob groaning from his injuries, in disbelief.

My job was to keep order, to ensure the smooth running of my team. I had seen cover-ups; I had been sickened by people getting away with attacks on others. I would not be part of any of that.

'You three go to bed. I'll sort him out.'

'What are you going to do about it?'

'Mate...I have to tell the truth.'

They were not happy. Not happy at all.

They were charged and shipped off to Colchester Military Correction Training but not put on trial until months later. I had long left but came back to testify.

They got off with it, possibly due to them having completed a form of punishment, possibly due to my evidence being a little sketchy, but at least my professional integrity was intact.

If only I could have let it wither, like others did, I might have been happier.

I certainly would have avoided some of the most challenging times of my life.

Chapter 13

My Corporal course and reputation for an easy temperament led to a recommendation for Section Commander at ATR Winchester. I didn't feel like I had an 'easy temperament' when I catalogued the aggressive incidents I had instigated, but I knew how to stay below the radar, how to push things as far as they would go without anything shattering.

The pregnancy was going well. The little fellow battled on, despite the loss of his twin.

Yes, I expected a boy again. We didn't ask for confirmation at the scans, but we never chose any girls' names, just like with Ben. Ben was always Ben and this one was always Jonathan Robert, for Tina's family name, Roberts.

I had such fun winding my mum up.

'We've chosen the name Fabian!'

'You can't do that!' (Apologies to any readers called Fabian!)

My parents and I had the relationship you would naturally expect. They visited us wherever we were stationed and we called each other up for news. My grievances about my childhood were packed away and labeled 'The Seventies'. It wasn't all bad – they had done their best as parents and, as grandparents, they were fantastic.

Generally things were good, apart from that major personality defect on my part: violent outbursts.

Occasionally Tina tried to talk to me about these, which manifested themselves in unreasonable road rage or throwing objects across the room, usually after drinking. This was now drinking every day and more and more at home, not keeping it to the pub. The wall-punching had never faded from my childhood; it was still the release of choice after I had wound myself up slowly over a period of time.

Never did I harm Tina or Ben, but she must have wondered how I would cope with the added pressure of a newborn in the house. I was not a morning person and had been away for Ben's newborn routine. How would she give me the space I seemed to need, allow me time to wake up properly, when we had a four-year-old and a new baby to look after?

I reported for duty as COS – Camp Orderly Sergeant – at ATR Winchester in the autumn of 1999, when we were heading for Tina's due date. Tina was ripe for the birth. We expected it any day and were both a little anxious after Ben's birth, which had been above average in its drama.

Before I could properly settle in with my new colleagues, I needed to be ready to drop it all and go to Tina. So, the night before the actual date, I thought it best to have a quick word with the Corporal, just to warn him.

'My wife's due date is tomorrow.'

'Yes?'

Here we go…

'I'm just saying, 'cos I might need to leave.'

'You'll still need to do your COS duty.'

'If my wife goes into labour, I am not going to stay here on COS duty! I will go!'

We left it at that. At 4am, Tina called the guard, who found me on the COS bunk.

'Your wife rang. She's in labour.' And he left.

I jumped out of bed, scrambled about for the number I needed and rang my replacement. He muttered some obscenity but ultimately came to relieve my post. I sped home, knocked on my neighbour Kev Lane's door to warn him, then carried Ben round.

Next I rang the midwife, Gill, who came to us at once. She ascertained that child number two was well on the way and we drove, in tandem, to Winchester Hospital Maternity Unit.

The highlight of Tina's room was the huge window, which faced the October sunrise. Once Tina was settled on the bed,

Gill and I turned to absorb the view, a kaleidoscope of the colours of nature, all touched by the golden hues of the rising sun.

'You can't beat that view, can you?'

'F**k the view!' screeched Tina. Needless to say, Gill and I turned round and attended Tina at once!

The birth went smoothly from then on and we found ourselves, on the 25th October 1999, with the second son I had anticipated: Jonathan Robert.

Our family was complete. We dealt with the new routines brought on by a new child, aware that Ben needed attention too as he adjusted to the new dynamics. Tina, as I had come to expect, coped brilliantly.

Or so it seemed.

We saw the year 2000 in at Worthy Down, just up the road from Winchester, at a family army do. We welcomed in the 'noughties' with enthusiasm and a dose of optimism, and I continued my work/home routine, oblivious to changes in Tina's perception of our life.

Jonathan's baptism took place the spring of the following year at St Barnabas' Church, Winchester. Much to my mum's disgust, I did not attend. Tina accepted this, as did everyone else. There was no point trying to change me; I was a law unto myself. Nowadays I was more upfront with my parents. I thought they were excellent grandparents, I really did, but they could like me or lump me. I didn't care. I certainly wasn't going to wear clothes I wasn't comfortable in and stand in front of a man dressed in a frock, promising nonsense to an imaginary being who had done nothing for me.

I stayed at home and prepared the food. The only picture we had of Ben on his christening day was in my arms, me sporting my Tic Tac T-shirt. We made sure there was a few more of Jonathan on his.

It was shortly after this that Tina's silent illness announced itself.

She was in church one Sunday. Jonathan was at home with me and Ben was enjoying himself at Sunday School, in a side room, when the first hymn was announced.

As the notes burst out of the organ and the congregation stood up, Tina could not move. Everyone towered around her and she felt panic as they hemmed her in, overwhelming her. Feeling unable to draw breath, she scrambled to get out, helped by the vicar's wife Esther, pushing along the pew to the aisle, all the way to the back and to the door and finally out into the foyer. Esther and the warden, Barbara, supported her until she calmed down again.

After a few minutes, Tina felt strong enough to go back inside, but sat near the back, feeling safer with the door in easy reach.

I didn't really get what the problem was at the time, just did what I could to be supportive. She had coped with Ben alone, coped with her dad's death, coped in Northern Ireland, coped with grandparents' deaths, coped with another birth. I was sometimes prone to fits of temper and drinking, but hadn't I always been like that?

What was the deal now?

Tina's health visitor, Christine, had been waiting for Tina to ask for help and, very soon, the GP prescribed antidepressants and recommended group counselling.

During this time, Tina didn't engage with anything, performed duties perfunctorily, without enthusiasm, didn't give me what I needed, and refused to go out without me except for the two-minute walk to take Ben to school (once to justify why Ben had told his teachers, 'Mummy takes drugs'). I couldn't grasp why. I took her shopping, accepted that I needed to do more at home, and did not expect Tina to run any errands outside the home, but it fell to Esther to be the emotional support. I was grateful to her, even if I thought she was a religious nutter.

When Tina improved, she started back at church.

'I wish you'd come with me, Neil.'

'It's a load of shit!'

And so it went on. We regained our routine. For Tina, church and caring for the kids. For me, a relatively calm two and a half years at work, albeit with a steady increase in my level of drink, and frustration and nightmares building up in my peripheral vision, kept at a manageable distance. For now.

I was training new recruits on a three-month cycle. We had a training timetable I knew inside out, so, apart from a few unexpected dramas, like in any job, it was simple. An added bonus was Ted Fields, with whom I had worked in 2LI. He also had a section and we were able to bounce ideas off one another.

Meeting a group of new soldiers and taking them through their basic training was fun and rewarding. My first view of them, their body language betraying their emotional turbulence, always took me back to my first day. I saw my friends in them, Wardy, Crabby, Woody and the gang. I don't recall ever having had the same nerves myself; I had been in the TA before basic and had developed an attitude hardened by bullying before joining the TA.

I did the whole 'mother duck' thing, taking the boys to try on uniform for size before sending order forms over to the QM. We followed on, allowing various elements of uniform to be thrown over the counter at us, along with a sausage-shaped kit bag and a grip bag, or hold-all.

It never went according to plan and the boys' first parade was a diffy/exchange parade, the aim of which was to have a group of men dressed more or less smartly: no 'sacks of potatoes'. The receipt of missing items depended solely on the QM's mood, as he was always sure the item HAD been distributed.

In the two and a half years, I met around twelve groups and was always surprised how many were clueless when it came to showering and basic cleanliness, even cleaning their teeth! The lack of ironing skills was less surprising.

Some poor sods were discharged almost immediately due to previously undetected medical issues.

'But I've jacked my job in for this!'

Bad luck.

Recruits' days are long; they learn so much. I enjoyed teaching all the lessons I myself had sat through, back in the day. Apart from NBC, I led them all. Most fun, however, was 'adventure training', or 'adventure drinking' as it had been cleverly renamed!

I had, at some point, passed a MLT (Mountain Leader Training) course and, due to my sniper training, my map-reading skills were excellent. I taught how to erect bashas, led patrolling exercises, demonstrated pairwork in fire and movement exercises (where one covers the other as they progress in turn), sentry duty, how to move at night without being seen, even how to get the best of rations (take your own flavouring, such as garlic granules). We had fun with the ration packs, motivating our lowest ranked soldiers to the higher echelons of power by displaying typical ration packs.

'For the senior NCOs, beer. For officers, we have… (imaginary drumroll as I removed the item from the pack)… wine!!!'

We swore a lot in these role-plays, demonstrating the importance of preparation, checking equipment. We made it comical. Porn magazines were whipped out of my pocket to illustrate the destructive influence of such distractions. We instructors role-played a range of scenarios where lack of attention to what was going on around us due to our overriding interest in the female form caused crises or death. In today's language, it was the equivalent of using a phone, just not as much fun.

When out on exercise, we had to teach the importance of responding to the 'Halt, who goes there?' question at the patrol harbor by using the correct password.

Training was fun but hard, engraining important knowledge into these boys' heads so they would be safe and reliable in battle. It had to be like this, or anyone could do it!

A lot of time had gone into the naming of the three main exercises: Exercise First Night, Exercise Halfway and… Exercise Final Fling. The middle exercise formed a major assessment, along with the drill that preceded it. The recruits' behaviour in the field was monitored closely.

It was a good laugh all round, apart from the beastings I

had to give to test the recruits' stamina and tolerance. The pressure I brought to bear taught them the importance of securing their belongings and following orders. The intense schedule made mistakes easy, as they had a lot to consider and little time. My acts of sabotage and unreasonable orders were 'measured and constructive'.

I was proud of my leadership in the 'adventure' and 'drinking' departments. I even kept out of trouble.

Except once.

Most of the two and a half years was calm. I suppose it wasn't calm when I was chasing French youths back into their block of flats to warn them off my recruits when we were on one of our regular tours of the battlefields of Northern France. I also suppose I should have expected recruits to gob off at the locals and start fights after a few drinks. After all, I used to!

Most of the two and a half years was calm.

When I was awake.

When I slept, however, I went on journeys, was taken back to roads littered with belongings, no longer needed, to bodies, slumped and twisted and useless. I watched scenes play out like documentaries.

Processed belongings. Photographs. Carrion.

Every night there was a time, between my calm day and the torment of sleep, when I drank.

Each gulp of liquid a prayer: Let my sleep be dreamless.

This prayer was rarely answered.

So my life was a cycle, where the answer to my inner torment was drink or denial.

The army understood that with trained killers, such as we were, aggression was always scraping at the surface, ready to break through if provoked.

Kev Green, a Platoon Sergeant at ATR Winchester, had not been as discerning. He had beaten up a recruit and had had to rejoin his unit until he had learnt his lesson.

I had resolved not to make that mistake and limited myself to the odd dig if annoyed by someone.

But one particular recruit, one special person, broke my resolve.

It was on a 'Final Fling'. He made the mistake of thinking I enjoyed someone else having the last word on me.

Big mistake.

I had been back to Bosnia in the night, had woken out of breath, my heart hammering to get out of my chest wall, and less than an hour later, this guy was giving me a mouthful because he didn't want to get his kit together.

So I grabbed his chin strap and swung his head round, controlling him enough to land a kick in his side and let him drop to the floor in pain.

'Ah!' he groaned.

'Don't you f**king 'Ah!' Get the f**k up and get going! You have messed up! What if this was a real situation? You could die! Your friends could die because of you! What do you think we are training for? F**king Disneyland?'

Yep. Disneyland. Where you can high-five a man whose wife is missing or a woman whose husband has just been decapitated to stop his soul from resting. Where you can scoop corpses out of the river, robbing fish of their food in the hope that a family can find some peace.

The recruit got up from the floor. Lucky him if all he had to worry about was a bruised rib.

I got away with that incident, which was just as well, as I didn't want to stress Tina out again.

Then came a change of pace which, ultimately, would almost be my undoing.

Chapter 14

My years of lifting heavy weights and Bergens meant a change was forced upon me. Some of my disks had prolapsed and healed again, and the pain of this was becoming too great to ignore. So far painkillers and my determination to keep hassle and restrictions at bay had worked. I would do anything to avoid being medically discharged, but things were getting too much and I knew something had to give, so I started looking for a role which would be less physically exerting.

I transferred to the AGC, the Adjutant General's Corps, in the SPS – the Staff and Personal Support Branch – although we often called it the 'Special Pen Service'. This was the ideal solution… I could still go out and do normal army stuff if I wanted to, and the skills I would pick up would definitely be transferable to a civilian job.

Okay, so I hated it. The administrative world is not my utopia. Claim forms, payroll, more forms. Brilliant…

My first posting was Osnabruck, back in Germany. Ben transferred to the school there, aged 6½. Jon was still a 2½-year-old toddler. Tina slotted into life there, as usual. Whatever issues I had, Tina was as solid as a rock throughout.

I joined an Infantry unit, which was useful whenever some jumped-up soldier boy labeled me 'only a f**king clerk' as I could accurately reply that I was more qualified then they were! In fact, bar one course (Education for Promotion), I was qualified to CQMS level!

Admin was a totally different side to the army. The AGC officers were welcoming but some lacked the backbone necessary to win my full respect. I wouldn't have trusted them to have my back, that's for sure!

My first op was to Poland with Sergeant Major Charles. I was there to provide his administrative support on an exercise. As ex-infantry and ex-platoon sergeant, I knew exactly what he needed and when. He received food, tea, evenly and accurately distributed ammo more or less the second he realised he needed it, and my pre-emptive provision of his needs meant a smooth operation. Needless to say, Charles appreciated me. He was an okay guy, so I didn't mind going the extra mile for him at all.

On a day-to-day basis, whenever I had to interpret army regulations, I generally did so in the favour of the soldier, not the army. There was a scheme called 'Satisfied Soldier'. This was less to do with services provided in sangars in Belfast and more to do with helping recruit to the army. Soldiers spent time in careers offices, to which they had to travel, and they often also had to stay overnight. I made sure they were amply reimbursed for expenses relating to travel and accommodation or PAR (privately arranged rates).

The document supervisor was Dougie, an ex-paratrooper who owed his enormous stomach to an op for stomach cancer. Dougie was a smoker, like me, and in the time between my arrival and his giving up his addiction, we hung out of the window of my office, fags in hands, 'kind of' following the No Smoking in This Building rule.

We got on extremely well, as neither of us was shy in expressing our feelings, and this openness created a real respect for one another. Our friendship was cemented by a shared outlook on life: If you don't like what I am doing, f**k off.

Another guy, Al, an ex-tankie (QRH), worked in an office across from me. He was a fun, no-nonsense guy who liked his booze, so it was no wonder I was drawn to him! We shared a healthy disrespect for the officers who didn't deserve respect.

I also liked Scott Jordan. He was similar to me in role and personality, except I was harder, more abrasive, and he was quicker-witted.

One day we were leaving for lunch at 12:28, when the Detachment (Det) Commander caught us out.

'It's only 12:28! You're two minutes early for lunch!'

Scott retorted, 'We can go back if you like, but we don't see you stopping us opening the office in the mornings, when we're unlocking a couple of minutes before our official start time!'

I laughed out loud and we went for lunch, leaving the Det Commander to chunter to himself, trying to save face.

We must have been a nightmare for management. Sergeant West was another, what I would call, 'tool'. When he first arrived, one particular soldier had an issue with pay. I had passed it to West's predecessor, Merv, to deal with, but it was apparently unresolved.

West rang me from his office to chat about the issue.

I was not having a brilliant day, either because I was hung over again, or because I was tired from more wandering through the darker landscapes of my mind when I should have been in a restful sleep, so I did not take too kindly to West suggesting I was to blame for the problem.

'Yeah, whatever!' I said and put the phone down on him.

I took a cigarette out of the packet and lit it before moving over to the window. This time I stood with my back to the window, leaning against the ledge.

I could hear West coming up the stairs and into my room, with his runner in tow. He slammed the paper down onto my desk and started to kick off. I listened for a minute, then suggested to the runner that he pop off and have a fag break for ten minutes. West was not amused.

'He's my runner! I'll f**king tell him when he can have a break!'

I thought it was time to let West know who was the real boss around here.

In the lull that followed, I heard office doors closing, including the Company Sergeant Major's door. They knew me well enough to know that their work was about to be disturbed.

'You can shut that door, if you like!' I ordered. West did just that.

I continued. 'Have you f**king finished now?' I flicked my cigarette at him.

'Who the f**k do you think you are, coming into MY office and speaking to me like that? Firstly, I am a relatively new clerk and I have not always done this shit job, so wind your f**king neck in, and if you ever come in here speaking to me like that again, I will f**king chin you! I will f**king drop you on your head out of this first-floor window! Do you understand?'

He stared at me, opened his mouth to speak, but I hadn't finished.

'Secondly, I passed this to your predecessor and he told me he had sorted it. Now...you tell me how that is my fault!'

West looked stunned. He could not speak.

'You f**king can't, can you? So there you go!.... How are you going to sort this out? Where is it wrong?'

He found his tongue and tried to explain where it was wrong but couldn't manage it and left, with me uttering the same word that had heralded this whole incident, 'Whatever!'

West went downstairs and related the conversation to Dougie, dripping indignation.

Dougie told him he was lucky to have got away with a mouthful, as I had a reputation for knocking people out if I was unhappy with them.

I was happy with that reputation. It was like having an invisible shield and sword on me, as I made my way through life. That reputation and the ability to find humour in almost anything were significant qualities.

Dougie, Scott and I laughed a lot at work, along with some of the women there, especially Jane.

I think I led Jane astray a bit. I think Jane would have followed all the rules if I hadn't been there.

One day we were walking off for a fag break, cutting across the parade square, when the RSM's office window slid open behind us and the RSM himself shouted at us to stop.

'Don't turn round, Jane!'

'What?'

I walked more quickly, and Jane matched my stride. The RSM shouted again. This time, he sounded very cross indeed.

'Don't turn round. He doesn't know who we are, or he

would have called us by name. Keep walking!'

With yet another scream from the RSM, telling us two to 'f**king turn round', our legs acted on our behalf and started to pelt over the other side of the parade square and into a nearby block.

Inside, we steadied our breathing and made our way back to our offices through the buildings, walking casually to throw off suspicion. A CSM walked towards us, asking if we had seen anyone who might have been on the parade square.

'No, sorry!' Jane and I said, in unison.

That evening's Part 1 Orders contained the words 'avoid' and 'parade square', funnily enough.

We all used to go out a lot and, on one particular Friday (POETS Day, or Piss Off Early, Tomorrow's Saturday!), the whole detachment was meeting up at 19:00 in a bar in town.

Scott and I decided to go to the pub straight from work, which was probably a bad idea, as, by the time the others reached us, we had downed eight steins of beer. This beer, Weißen, was not for the weak and by the time everyone got to us, we were bladdered. Apparently I am hilarious when I am really drunk. It was a good night; I just wish it wasn't such a blur.

Jane was there with her partner, Mark, and her parents. An argument ensued, arising from the accusation that Mark was not making Jane happy.

These notions floated over to me in my haze and an idea for a hilarious joke came into my mind, which I whispered to Scott. 'Obviously you didn't see her sucking on his bellend last night, did you?'

My eyes screwed up as I was laughing hard at my own joke and, when I turned to face the crowded table again, I opened my eyes to find everyone staring at me in silence. Mark looked angry.

Whoops.

'Did I say that out loud?'

The silence had entrenched itself and was threatening to spoil the evening, when Jane burst out laughing. Her parents joined in and Mark had no choice but to let it go. Even today,

Jane's parents ask after me. I certainly made an impression.

I may have been smashed, but I still knew when I had got away with something. I could still sense relief, and this stayed with me throughout the rest of the night, the beer, the shots, the increased oblivion. Maybe I would sleep well tonight? I don't know what time I got in to Tina. As usual, the boys were well cared for, tucked up in bed.

Tina was a good wife to me throughout all this. She was still in the Wives' Club and, by now, had started up a child-minding business to earn extra cash and to keep her mind occupied. Her first clients were Dougie and his wife Magda, who had a daughter. Tina soon became an outstanding child-minder, certified by the British Forces Early Years Service, the equivalent of OfSted.

Tina was patient with me. She knew the army had a drinking culture, knew I would go out 'bonding' once a week at least, knew not to try to stop me drinking. I was alcohol-dependent, for sure, but my bouts of anger occurred at work and less and less at home. I tried to leave my work at work, and at home I was the husband, the dad, until it was time for the drink.

The drink and my nighttime journeys into hell.

I drank, relived the worst moments of my life, watched new scenarios unfurl before me, woke up with a start, out of breath, lay awake, forcing all my fears deep inside of me. Telling no one.

Towards the end of 2002, Scott and I were left in Germany whilst many of our gang went back to the UK to participate in Operation Fresco, which was brought about by the firemen's strikes over pay. The army was on standby with its Green Goddesses, should the public need a fire putting out.

One day, Scott and I were at a loose end. We were in separate offices, working through our work at a steady pace, but it was no fun at all. The way the UNICOM email system worked, we had to open each email as it came in before we could see any of the others. Unopened emails just stacked up and the only way you could clear them was by opening them.

In a moment of boredom, my eyes ran over my screen. Suddenly I had an idea.

I would send Scott some emails.

20-30 would do.

Create, click, send, create, click, send, create, click, send, create, click, send, etc.

I sat back in my chair and waited. Through our half-open office doors, I heard him groan and sigh. I stifled a snigger.

A few minutes later, my computer pinged the arrival of Scott's revenge.

Over sixty times!

I laughed and opened each email in turn, which took a while, as you could only open one every six seconds.

I plotted.

It took a bit of thinking and working things through, but I managed to work out how to send a short email (8 letters) to one recipient 800 times with the push of two buttons. Then, with the use of a finger on each hand, I repeated the process a few times.

Scott yelled.

Was it possible I had gone too far?

200,000 emails? It would take two whole weeks, without pausing, to open them all!

Scott and I met in the space between our offices, doubling up with laughter. This was hilarious! What had I done! I had proper f**ked up, and knew I would have to own up.

I told the Det Commander and the RAO, Captain Crowley. They were not impressed but didn't react too badly.

Until that afternoon, when they realised the true implications of what I had done. We were 'sent for'.

Apparently (and how was I to know), you can only fit 200 emails into an inbox before the whole system crashes.

Whoops!

IT experts from Worthy Down had to come and remove all emails, not just my 200,000, but also any emails wrapped up in them. This included Operation Fresco instructions, which meant the unit had to request them to be re-sent.

I was not popular, to say the least.

As we awaited our fate, Scott rang his brother, a Military

Police Officer, asking for advice. All we needed to do was begin our punishment, or 'extras' as they were called, whatever they were, immediately. If we started them before they were documented, they would be illegal and no further action against us would be permitted legally.

Captain Crowley ordered us to do one day on, one day off until further notice.

'Do you accept my award?'

We most certainly did and we took it in turns, with immediate effect. The emails died away the next morning, the burden passed to some poor sod at Worthy Down.

Within the next few days, two things happened.

First of all, Captain Crowley had her leaving do. 'I would love you two guys to be there, you are such a laugh…'

Cue us diverting some other soldier's 'extra' to Friday, which released us to join the party. Result!

Secondly, Worthy Down called and demanded we be charged and thrown out of the army.

Unfortunately for them, we had started our award, so their request just had to be denied. On top of that, the awards were now illegal and Captain Crowley was leaving anyway, so we really did get away with it!

Meanwhile the 'poor sod' at Worthy Down was so unhappy with his lot that, even six years later, he was still furious. We had met up and got on really well, without knowing much about each other, when he told me about this nightmare job he'd had and how the perpetrators had been kicked out of the army.

I did disabuse him of the notion we had been punished. I even proved it was me that had sent the emails. 'I can even tell you what was in them….I wrote simply, "Hahahaha!!!"'

He went very pale, told me I was a knob and never spoke to me again.

I can't say I blamed him. After all, he was the one who'd had to open them all.

Chapter 15

I was desperate to go to Iraq when it all kicked off again over there in 2003. I wanted to be where the main action was. There was not much point being in the army if you weren't ready to get your hands dirty in a warzone, so I asked the RAWO (Regimental Administrative Warrant Officer), my boss, if I could go.

The answer was no. 'But I'm glad you came to see me, Neil, because I do have something I want you to do.'

I wasn't expecting Kosovo.

If I had known my unit would be going to Iraq a short while later, I would not have gone to Kosovo so freely. As it was, I accepted my new posting. I moved from A Company to Support Company and slotted into the BSP: the Brigade Surveillance Platoon. They needed HR and the physical intensity of the posting meant I was the only one capable. Despite my back not behaving itself, I was still the best at PT.

Tina and the boys stayed in Osnabruck whilst I travelled to Kent to refresh the surveillance and photography skills I had originally learnt on my sniper course. I was updated on the top-secret aspects of photography too.

Part of this course was a Combat Fitness Test – eight miles carrying my kit and rifle, etc, over shale in one and a half hours. I took it steadily and was overtaken by the others at the start. No doubt they saw me as an older guy, as I was well into my thirties and considerably above the average age.

I overtook them one at a time and came in third overall. Result! I was proud to still 'have it' and looked forward to being properly useful again. Maybe part of me hoped that a more active role would dissipate my night terrors.

Kosovo was a peace-keeping mission. It wanted

independence from Serbia and its issues had not really been dealt with. Not even the horror stories from the nineties had been enough to stave off its dissatisfaction.

I spent five or six months based at the Slimlines Barracks just outside Pristina. The difference between this and my last stay in the region was palpable. In Bosnia we had felt like scavengers, queuing for toilets, showers and phones, whose services were below par, to say the least. In Kosovo, we slept in portacabins with our own lockers. The washing facilities were excellent and phones were easily accessible, as were computers for emailing, televisions and even DVD players. Luxury!

I mainly worked with a guy from Fiji, Mr T, so-called for his black skin and his huge frame. He was a good junior. However, I also went on sorties with HUMINT – Human Intelligence. These guys worked in plain clothes, recruiting on the ground for information gathering. My role was to oversee the use of secret documents, ensuring they were used properly and never unaccounted for, or sometimes I went out with them just for the ride. I knew a few of them from previous postings, so it was always good to hang out with them.

I enjoyed this time, as far as I could enjoy anything, I suppose. The change of scenery and new focus had not dispelled my nightmares, which were never far away. They waited until my brain was processing images of my everyday, the acceptable destruction of buildings, fences warning us to keep away for fear of a carcinogenic atmosphere or unexploded bombs – the things I could live with – but gradually other scenes overlaid these, infusing them with death, with misery. They played out on a loop, increasing my anxiety each time.

I fought to keep the nightmares at bay by excessive exercise and alcohol. I bench-pressed and squatted huge weights. I ran. I drank as much beer as could be poured down my throat. I started it all again. Exercise. Alcohol. Sleep. Work. Exercise. Alcohol. Sleep. Work.

So my demons, which had travelled with me, had not allowed me to escape, but they were controlled.

Just about.

I was eventually called back to Osnabruck for a big inspection, cutting short my tour in Kosovo to ensure boxes could be ticked and pen pushers satisfied. As the HUMINT guys shouted goodbye, they encouraged me to come and join them permanently, told me to apply. I nodded and smiled but I never did, because of my back problems.

That decision was the best and worst of my life.

Chapter 16

As always, Tina had held the fort without me. Caring for our sons, running the household brilliantly. She and Ben were pleased to see me, as ever, but Jon was a particular source of joy for me at this time. He had always been closer to Tina, for obvious reasons, but he had missed me when I was in Kosovo. His face lit up when he saw me for the first time and he actually wanted to spend time with me.

I was incredibly happy about that.

Back to the office drudge, I discovered that none of the admin I had sent back from Kosovo had been dealt with. Months' worth of processing had to be done! Apparently they had been busy in Iraq. I was annoyed at not being warned of this, but set about rectifying the situation, finishing it all off on the Friday afternoon before the Monday morning inspection.

As you can imagine, I was not particularly good company that day. So when some jobsworth, some Financial Services Administrator, some Warrant Officer class 2, some right knob, came to complain about my files being different heights and thicknesses, I was less than impressed.

I had taken a break from catching up on other people's work to write personnel rates up on the board for the inspectors. He came in and began his monologue. I did not stop writing, just listened, becoming increasingly more incredulous the longer he spoke.

Eventually, I was so dumbfounded, I had to stop writing and turn and face him.

'I am preparing for this inspection! Why the hell does it matter what size the files are?!'

'Come with me, Corporal Obbard!'

I threw my pen down and followed him, cursing under my breath. He disappeared into Al's office. I followed suit.

We stood there, side by side, looking at Al's shelves.

'What do you see, Corporal Obbard?'

I so wanted to say something sarcastic, but I was genuinely trying not to lose it with him. Didn't he know how busy I was?

I did try, honest, but it was too much. I answered his question. 'Al? A couple of people?'

Jobsworth continued, 'Do you know what I see? I see professionalism!'

Okay, so the files looked like they had been arranged by someone with OCD. If the inspectors wanted mathematical precision, symmetry, colour co-ordination, then Al would pass and I wouldn't.

'Surely it is what's in them that counts?' I dared to suggest.

'The inspectors don't look at that!'

This was too much. It had to be said... 'Then what's the f**king point?'

He went on, spewing forth a stream of all kinds of shit I didn't give a f**k about. I told him so.

He changed tack and suggested we look at my 'amazing' files.

Bring it on. I led the way back to my office.

He flicked through a few of my files, asking me why this person and that person weren't paying food and accommodation, addressing me as 'Mr Perfect'.

'Because they are away on ops, and you don't pay for food and accommodation when you are away on ops!'

I addressed him as 'F**king Tube'.

'What are you going to tell the inspectors when they ask?'

'I will tell them exactly what happened, that I have been busy catching up with the work you were too lazy to do when I was in Kosovo. Surely, if the work was that important, you would have done it?'

Point made, he stormed off, with me shouting obscenities after him.

The inspection went well and my files were instrumental in promoting me to sergeant.

Time for another move!

I put forward two posting preference forms, both requesting, quite clearly, Germany, and specifying that I did not want to be in the UK or attached to Special Forces. Surely I can't have filled TWO forms in incorrectly?

The Staff Officer informed me I had been selected to go to Hereford (UK!) and work with the SAS.

I did not want to go but I had no choice.

It was the start of the worst period in my career and, in fact, of my life. What was supposed to be the highest pinnacle turned out to be the deepest abyss.

Chapter 17

By the end of 2003, we were in Hereford, settling into another home. The boys were enrolled in the local school, Tina was establishing a new routine for the family and I was learning how they did things over here.

I had never been particularly interested in joining the SAS, despite being fit enough for the job when I was younger and covering many of the courses they have to do. I was put off by their need for a disconnect from normal life; I treasured my family life too much to be away from them, without any contact whatsoever, for indefinite periods of time.

I was told this position was the pinnacle of my career. I should have felt proud, but I couldn't quite feel it. I didn't tell my parents anything about the job, since they didn't understand the need for tact. When they visited me in Northern Ireland, my dad had forgotten that he was supposed to keep quiet about me being a British soldier and included this fact in chit-chat at a local shop.

In any case, if I had tried to explain my role, they might have thought I was actually SAS, rather than *attached* to the SAS. I had been chosen for my resilience (someone had clocked me helping a woman in the CFT we'd done during the inspection, carrying her kit as well as my own on the eight-mile run), but basically I was a pen-pusher for the SAS guys.

So there was no family celebration or proud phone calls. I took the arrival at the 'pinnacle of my career' in my stride, and for a short while, it all went smoothly. I settled in, got to know names and office procedures, found my way around.

I was a few days away from an exercise in Brunei when three of my co-workers, Bill, Jeff and Gary, invited me out for a drink. As usual, I said, 'Yes, please!' I was always up for that!

We got a round in. I gulped down the beer, felt the familiar taste slide over my tongue and down my throat, sending the first signals to relax to my battered brain.

It was all going smoothly, and I was congratulating myself on a new job with drinking buddies, when Bill disappeared and I was left with just Gary and Jeff.

I laughed when they told me they were going to inform me how things really worked in the office. We all knew that there was the official and the unofficial way of working, same as in every workplace. This would be a laugh! I couldn't wait!

But this was different.

The words flowed over me. I struggled to take it in. It was like hearing a string of threatening vocabulary without any warning whatsoever. Was I really being told that our real job was to make money on the side for ourselves and for the squadrons?

I laughed, looked cool about it, battled inside to know how to react.

Was this a test? Was I undergoing some test of my psyche?

How was I doing?

When Bill returned to the group, it was clear he was in on all this too.

I decided it was a test. The alternative, that they were on the make, was unacceptable. I would go with the flow until it all became clear. I didn't want to freak out and make a fool of myself if it was a test or a wind-up.

I went off to Brunei and followed Gary's instructions. Whenever I bought anything, I asked for another receipt, thus creating accounts based on much higher amounts than we had actually paid. The expenses claims therefore provided me with a huge profit, which I had to share with the others, those in the know.

Apparently the £1,500 was more than they had received before.

I took the praise and waited for some clarity. It felt like I was in some kind of fog with a crowd of people. I could see

Gary and Jeff, possibly Bill, but the others were indistinct and I could not tell who they were, whether they knew. I saw hints of corruption, but they faded quickly, so I doubted myself.

I participated in conversations about making money, conversations where I was told I could take half.

Really?

Once, right in the middle of a conversation where it felt like I was being told to rip off the British Army, to steal from the British public, Gary mentioned that I would be killed if I tried to sabotage this operation.

I wanted it to be one big wind-up, but it felt more like a threat.

I was sickened by this theft, especially when I thought of the ground troops in Iraq, missing body armour due to lack of funds. I was lost for an answer, a way out of this, unsure what my next move should be. The only point of absolute clarity for me was that I would never take any money at all for myself. After Brunei I never made the profits myself, never did anything to defraud the army; all I did was witness what others were doing and go along with it, for want of an escape.

There was no room in my life for rest anymore. If I wasn't having my nightmares, I was wide awake, wondering what to do.

This was a new level of torture.

I told Tina. I really didn't want her to share my anxiety, but I was so desperate to find a way of coping, a way out, that I had no choice. She was disgusted by it all, and worried for me. She knew my high standards would not tolerate all this. She wanted me to report the issue, to get some help, but I was too afraid of the consequences for now.

Every day I wished I loved money more than my morals.

Throughout 2004, one of my jobs was to go into Iraq for three or four days at a time for 'replen', or replenishment. I took money out with me – usually about a quarter of a million dollars, which I naturally had to sign for – and exchanged it for receipts. I also dealt with admin connected with home, problems with pay, expenses and so on.

Occasionally that fog cleared patchily, revealing a new link. Dan, another guy just like me, a guy I knew from Winchester, referred to an exercise known as the 'Aztec Armour' in South America, and how he had run rings round the RAO Ted Clark.

'He hasn't got a clue what goes on! I made £28, 000 on that op, just through double receipts!'

Dan educated me, gave me a cut for myself. I didn't ask the questions I should have done. I was stunned.

I put the money in an envelope. I could never spend it.

I hated my work. What was already a high-pressure posting was now unbearable. Sleep was a rare beast and, during the times I managed to cut out the present, I was cannoned into the past, where I was haunted by what I had seen and done.

My life was intolerable.

Tina suggested I write everything down, so I started a log of events: names, places, dates.

I suspected other scams. Unscrupulous characters wove in and out of the fog, gathering contraband from aircraft, selling it on, swapping cigarettes, even weapons for cash. Whispers of huge sums of money made in Iraq echoed in the fog.

When on replen, I would fly to Qatar, change plane, and continue on to Basra, the British stronghold, before ending up in Baghdad, which was held by US forces. I was always met at the airport by at least two of the SAS, always given a weapon – usually a Deimaco rifle, nice to handle. I was always reminded of the drill if we were attacked, always escorted by car to a safe house in the Green Zone.

I listened but I already knew the drill. It was similar to the COP drill.

The road we travelled was the most bombed road in the world. The U.S. Army had cleared about 250m on either side of it, ridding the area of buildings and vegetation, to reduce the risk of attack. At any hint of danger, anything in the slightest bit unusual, even what appeared to be rubbish lying in the road, we took no chances, in case it was an IED, and sped away.

The Green Zone was deemed a safe area, if by safe you mean an attack was unlikely. It was not safe for me. I felt vulnerable. I was 'fitting in' when all I wanted to do was abandon everything and go home. I didn't know whom to trust, so I trusted no one completely.

I left a few days later feeling impure and weak, but mainly powerless.

Where was that outspoken, confident soldier? Where was the man who had conquered bullies, who'd had the resilience to cope with incessant attacks on his person, who did not need anyone's help?

The most I did was collect up my log and the little money I had been given and place them in envelopes. I passed them on to a friend who was a Justice of the Peace, and he, in turn, placed them with a solicitor.

'If anything happens to me, open the envelopes. Call the police. Do not let it drop...involve the media...do all you can!'

In the weeks between my trips to Iraq, I played a role in the offices. I played at working. I turned up, went through the motions, messed up time and again, didn't care. My heart was not in it.

I went home, played at being a husband and father, drank, lay in bed waiting for the images to fill my head. They were the most realistic they had ever been and were becoming harder to control.

I am running along a road. It is deserted but for the piles on the edge of it. As I get nearer, the indistinct becomes clearer and I can make out objects forming some of the piles. They are everyday objects that mean something to someone: clothes, bags, toys, photographs.

Other piles are different. They contain clothes too, but these clothes are wrapped around their owners, who lay, bent and twisted, around others still. I can't tell where one body starts and another ends.

Sometimes the heads are severed.

The faces look peaceful. I tell myself they are asleep, but as I get nearer, their eyes fly open, their blue, green, brown, grey irises, with pinpoint pupils, already staring at me.

The piles unfold, untwist, each individual body unravelling itself as I pass it, on my lonely road. Once upright, they follow me, so that soon I am pursued by an army of the dead.

What do they want?

Sometimes I would wake up breathless, exhausted from being hunted down by a target, a target cut down as dawn broke, perhaps?

Or, just for a bit of variety, I am hiding, as a faceless man searches for me, getting nearer and nearer, until I feel his hands on my shoulders, dragging me out, shouting at me, reaching for indescribable instruments of torture.

There was no escape from the nightmares. My whole life was a permanent nightmare. I was a prisoner with no hope of escape. I felt like that small child, trapped in a house by his mum, unable to break out and be myself and live the life I wanted.

Gary had been promoted, so we got a new colleague. Jeff and Bill told me to brief the new bloke about Brunei, synonymous with corruption training.

We all went to the pub, the new guy smiling because he thought he had reached the pinnacle of his career and had friendly colleagues who wanted to buy him a drink. I did not want to be there. I did not want to be wired up. I did not want to record the conversation to put an end to the whole situation.

I did not want any of this, but recording the conversation seemed a good way to protect myself.

I followed my script, improvising only to tell him, 'You don't have to do this, it's up to you!' Just enough to sow that seed of doubt, but not enough to unsettle Jeff and Bill.

'Yeah, yeah! Cheers, Neil!'

I knew he wasn't happy, could see the signs. I knew a lot about 'tells', had learnt about them from the HUMINT team.

No…he was not happy.

After the meeting, I removed my wire, checked the recording and slid the cassette into another envelope to be passed onto the JP for safekeeping.

Then I carried on with my routine. I felt sick most of the time. Work did not go well.

Bill was older and was liked by most people, just not me. He was a pleaser, but I saw straight through him. Maybe he sensed that in me and picked me up on every detail of my work. Maybe he knew I was not committed to 'the cause'.

He wanted me out but I wanted to leave on *my* terms. Dougie thought very little of him and encouraged me to land him one, but I couldn't, as he was too old. So I tried talking to him. 'Where am I going wrong, Bill?'

Bill said he didn't have time to show me where I was going wrong. The job was too fast-paced.

Truth is, I *was* making mistakes, was sloppy. I was not in control of my life, just getting through each day as best I could. One day I found myself in the office of John, the regimental accountant. He was not involved in any scams. I don't even know why I was there.

'What's up, Neil?'

I don't know what I said exactly, but it was something about theft, something about not wanting to be a thief, being forced.

Had I gone to him to tell him, to finally unburden myself, without making that conscious decision? Or was it his intuition that made him ask? I watched his face as I told him. He was horrified, shocked, almost, but not, incredulous.

'F**king hell, Neil!'

That was in the morning. I left his office not 100% relieved. My thoughts and feelings were turbulent. Somehow I managed a few more tasks, waiting. A short while later, John told me he had told someone else. I was not happy. 'For f**k's sake, John!'

'Sorry, Neil, but I had no choice!'

The WO1 John had informed sought me out. Even he was out of his depth with this information and suggested we talk to Ted Clark, the RAO. Reluctantly, I agreed.

Later that day, Ted called me casually for a job which happened to be away from everyone else, in a quiet corner of the building.

'I understand that you need to talk to me in private and it is important I listen?'

I had spent months repressing my fears, guilt, anger. Telling

John had been like a trickle of water through the tiniest of cracks in a dam. And now my defences were totally destroyed.

The words spilled out of my mouth, as well as the tears from my eyes. It was the first time I had cried in years, since a moment alone one night in Bosnia, when I had been drinking.

Ted listened, uncharacteristically shocked, listened and listened, until he knew all I had to tell him. 'I want to move, I want to go to Regimental HQ and ask for an immediate transfer,' I finished. I must have sounded desperate.

Ted told me to hang fire. He looked thoughtful, obviously weighing it all up. 'You're due to go to Iraq next week. Are you still good to go?'

I agreed reluctantly. He probably needed some thinking time.

This was big. When I had first been briefed by Jeff, he'd told me to keep two books and to deny everything if caught. He said the Royal Military Police and Special Investigation Branch had never had a conviction without a confession. I told Ted about my envelopes with the money and logs, and the recording. He understood that those envelopes were my security.

Then I went about my job, leaving him to work out where to go from there. I learnt later that the CO was not happy knowing about the evidence locked away by the JP, but Ted insisted I keep it there, if it helped me to feel safe.

I continued as normal. What else could I do? Tina was relieved I had confessed, that someone was taking things into hand. We hoped it would be the first step to a return to normality, where we could appreciate the insignificance of household bills or everyday ailments, children having a bad night's sleep or boilers breaking down. A million of those things would be preferable to this burden.

In preparation for Iraq, I collected the money as usual, except it was an unusual amount: $50,000 more than I had ever taken before. I was so tense that any deviation from routine felt like a threat.

I signed for the cash, every nerve wired, and made my way

to the plane, mixing into the 200 or so uniforms filtering through the airfield to the Hercules bound for Qatar.

'Remember, we know where you live...'

I swung round to find the owner of the voice, but all I saw was a collage of faces, none of which engaged with me, just focused on the path ahead, on climbing into the plane.

What made me climb onto that plane after that?

I felt my pocket for the Nokia Triband I had bought. This was some comfort to me, as I knew it would work in the Middle East, wherever there was no satellite, such as in the British area. It would bounce off the US signals in Baghdad. I could ring anyone, anytime. I would never really be alone.

The flights and links were, thankfully, without incident, but I can't say I relaxed. At Baghdad airport I met my contacts and slid into the back of the car, as usual.

But this time they did not give me a weapon.

I was mulling this over, convincing myself that paranoia is an uneasy travel companion, when we deviated from the traditional route to pull into an underground car park, marked by concrete pillars and very few other vehicles standing idly in the gloomy corners.

My escorts got out of the car, told me they would be back soon and left, slamming the car doors behind them. They didn't say where they were going or why or how long they would be.

My heart picked up its pace. My breathing became shallower. This was not right.

I looked around, waited a moment, then got out of the car myself and moved into some shadows, away to the right. From there, I could see the car and both the entrance and the exit to this storey. I calmed down a fraction, but my entire body was on high alert.

I waited.

A couple of minutes later, I heard a car arrive, slowing down on the ramps, pulling round to face our vehicle a little faster than necessary. The driver braked and two local men got out, one from either side, and moved to the car I had just abandoned.

They bent over to look inside, checking the front and rear seats. Finding it empty, they scanned the car park.

I pulled further back into the shadows.

They did not see me.

I saw their pistols.

I saw them looking for me.

They did not see me.

I watched them shrug their confusion and get back into their car and reverse away.

What had just happened?

The SAS escort returned, so I stepped out of the shadows and returned to the back seat. They looked surprised to see me out of the vehicle.

Were they just surprised to see me there, or to see me alive?

I acted as if I were oblivious to what had just happened; this was my defence. I just made out I had been for a pee behind a pillar. My mind created suspicions that made me vulnerable, destroyed my trust, made me question everything. I was still fit; I had my sniper training, my fighting skills. One-on-one I could survive, and this gave me some confidence, but that was not enough to stem the fear building up in me. After all, I might be outnumbered…

We turned back to the airfield we had just left. Apparently we were jumping aboard a helicopter. The route was going to be dangerous, so this was the best way to get to the safe zone.

I was thrown again by this sudden change of plan, but went with it, following my escorts, seemingly calmly, but always alert.

Odd, the moments of unexpected and sudden tranquility in the centre of a storm. My general existence was in turmoil, and this particular trip was unusually threatening, yet I could look at the view from the helicopter and marvel at how beautiful it all was out here. The landscape, the river winding its way through this city, even the island on the middle of the river looked stunning, if you forgot that it was the seat of Saddam Hussein's sons' palace and they had allegedly used it to rape and kill women.

Suddenly the helicopter started to perform manoeuvres and the flares on the sides came out, which meant we had been 'locked on', that someone was aiming to kill us. We twisted so far round that we were at right angles to the ground.

The doors were wide open.

I was not belted in.

Had I forgotten for a reason? Was I meant to let myself fall into the shiny river below? It looked so calm, almost welcoming.

Believe me, I was tempted to let go, had been tempted by the sweet nothingness of death before, but if the scrawny boy I had once been had never given up, why should I?

I held onto the netting that made up my seat.

It felt like everything was sent to intimidate me, make me throw in the towel. Was that the point or was it all just horrible coincidence?

The helicopter righted itself and brought us in low to land. I climbed out, hoping my legs wouldn't give away my nerves, and managed to reach the safe house. There I did the job I had come to do.

They were surprised I still had the extra $50,000. It was no longer needed, apparently; I could take it back with me.

The safe house was filled with guys on normal ops, but luckily I had a room to myself. I barricaded the door with the largest piece of furniture in the room and tried to rest, counting the minutes until I was back safely at home.

I missed Tina and the boys. I didn't get much sleep at all, just thought about them and how wonderful it would be to live a normal life with them.

If all this ever settled down, I would appreciate the everyday forever. I might even cope with the hauntings. My life had deteriorated drastically: the nightmares were the least of my worries.

The next morning, I got ready to leave as normal, but when I stepped outside, there was a commotion, a small firefight, which was highly uncommon in the Green Zone. I was unnerved and felt for my Nokia, stabbing at the digits wildly.

'Tina? Is everything okay?'

'Neil? Yes! All okay here! What's that noise?'

'A bit of a firefight.'

'What are you doing on the phone!!'

'I just needed to say hello, Tina...'

She must have been sick with worry. I tried to sound controlled, but my voice might have betrayed me. We spoke briefly, then I said a quick goodbye and climbed into the helicopter, buckling up this time. Before too long I was on a plane to Basra, where I relaxed enough to sleep for a while, twisted round in my seat.

At Basra airport, I was picked up by a young guy in civvies, who escorted me to a building to wait for my next connection. I had never been to this building before, had always waited somewhere else, the same place each time.

'Just wait here!' he said cheerfully. 'The helicopter will be here in a minute. You'll be the last one they pick up.' He left me alone.

By now it was dark. I was really on edge. My instincts told me to move away, hide myself again and watch for my connection from somewhere I felt safer. This small act, which had worked yesterday, gave me a sense of control.

As if I was watching an action film, I saw a car draw up to the building where I had been left. The occupants got out, looked around (for me?), got back in and drove away.

The young lad was returning, so I quickly recovered the position he had left me in. 'Are you still here?'

'Yes, I'm waiting for the helicopter!'

He raised his head slightly. 'Hasn't it been yet? It will soon be here.'

I wasn't sure if he asked questions with obvious answers to make conversation or to cover his confusion.

I returned to my 'safe place', the same car returned, the same people got out and looked around and went away again.

Was this a coincidence?

Eventually a Chinook swung in and I got into it. I was the only passenger. It took me the whole twenty minutes' journey to Basra Palace for my breathing and heartbeat to regain their regular rhythms.

There I found myself with some SAS guys again, ones I knew. I trusted these men more and felt myself properly relax for the first time that trip.

That was my last trip to Iraq. I arrived home shattered. I hugged Tina, hugged my boys, told Ted everything. He promised it would be my last trip out there.

In the following few days, in the office, there were hints of what was going on behind the scenes. In meetings, we were told to cross our 't's and dot our 'i's, to check all our accounts, because Ted was on the warpath.

Ted made a show of moving me quickly, as if I had messed up somehow and he wanted me away. Part of me was pleased to no longer be there; another part of me was annoyed. It was humiliating that my colleagues had been led to believe I was corrupt.

Despite this, I still felt that Ted was a brilliant leader. He showed me the true value of morals and integrity, of leading by example and standing up for what you believe, even if it is not easy.

It took me three whole days to tell the RMP (Royal Military Police)/SIBs (Special Investigation Branch) everything. Staff Sergeant Lovell came to my home and Tina provided us with endless cups of tea. I passed on the JP's number and called him myself to ensure he passed on the evidence and the money.

It was the biggest SIB investigation into fraud ever. How would it end?

Chapter 18

At the start of 2005, I was back in Winchester as a Platoon Sergeant of mixed sections. Initially it all went reasonably well. I was back in my comfort zone, enjoying the mundane everyday. I slept a little better; my dreams were manageable.

Building a soldier is always enormously rewarding, but one recruit I am especially proud of from this time is Mary Morris.

Mary was in one of the first mixed intakes. She suffered from a lack of self-confidence and there were signs on more than one occasion that she wanted to leave the army. This would have been a huge loss to us. Mary was enthusiastic, and she had something 'extra', so I persuaded her to stay in and persevere.

It was the right decision.

On 11th June 2006, in a fierce battle at Al Amarah, Mary rescued her vehicle commander under fire. She was the first female to win the Military Cross.

During that first year after my removal from Hereford, I was visited by SIB at Winchester. There were anomalies in my accounts.

I studied them. They were not my handiwork. Someone must have altered them.

I was going to be charged. They thought it would help if my role were brought under scrutiny before the trial. I was devastated. I was under investigation and it looked like only Gary would be punished. My sleep patterns suffered; my drinking increased.

When I attended a six-week course, 'All Arms Advanced Drill Instructors', I got bladdered every single night and still passed. This was normal behaviour on this course, so I fitted in. The difference between me and the others was the reason: they drank for fun, I drank to cope.

Tina was worried about me.

I was worried about Tina and the boys.

My mental state deteriorated. The rota threw me up a three-month stint without a platoon. I was told to report for duty at the barracks at eight in the morning, but I had little to do and nothing to care for, so this was the worst thing for me, as it gave me time to dwell on all my troubles. They were enlarged and accentuated, their potential for harm magnified. I tried to avoid this time alone by turning up at nine, but this was frowned upon and I was reminded that I started at eight. Somehow I managed to arrive by eight, just in time to pick up the phone and immediately replace the handset when they rang to check I was there at one minute past eight.

I spent my days dwelling on every issue in my life. The nightmares played out in my mind even when I was awake now, punctuated by new episodes. Episodes which had waited in the wings, biding their time for an opportunity to display themselves, to torture me.

Piles of headless bodies, flashes of blue nylon rope and faraway laughter, flying petrol bombs and the grimaces of rioting men, the sense of starvation, whole dialogues where I was battered into submission, the feel of burning on my head. The intimate noise of street fighting, the questions about death on board an old tractor, the sound of gunshots, mixed in with shattering bone and spattered blood, the apparent threat of strangers on your side in a warzone. The personal attacks brought on by fear, greed and the need for domination.

Words such as 'Remember, we know where you live' played over on my mind on a loop.

What about Tina?

The boys?

I did not eat, was incapable of work, could not connect with the world around me at all, felt comfort only from a beer bottle.

Tina saw the shell I was. Even my anger and aggression had disappeared somewhere. Speaking to me was a worthless effort. I retained nothing of what she said. She was the alpha. She called me a few times a day, even popped in to see me, prompting me to eat, to drink tea. It saddened her to see me just sitting, existing, my life playing out in technicolor on a loop in my head.

False profiles sprang up on dating sites for me. If someone was intending to drive a wedge between me and Tina, they would need to do better than that.

And they did try to do better than that.

Emails stating they knew where we lived, that they could take us out, they could track us on the military computer system, we could never hide.

SIB brushed it all off, failed to take it seriously. They just told me to change my email address.

Tina turned to Trevor and Esther, the vicar of her church and his wife. She told them everything. They offered to set up a safe house for us, off the grid. And in the background, people were investigating anyone who had anything to do with money, buying, selling in Iraq. Integrity was questioned, checked, evaluated.

It got so bad, the civilian doctor arranged counselling for PTSD for me with the Community Psychiatric Nurse, but this illness was still seen as a weakness and vastly misunderstood by society, especially in army circles, where men still had to be men.

I was so ashamed of myself.

The doctor also gave me anti-depressants and told me to go home, but I was determined to finish my working day, which, on this particular day, was on the ranges. She must have told the OC and the Sergeant Major, as they were at the ranges when I got there, presumably to check I wasn't going to finish myself off, or maybe to check my work ethic.

A bullet in the brain would have been the easy option, but something stopped me. I thought about it often, but I couldn't do it. It would be a while yet before I understood why.

So I went home. I had been given more time for my ghosts and my thoughts on the investigation.

Still no news from SIB on this, but in the summer of 2006,

my own case came and went and, thankfully, it went as I had been promised.

An island of optimism in an enormous ocean of pure shit.

I was the loneliest I had ever been. I felt as if no one understood me, not even Tina, whom I had known since I was sixteen. I didn't even understand myself.

I returned to work, was signed off, returned to work, was signed off, on a cycle. Despite being still so delicate, they expected me to work as normal. I could only just about manage to get myself out of bed and dressed for work; the requirements of a working day were still well beyond me. No one seemed to have a clue how I was feeling. The RSM still hassled me to go to the mess, bullying me to attend a mess do for some irrelevant award ceremony. I didn't go. I wasn't in the right frame of mind, and was worried I would kick off at someone for no good reason. Plus, I had to go and see Ben's teacher that evening. My behaviour was affecting him. He was becoming a 'problem'.

Apparently so was I. The RSM let rip on me one day. If he told me to be somewhere, I had to be there. I rolled my eyes, but said 'Yes, sir!' This combination didn't go down well with him. He told me I was shit and to leave his office.

I turned to leave, but something of the boy who had learnt to answer back sparked within me.

I shut the door, removed my stripes and said, 'Anytime you want to leave this outside, I will f**king kill you! I f**king hate it here. I have got a lot going on at the moment and I can't cope with this extra bit of pressure you're putting on me! So just f**k off, you bellend!'

Something in his attitude shifted. 'What's going on?'

He must have sensed something was really amiss. I opened up to him, explained everything. He listened sympathetically. I told him I had asked the OC to take me off post, which she did.

I went home to be told that Trevor and Esther had arranged a holiday for me, Tina and the boys at the YMCA Sandown, on the Isle of Wight, in a few months' time.

'You go, Tina, you and the boys.' I really didn't want to spend any time with Trevor and Esther and a bunch of religious nuts. Life was bad enough as it was!

'Neil, we all need a break. We will all go.'

'Okay,' I said. 'But none of that Christian shit!'

I put it out of my mind and continued my existence, trying to work, trying to be a husband and father.

This period of time is a blur. I was not connecting with the world at all, was going through motions at best. In the spring I was training in Wales and, as usual, could not sleep. I ended up wandering outside.

I sank against the building, into the shadows cast by the moon. I was aware that one of the female cadets was striding confidently over to the outdoor smoking shelter, but my mind pulled me back into other scenarios, ones that had passed a long time ago or maybe a few minutes ago. The cadet disappeared from view, just as a pile of bodies appeared in my vision and distracted me. I had passed into a riot, reliving a particularly stressful attack, when I sensed one of the PT instructors following in the cadet's footsteps. I was drawn back to the big window of my childhood, the hairdryer, the street fights, the tractor ride, the failed suicide attempt, the fraud, the death threats…

I was horrified to learn that the PT instructor had sexually molested the cadet that night. That night, with me a few metres away. I had seen them. I should have known something wasn't right. They were in there far too long for a cigarette.

Another black hole appeared in me, sucking in the last vestiges of self-esteem I had. How could I have let that happen? I should have known, intervened, rescued her!

I was not good enough. I had lost it. I was not the man I used to be. I was useless as a soldier and my seniors agreed.

I felt the weight of even more guilt on me.

I continued the counselling and the medication, but I was too broken to mend. I asked to be removed from post again. The army seemed to abandon me: I spent a few months at home.

Until the holiday that would change my life.

Part 3 – The Answer

Chapter 1

The time between agreeing to go on the holiday and the actual date of it had passed in a blur of unpleasant, foul, distressing images. My life was happening around me. Nothing afforded me relief.

My life was simply not worth living.

I could not connect with Tina or Ben or Jon.

That morning, I got in the car, or rather was bundled in and reminded to put my seatbelt on. Poor Tina! She must have felt as if she had three children to care for!

The journey passed with no help from me. I couldn't drive, couldn't navigate, couldn't even engage in meaningful conversation. I regretted agreeing to go and dreaded my arrival, so when I saw the building, I was overwhelmed with the compulsion to flee. I sat in the car for a full twenty minutes. Tina spoke firmly to me, cajoled me, tried every resource available to persuade me to leave the car and go inside.

I was too afraid. I felt as though eyes were watching me from the window, as if there would be a crowd of people waiting the other side of that door to evaluate me and find me lacking. Paranoia makes you feel very lonely.

Finally, I submitted to Tina's persistence, responding at a basic level to her plea on the boys' behalf. They were hungry and tired.

We entered the hostel, registered and found our family room. I say 'we', but it was all Tina. I just followed, swaggering through the building, glaring at anyone who tried to make eye contact, rejecting any attempts to make me feel welcome there.

I was here. I was not to be messed with. I exuded arrogant confidence but I in no way intended to allow any of these people in. They might believe in all that mumbo-jumbo God crap, but I did not. Church was full of hypocritical do-gooders and, in all my days, I had seen nothing to convince me otherwise.

The building had been donated by the Mothers' Union. It was not an ugly building by YMCA standards; it had balconies and gables painted white. It overlooked the sea. In another life, I might have liked it. As it was, I didn't care and I didn't appreciate anything about it. I could see no beauty in anything at all.

It was attached to a chapel, which could be reached internally via the ground floor corridor. The week consisted of a series of events in the meeting room and chapel, as well as outside, including on the beach.

There was nothing about this holiday that appealed to me. I disliked everyone and refused to engage with them or their ridiculous activities. I sat apart from everyone and, despite the drinking ban, continued to soothe my soul with alcohol, which I bought in a shop down the road.

If I wanted to drink, nobody would f**king stop me. No one here would be hard enough anyway!

If anyone tried to interact with me, I was thoroughly unpleasant. I treated the staff with contempt and rebuffed anyone's kindness with a sharp word or an ugly look. An older lady called Benni joined our table at mealtimes. I suppose she was being friendly, trying to make me feel welcome, maybe help Tina a bit with the boys.

I tried to get rid of her. She began conversations full of kindness and good intentions and I twisted them until they became tarnished and repulsive. I swore, shocked her, placed horrendous images in her head, anything possible to repel her, make her go away.

But she kept coming back.

Another one, Steve Mann, tried to engage with me too, tried to build a bridge to me by saying he was from a military family.

I tried him out, opened up to him, described details about some of my operations, filled his mind with gruesome intricacies, scenes he had never imagined, delivered in my foulest language: bodies, rot, a face destroyed by my hand, gun at my head, failed suicide, bullying, lies, another face destroyed by my hand, another, another, another...

I saw in his face that this was nowhere near a normal discussion for him. I apologised, unusually aware of someone's image of me and of the pain I could inflict. His attitude surprised me. He seemed okay for 'one of them'.

'Don't worry, Neil. That's who you are!'

Exactly. This was me.

Between my displays of nastiness to all these people who knew nothing, and with whom I did not belong, I spent the first few days looking out to sea, thinking too much, or running on the beach, trying to escape.

However far or fast I ran, I was still me when I stopped. The thoughts caught up with me and swirled around in my head, forcing me to deal with them, trying to process them again and again.

There was one event I managed to show a vague interest in. Bill Legend was a volunteer at the camp that year. I knew him as the last surviving member, the drummer, of T-Rex. I showed up for his Q&A session in the chapel on the Monday evening, but didn't feel motivated enough to engage in conversation, just let the event flow over me. I suppose it must have given Tina hope that I was starting to relax.

The following day was Visitors' Day. Esther was there, participating in extra fun events. Around me people of all ages were laughing and joking with each other, relaxed in the summer sun.

I couldn't recall my last smile and found their laughter annoying.

'Hi, Neil!' Esther smiled at me. 'You'll be good at today's activities! Why not have a go? You and Tina can both find a race, you'll fit right in!'

Me? Fit right in?

I glared at her with disdain. What the f**k was she on?

Something hit me at that exact moment. Maybe it was the glittering sound of happiness in the air, or the warm sea air and the summer sun, maybe it was being far removed from any physical reminders of my crippling existence, I don't know. But in that moment, on that Tuesday, I felt what an utterly horrible person I was.

I was a lying, cheating, murdering scumbag.

I was like a stain on this world.

I was not the hero that people imagined I was, just because I was in the army.

My new perception of myself served to lower my self-esteem even further and, the next evening, I was drinking a little earlier than usual, having bought my beer at the shop up the road again.

For some reason I was sitting on the floor near the chapel door. Tina was in our room, settling the boys down to sleep. The drink had taken the edge off a little. I was enjoying the fuzziness it gave to my bitter thoughts, how the images in my head were made less sharp, though not so much that I could pretend they were of something else.

After a while, after I had spent some time trying to obliterate this new vision of myself, to blur the comparison between me and the people around me, the guy called Steve wandered up the corridor. He stopped near my feet and bent slightly to make eye contact.

'Are you coming in?' he asked me, pointing to the chapel door, which was slightly ajar.

I laughed bitterly. 'No! People like me don't go in there!'

I heard the vicar's voice float out into the corridor. I recognised it as belonging to the woman who, on our first day there, had formed a pig from a banana. I remember wondering why she couldn't just eat it.

Steve hadn't moved. He was waiting for me.

I stood up, a little unsteadily, announcing, 'I am thinking of throwing myself off the cliff.'

Steve didn't look shocked, just concerned. He encouraged me to come with him into the chapel. We could sit at the back, we could just watch.

What did I have to lose? I felt like I was staggering around in the depths of humanity, ridiculous, hopeless, worthless. Why not spend a few minutes in there? What did I have to lose?

I followed Steve in and we sat down on the pews nearest the door. I could leave easily at any time. A few people looked over at me, but their focus was on the vicar, who was about to start the 'Reflection'.

Candles flickered and soothing music rolled through the air, but I was still restless. Beyond that chapel wall was a high cliff. There were rocks underneath. I knew I could still go there and be at peace in a matter of seconds.

'...and take one...'

Steve had stood up. Everyone in the room was standing up to go and collect something from a bowl in the middle of the room. He waited for me longer than I thought he should. I didn't want to go. I didn't want everyone looking at me. I didn't want to take part.

Steve waited some more, until I reluctantly stood up and went with him.

We approached the bowl. It was full of pebbles. All shapes and sizes, all colours. I grabbed one and followed Steve back to the pew.

I looked more closely at the pebble I had taken.

Here I was, sitting in a church, holding a pebble. A small frown formed on my face. I waited.

What was all this?

The vicar's voice rose steadily and filled the silence. Everyone listened.

'Come to me, all you who are weary and burdened, and I will give you rest! This is Matthew 11 verse 28.'

She said more, but I was staring at the stone in my hand, really thinking about what she had just said, allowing the significance of it to sink in.

Something was connecting within me.

'This pebble represents all that burdens you, all that makes you weary. When you are ready, come and place it at the foot of the cross. Take your troubles to Christ!'

I focused hard on the pebble and, as each of my burdens

paraded through my mind, one at a time, I imagined them pouring into it – the bullying, the killing, the trial, the fights, the lies, the pressure to be a good father, the guilt and the general worthlessness of my existence…these things all poured from me and into that stone in my hand.

I looked up at the cross, watched some of the congregation walk to it, place their stone at its foot, glance up, mutter a silent prayer and return to their seats.

'Okay,' I thought, addressing God, 'If you are there, I really need you today, I need you *now*.'

After what seemed like an eternity, but was only a few seconds, I tried to stand up.

But I was weighed down.

I was a strong man, used to lifting massive weights, but I could not lift this little pebble. I struggled a moment, determined to manage this small task, but it was so difficult. Then, somehow, I managed to lift it, carry it to the front and place it, full of my burdens, my worries, my guilt, at the foot of the cross.

I felt, in that very second, the most incredible love and the unfamiliar lightness of an existence free of worry.

The relief was instant and complete. I felt cleansed of the residue of all I had ever done wrong. I felt forgiven. I felt at peace.

I felt the unconditional love of God the Father for the first time!

The brief moment of my true understanding extended in my mind for a long, long time. Clarity pulled me into another dimension of time and space. I was changed irreversibly for the better, I knew that, and the unique sensation was the most truly awesome I had ever felt.

I would never forget that feeling. I wanted it forever. I wanted everyone to feel like this!

I looked at Steve. He was smiling. He knew I was at peace, at last. He could see the difference in me already, was witness to my first moments as a new man, finally breaking free of all that was harmful and negative.

That night I slept a dreamless, deep, refreshing sleep for the first time in many, many years.

Chapter 2

Tina was asleep alongside the boys when I went back to my room. I slid into bed quietly, my soul calmer but my mind wondering, excited, in awe of what had happened to me.

As soon as I woke up, Tina could see a change in me. It was if my brain had fired up again after months and months of sleep.

I chatted away, looking forward to my day, helping get the boys dressed, looking forward to breakfast, hoping to see Benni. Tina listened, watched me, thrilled at the changes in me.

'You're back, Neil!' Her joy was palpable. I couldn't yet find the words to tell her what had happened, but, that morning, normal interactions with my family brought me great joy.

I saw the world differently. On the way to breakfast I saw everything and everyone as if for the first time, as if I had been blind and had been suddenly given the gift of sight. I engaged in conversation, was kind and welcoming to dear Benni, felt amazed at the love I felt in the room.

I smiled a lot.

I didn't speak about what had happened in the church the night before, but at some point, in the day, the vicar and I found ourselves together, in a quiet corner. I drank in her words. This was the first step towards learning about my new world.

'We all have a God-shaped hole in our heart, Neil. Some people try to fill it with money or violence, sex or drugs, or drink…but nothing can fill that space but God. To be forgiven, it is enough to be sorry and to make Jesus Christ the Lord of your life.'

These words started to make perfect sense to me. I had

finally found the answer! The image of me as the heroic soldier was being stripped away to reveal the truth.

We prayed together. I confessed and repented of all my sins. These acts became a shocking list in my head. I saw my younger self in unpleasant conversations, fighting, bullying, saw each of my 'targets' in turn. I pledged to turn away from these sins and to accept Jesus Christ as my Lord and Saviour.

Each scene in my head, each sin, dissipated and was washed away, forgiven. I was cleansed. The weight had gone.

I thought about my life. A lot. I played back scenes in my head, times I had made certain decisions, times I had been moved in certain directions. I felt that my vision of God had been obscured by the influence of others, by the way He had been represented by people who were almost as blind as I myself had been: the hypocrites who had stood between me and God before.

With absolute clarity I recognised the hand of God, His role in my life. He had been there all along, the friend I had not seen.

For the rest of the week, I took part in lots of activities, slept well and didn't drink at all. I felt that I was re-connecting as a husband and as a father, that I was a new human being, a valued part of the group. I had the time of my life!

On Friday afternoon, we had a Thanksgiving Service to say what we had done that week. I went without any pressure at all and sat with Tina and the boys, looking at the cross, looking at my pebble, still at the foot of it.

People stood and spoke about their activities, what had made them happy, the joy they had felt in the community. I listened and appreciated their comments without a hint of the contempt I had been feeling when we first arrived. I, too, wanted to share my appreciation of the week.

I rose from my seat.

'Neil?'

'Thank you! It has been a very good holiday!' As simple as that.

I could sense Tina's surprise as she adapted to my new view

of the world, to the new me. I saw one or two members of the congregation look at each other.

Was that Benni smiling?

Even I found my transformation difficult to believe! Where was that nasty, malicious man from a few days ago? Where was that man to whom hope through religion was inconceivable?

That night we had a fancy dress party. I dressed as King Canute, dancing around, being daft, carrying Jon on my shoulders, joking with Ben, laughing with Tina. I chatted to people I had formerly glared at or even ignored.

I began the rest of my life.

Happy. Fulfilled.

Full of the joy of Eternal Life.

Chapter 3

I attended church from the following week after our return home. The community was really happy to see me there and welcomed me warmly. Trevor, whom I had previously rejected, became my link to all this new knowledge. Tina had filled him in on my transformation and he approached me and offered himself up to help me. He spent evening after evening with me at the Mayfly, a local pub, leading me, a willing follower, down a new path.

I was desperate to know more and sorry I had not been kinder to him before when he had tried to reach me.

I returned to the counselling sessions set up by my doctor and was amazed that they actually started to work for me. God was working with me, always had been, it was just that I had not recognised it or accepted His help and His protection.

I was posted as Chief Clerk to Worthy Down, which was so close we didn't have to move house, I could still see Trevor for our informal discussions, and I could still attend the same church on Sundays. Tina, the boys and I went as a family now, a highlight of our week.

Tina continued to be relieved and delighted with the changes in me. I slept better, I had stopped drinking to cope, and I no longer needed to thump walls to release tension. The new me was the best I had ever been and then some!

This period was calm and happy. My only concern was the outcome of the trial, which was still a blot on my landscape.

I was told the delay was due to the wait for the outcome of the Baha Mousa trial, where soldiers of the British Army were accused of torturing an Iraqi to death. Apparently the legal outcomes of this trial would have a bearing on ours.

I waited patiently. My prayers helped me and were a huge source of comfort and guidance for me. I was in awe of my new ability to cope.

I was so in love with this new attitude, my new life, and I was so committed to Christ my Saviour, that I began training to be a licensed Lay Reader at St John's University, Nottingham, in my spare time. This course was to last almost five years, during which time I would learn something new every day and would develop a wider and broader understanding of the Word of God. Early on I learnt that the rigidity of the Church of England did not embody the will of Christ and I wanted to do my part to change that. After all, this rigidity had played its part in keeping me away for so long.

Finally, in 2008 a court-martial took place. Gary was the only defendant, as 'they could not put everyone on trial'.

I was not asked to bear witness.

Investigating officers had found approximately £100,000 in plant pots at Gary's home. He said, under oath, that his profits were made by selling luxury items to the servicemen, such as Viagra, cigarettes, etc.

In short, his books balanced.

I was informed of the outcome as I was leaving Worthy Down for a new posting in Höhne.

He was proven not guilty.

So that was that! We had had a trial and Gary had been found innocent! He was proven not guilty and promoted shortly afterwards.

The result tested my faith both in the army and in God's plan for me. I must have been mistaken about everything. Many of us must have been mistaken, even some high-ranking officers. Why had I gone through all that pain and anxiety?

I realised that the Army (which had been, up until this incident, my family) had been my support. Its ethos had helped me with my issues until this. The trial had threatened that sense of family and this had led to my breakdown.

It had broken me.

Could I regret that, now that I was a better person, now that

I was learning to act selflessly, help others at last?

Later, I was invited by the Brigadier of the Army Prosecution Service to go to see him. This was an unprecedented move and highlighted the enormity of the case. I like to think it was also an acknowledgement of what I had suffered because of it.

The 'new guy' was also at the meeting, along with a host of the SIB men who had worked long and hard on the case. The Brigadier explained it all, told us how hard they had tried, told us that they had, at one point, considered putting me into witness protection, me and the 'new guy' who had also not taken part in any of the dealings back then. At least I had saved him from the same fate as me. He was grateful for that.

At the meeting, I questioned the lack of concern over the email threats and the fact that they had simply told me to change my email address.

'Do you think that was an acceptable answer?' I challenged.

Silence.

I was obviously very upset about all I had been through, and resolved to stay away from anyone involved from then on. Whatever had happened, there would be no good feeling between us.

Others had been investigated, action had been taken where it could be, but National Security was paramount and this had dictated the outcome. It had all been dealt with satisfactorily and the army had moved on, altering the financial procedures that had been highlighted as exploitable.

Because of my love of Jesus Christ, I had the strength to accept the situation and to simply crack on with life. I needed to make up for the time my stress had stolen from me and work towards another promotion.

If you are expecting that I was now perfect, you would be wrong. The ingrained habits of my entire life needed to die away a few at a time. I did remain blunt. I still asked people, 'What do you expect me to do?' I still walked away if I was unhappy with how I was being spoken to. I still didn't take any nonsense. My intolerance of financial misrepresentation did not lessen. My faith and hopes for a better world highlighted a whole new range of issues, which I took on, questioned, contested.

Only once did I revert back to the physical aggression of the former me. This took place in 2009, when I was working in Höhne, in the Regimental Finance Department. I had never regained my attention to detail after my breakdown. There was too much unnecessary paperwork arising from the army's antiquated systems. On a good day, I was average and worked 12-hour days, so my mood was not at its best.

I was with my friend Darren, an FSA, in my office, when we heard one of the juniors mouthing off to another of my colleagues. I went out. The Det Commander, Bob Howard, was there too.

'What you doing, OC?' This was short for O'Connor.

OC went to remove his hands from his pockets. He was so wired, I thought he was going to hit me. I was so wired, I made a pre-emptive strike.

I grabbed him by his throat, by his windpipe, and banged his head against the door about three times. He was almost choking.

I could have killed him!

'F**king hell, Neil!' shouted Darren. I dropped OC, who staggered away, threatening me, between gasps, with disciplinary action.

I didn't care.

Bob Howard spoke to OC, telling him he had been out of order. It was not quite 'You deserved it!'

I could have got away with this incident, as I had so many times before, but it was no longer about avoiding issues at work. It was about far more than that.

I was devastated at my 'relapse'. I prayed a lot about this. Soon, I went to see OC, but he spoke first. 'I'm really sorry, Neil!'

I was surprised and said, 'Me too, OC, I should have known better.'

OC and I had a good heart-to-heart and I explained exactly why I was sorry. I told him how much I had changed and, over

the course of our conversation, I introduced him to the love of
Jesus Christ. OC listened to me and I was overwhelmed when
he changed his life at that moment and began his own path
where he also changed his own negative ways and came into
Christ's Light.

This was awesome – I had led someone to Jesus!

Naturally I regretted my violence, but I had to see it as part
of a journey. As long as we are truly sorry, we can be forgiven
and we can continue on our way with renewed good intentions.

Only once did I revert back to the physical aggression of the
former me, and it led to a saved soul!

Throughout this period, I returned to the Mothers' Union
holiday each year, growing from 'scum of the earth' to a
confident member of the 'family' who had fun and made the
day fun for others.

My life in the church had become my main focus. In my
normal everyday, I followed two paths, one where I was
learning about God, developing my knowledge through my
course and conversations with members of the church, and
one where I seemed to be stuck battling the same dishonesty
with certain members of the army.

From 2009 to the start of 2011, I was with the Queen's Royal
Hussars at Sennelager, Germany. It started well, but I soon
found that I didn't get on with the RAO there either and ended
up having a disagreement with him and the RAWO about their
work practices. The RAWO was called Graeme Gordon (from
experience I knew he wasn't keen on being called 'Flash'). To
top it all off, there was another guy called Billy who tried to
undermine and manipulate me at every opportunity.

The mutual dislike had started almost straightaway, fuelled
by a disagreement about an email. I had chosen to ignore the
instructions in it because I didn't think staff welfare was at
the heart of it. Graeme felt a more compliant approach was
needed.

Also, from the disrespectful comments that fell out of his
dirty mouth about a woman in the unit, one I worked with in
the gym, it was clear he had sexually harassed her. It was also

clear that the RAO had turned a blind eye.

I was desperate to avoid confrontation but could not bear the injustice, so was quick to defend her. 'You can't do that sort of thing! You are such a dick!'

'If she had been in a commando unit, she would know what sexual harassment was!' This was Graeme's answer, but it was no defence.

'That is not the point!' I yelled. 'Whether you meant it or not, if she feels it is sexual harassment, just stop it!' I was incensed, simply could not understand how anyone could treat someone like that.

In addition, Graeme and Billy were committing documentary fraud, covering up errors, which could have repercussions further down the line. We held a General Procurement Card to order stuff for the unit, and the transactions went through public accounts. This was being misused and the transaction accounts doctored. Now, to me, if anyone makes a mistake, they should admit it. I would personally help anyone rectify their error, as long as they were honest about it. The British Army Code of Conduct is clear: minor crimes reveal a soldier's lack of integrity.

So my sense of justice and integrity rose again and I challenged the culprits again, which led to me being ostracized and eventually forced out under a cloud. Some of my work was manipulated, altered to reflect badly on me. My working environment was made untenable by the bullying. Stress started to claw at me again and I requested that I receive no more finance positions.

I basically left work. I refused to be bullied there and was determined to put my health first, for my own sake and for my family's. In short, I was at home from January to August 2011, awaiting a new posting in any role but finance. If the difficulties of the system made temptation too much for some people, at least I wouldn't be put in a position to have to deal with it. I was told to see a psychiatrist, but was judged 'normal', and when I complained about my 'dismissal' from this role, the RAO was asked to make a statement about me and about the situation. He stated that it must be a burden for me to always have to be morally right, but, for me, this was not a burden. This was the right way to live. My esteem for the army was being eroded again.

While I was off, they forwarded me my mail in the married quarters and, by accident, I received the Visa statement for the General Procurement Card.

Graeme had been buying personal stuff on the account! It was there before me in black and white – dates, items, all personal. I was disgusted. Graeme's bad habits had finally led to theft.

I didn't take long to decide what to do with the Visa statement.

When I was posted to Divisional HQ in Herford, Germany, in August, where I went on to spend three years, I showed it to the civilian accountant there. The situation was investigated. I had no regrets.

Chapter 4

Privately, I had started to feel the call to a greater role in the church and had been looking for guidance in this. As I was thinking this through, searching, a regret germinated in me. It grew and grew, until atoning for it, rectifying my mistake, became all-consuming.

Tina is beautiful inside and out. She had been my rock since we were children. She is a fantastic mother and a wonderful wife. And I'd made her choose between a church wedding and baptizing our children...of course she would choose her children over her own self!

I had to put this right!

On the way to the 2011 Mothers' Union holiday, we attended our niece Isabel's wedding in Stourbridge. I wore my number 1s: full dress uniform. Tina had bought a new dress, and the boys had sported waistcoats, shirts and smart trousers. We brushed up really well!

So, having driven directly to the holiday, we had appropriate outfits, which was one less element to worry about. Now for the rest...

This year we were at Pilgrim Hall, a rather grand venue in Uckfield. All carved wood and beautiful staircases. Perfect for a Marriage Blessing, if not for our sticky-fingered gang of children!

I enlisted the help of the team, especially Ernie and Claire. I explained why this was so important. 'I made Tina make a horrible decision when I was not the person I am today. Now I want to make up for that. Can you help?'

Everyone on the team was touched by my love for Tina and desperate to help create a memorable day for us. Claire agreed to sing at the service, Ernie felt honoured to be my Best Man, and the vicar, Kate, agreed to perform the blessing. It was all going to be perfect...apart from the fact that the only available spot for Kate and the chapel was just before the fancy dress disco!

On the afternoon of the Blessing, I told Tina to put on the dress she had worn at Isabel's wedding the weekend before. At this point, she started to question me. I don't think it helped that the boys were confused about their own posh outfits too! After all, everyone else was going to be wearing fancy dress!

I had to come clean.

Tina was so happy! She had known something was going on, because I am an open book to her, but when she heard what we had all planned, she was delighted! We talked it through with Kate. I explained how I wanted to mark our marriage and the importance of this holiday at the same time.

We arrived at the chapel, along with the other holiday guests, who were in various hilarious costumes. Snow White was there, with a green face, as well as Abraham Lincoln.

Kate announced to our friends what was happening. An excited murmur rippled through the chapel and the ceremony began.

The moment was truly magical for me and Tina. Our marriage was blessed before God as we were surrounded by all our dear friends. There were smiles and happy tears, the mood totally incongruous with the clowns and pirates and animals their outfits were portraying. It was a truly great day!

Soon after this holiday, the solution to my need to do more for the church presented itself to me through Tony Anthony, who'd inspired me from our first meeting in Germany.

The church I attended at that time, and whose services I sometimes led now that I was qualified to do so, had invited Tony to talk to our congregation. I was asked to help organise the event and form part of the welcoming party. I was happy to help.

Tony and I hit it off immediately. He'd come to Christ whilst in prison in Cyprus in 1991, after a life of extreme violence.

His biography, *Taming the Tiger*, has spoken to millions of people: the turn-around in his life was titanic, the change in him through the love of Jesus Christ dramatic, mirroring my own.

I wanted to do the good that Tony was doing.

Tony was a founding member of a global missionary organisation whose aim was purely evangelistic: to spread the Word, to share the Good News about Jesus Christ. A passion for telling others, a love of helping others to be saved from their mediocre path and raised to greatness, was something I shared with Tony.

I jumped on board, thrilled to be moving my work for Christ forward. The first thing I learnt was how to harness my enthusiasm and share my testimony effectively and considerately.

I loved taking part in the missionary work. I was on their list of speakers and, through this work and by listening to others, I grew as a Christian and became increasingly more empowered. The work I did during these few years certainly satisfied my need to do more for the Church. The army was my second priority now. I left the office as soon as I could and spent my spare time and my holidays spreading the Word.

I still had my trials. They were just far easier to cope with now. Another example of this occurred a few years later.

Accommodation was provided by the army, but we'd had half an eye on the day we would need to buy our own house and had bought a house in Anglesey back in 2005. We rented it out to cover the mortgage, which we had arranged through Blue Forces, a financial company promoted by the Armed Forces. It even had a military phone number. We had an option to save with Blue Forces too, so we overpaid on the mortgage, building up our savings.

In 2012, we requested the balance of our savings in order to provide a deposit for another property, where we would live when leaving the army. A week passed, then bad news: the company had gone bust. We, along with countless others, had lost all our savings. In our case, this amounted to £17,000. This was a major blow to my family.

I was absolutely devastated but turned to the army for support. After all, the company had been promoted by the army, hadn't it? Surely they would rectify it?

I had no doubt, but I was wrong. The army washed its hands of us.

I prayed.

Through prayer, I searched for guidance and found that I had been given perspective. It was only money, after all, and there was no permanent damage to my family. I felt some pity for the owner of Blue Forces: he had submitted to temptation.

That was between him and God.

I did pursue a claim against the army; I felt I owed it to my family to try. I was interviewed by *Don't Get Done, Get Dom*, a consumer rights programme. I provided what I thought was adequate proof that the army was liable.

No good. I had to settle for a couple of hundred pounds from the receivers.

Workwise, I had asked never to be given a finance post again, but I was forced back into the same old antiquated mix of systems when sent to Chilwell in 2014. My mind froze around the figures, almost panicking at the idea of involvement in this area. The systems still seemed to invite fraud and corruption, they were so inconsistent. The fear of discovering someone's misdemeanor, leading to past stress, was too much. So I spent some time floating between departments in Grantham, attaining the rank of Warrant Officer, which is the highest rank a non-commissioned officer can achieve.

I should have been proud, but it was nothing compared to my achievements for God, my work with those in need in the world, so instead of embracing the opportunities this new rank afforded me, I undertook resettlement courses in skills such as tiling and the art of a locksmith.

It was time to move on, so finally, after twenty-two years of regular service and three years in the TA, I left the army. What would happen now?

Chapter 5

My Mothers' Union holidays were still going strong. I had become team leader, working alongside the wonderful Dougal Rose, Steve Mann, Sue B and Claire Lymer, to name but a few. All of them had witnessed my transformation back in 2006. We have done lots of good and had lots of laughs. I have worn a variety of costumes to amuse the children. Once I encouraged Ernie to sing Queen's 'I Want to Break Free' with me, dressed as women and using balloons for breasts! I am game for anything that entertains and helps. But over the years I have also worked with young people whose carers had exhausted many avenues in an attempt to 'save' them from a life of crime, drugs or emotional handicap.

Doreen arrived with her foster son, Kevin. His mother was absent, his father in the military somewhere. Kevin was Trouble.

Kevin was so disturbed, so incapable of quiet relationships or being alone without causing havoc, that Doreen was struggling to know what to do with him. He had attended clubs to keep him occupied and focused, but we were in the school holidays and Doreen was at a loss, so she asked to come with us. There were men here; maybe Kevin would benefit from some masculine role models?

I met Kevin and we hit it off. I was still a muscular bloke, with tattoos, and probably reminded him of his father, who had become a legendary army hero in his mind. I soon learnt that he had emotional, behavioural and learning problems, but that he was physically fit and had a certain intelligence, matched with a penchant for manipulation. I could see why he had been excluded from his primary school, not accepted into the mainstream.

We harnessed Kevin's energy through physical activity. If he acted anti-socially, we talked it through calmly, helping him to see a better way to be. I prepared a comic strip version of my childhood story for him, so he didn't feel so isolated, didn't feel he was the only one to feel out of place in the world. I knew how that felt.

I heard he was excited about coming back to the camp the year after. I heard that the comic strip was one of his treasured possessions. He has a well-adjusted life now and I am happy to have helped in some small way.

Through this work, I was able to see that we are all the product of personal events; that parents are not perfect either; that we should not imagine our parents' mistakes are because of us. Sometimes they can't cope, and that doesn't mean we are not loved.

Despite the successes of the annual Mothers' Union holiday and my everyday church work, I still needed to earn money. When I left the army, I scanned the civilian world for opportunities, armed with my new skills.

My first civilian role was as the owner of my own business, as a contract locksmith. It was successful, and I won some solid sub-contracts. I did a good job, removing broken locks carefully without damaging the doors. However, my high moral standards would not allow me to charge customers the rates necessary to please my contractors and feed my family without guilt.

I looked for something new. Early in 2016, I heard about the need for people with my background to support children in local education. After successes such as Kevin, I thought I would give it a go. I felt I could bring into my working life some of my interpersonal skills and really do some good.

This is where I am now.

I still don't tolerate lies or a lack of moral fibre. I challenge them and, if nothing changes, I walk away. And, however rewarding my 'day job' is, my main role in life is my work for the Church.

Since placing that pebble at the foot of Jesus' cross, I have come a long way. I am a much better person for Christ in my life. I try harder and have even made amends to individuals, such as writing a letter of apology to Mr Duncan, the physics teacher who had got into so much trouble because of my drinking at the conference.

My passion is mission work.

The Great Commission Society is a global movement that seeks to communicate the Gospel message to every person in all the world, responding to a wide range of humanitarian needs, and promoting human welfare and social justice.

In the last ten to twenty years over 40,000 people have come to Christ in South African prisons alone. They have undergone discipleship programmes in prison. If they are up for parole or leaving prison, these people do not re-offend. We teach how to actually be evangelists too.

We carry out mission work in many different countries. I have visited Italy. Despite being a Catholic country, there is a destructive undercurrent. We have visited Turin and spoken to those people on the edges of society, such as prostitutes and the homeless. We also spoke to those such as the police and the security services, to those who feel isolated, aggressive, unloved.

I also visit many areas of the UK, usually the big cities, impersonal in their nature, the kind of places you can get lost in. We talk, we pray, we sow the seed of the Gospel. I take sweets, toothpaste, gels, wipes, bottles of water. All these things are needed by the homeless and give me a start to a conversation, for which they are so grateful.

I love to speak to those that no one else wants to speak to.

I am not afraid of going into the Lion's Den. Christianity is important to me, but helping men to deal with their issues with or without acknowledging God is vital too. I try to engage with everyone, regardless of their background. I speak out in pubs, using our shared vocabulary. I am open about my past, let them glimpse my dark history, so they can see how changed I am. I draw in my audience of men, who may be hiding behind their image, their pints of beer, their bravado.

I know all about that.

And if I sow a seed that makes them talk to someone, or seek help professionally, I am glad. If they turn to God, I am even happier.

One example was a co-worker whose life was a series of panic attacks, anxieties, redundancies, loneliness and darkness, a co-worker with no one to turn to for help, who was not coping. I spoke of Christ and was ecstatic to find that my love and enthusiasm caught them up; another lost soul was saved, another life given strength and meaning!

I now lead the Mothers' Union Holiday every year and am an AFIA holiday team volunteer. I owe them so much. They are my family, and this is the least I can do for them.

Every year I see miracles, and people healed in God's name.

Prayers are often answered in an explicit way. Migraines disappear in the blink of an eye, back pains subside with the touch of a hand, troubled souls are cleansed and liberated. When God is working through me like this, when I am trusting in Him and not myself, when I am following the Word, doing as He wishes, there is no power on Earth to match it.

One miracle that stands out above all others happened to someone like me, to someone who had led a life in three parts.

Just like me.

He was an Iraq veteran. We got chatting on one of the AFIA holidays, but I did not tell him I had been in the army.

He told me he had been abused physically as a child. He was an alcoholic. He was plagued by his actions in Iraq: when the fighting started, his body reacted as if he were still the abused child. He ran away. He left his team and ran away. Scared out of his wits.

One night, on the holiday, he had an argument with someone, and I saw him run crying into the woods. His loneliness and anxiety were like a beacon to me. I saw something of myself in him, of me from ten years ago.

I followed him, spoke to him, prayed with him, enveloped him with the love of Christ, which he accepted into his heart.

He is no longer an alcoholic. He has a fulfilled life, free of his demons. He is getting married soon, leading a meaningful, complete life.

Not bad for a scrawny lad from Bridgnorth.

Epilogue

The early morning light alters almost imperceptibly. Wildlife stirs, unaware I am there, quietly waiting for the everyday world to catch up with me. I revisit old scenes in my head to pass the time.

Moments pass.

Stillness concentrates the mind, makes you focus on this moment.

Makes you focus on who you are.

We are the sum of events. We are formed by what happens to us, like pebbles on a beach, knocked and pummeled and shaped into what we are.

Knocked by piles of headless bodies, by blue nylon rope, by petrol bombs and rioting men, by starvation and control and everyday weapons. Pummeled by street fights, a tractor ride, a failed suicide attempt, strangers in cars in warzones. Shaped by other people's greed, other people's love, other people.

It is not their actions that change you, it is how you perceive those actions.

I smile again, thinking of that real pebble in my hand that changed my life for the better, that, in one everlasting second, showed me Jesus had wiped out my sins and the damage caused to me by the sins of others. I forgive them, even understand them.

I run through the list of people I have helped to find Christ, helped to find a better, happier, more fulfilled life.

This, this is the evidence I have been there.

Afterword

Now, as I look back, as we all do, I can see all of the things that I have done, what I should have done, what I might do if I had the time again.

The major turning point for me was understanding the Gospel and the love of Jesus Christ. I saw everything differently after that. I am not saying I stopped counselling straightaway and I was off the antidepressants straightaway, but I saw things differently in such a major way: I started to see people through love instead of suspicion.

The thing is that you can forgive. I love my parents. I have highlighted some of the bad times, but there were many good times. I have highlighted the bad in hope of helping people in similar situations. My message to them is 'It doesn't matter what has happened to you, you are strong enough to overcome anything!'

I loved my time in the army and all the people I served with. In fact, I loved all of it. I know there are people who have problems forgiving and who want to respond with hatred and violence. I really understand it, but forgiveness is for you, not them! Recently, a close family member died and left everything to me. Another close family member knew of this, as he had told him. However, when the inheritance turned out to be a significant amount – he kept it for himself! Yes, he kept it. I was very hurt; my children find it very hard too. His excuse is that 'it was not written down' – he told him with his own lips. However, I have to forgive him. It is hard to forgive; sometimes it's a journey.

I love going to speak to the homeless, the prostitutes, the prisoners, the addicts; basically people who rarely see other people outside of their social group. I love telling them that there is more for them, there is a way out, you can do it, and that Jesus loves them. I love speaking to the guys who are in the police, fire service, ambulance, armed forces, all those who keep us safe. There will be times when they go out to do a job and may not come home, as they die protecting innocent people. I want them to know Jesus. I want them all to know that they are loved.

A portion of the profits of this book is going towards The Away From It All Holiday in order for the holiday to be able to continue. I would love it if we could have a permanent home for everyone in the UK to be able to come to. If anyone wants to donate an old hotel or similar on the coast, that would be awesome! Then we could change people's lives all year round and not just for one week per year. A portion of the profits of this book is also going towards The Great Commission Society, so that we can continue to go and preach the Gospel whilst offering humanitarian aid, education against human trafficking, anger management and PSHE in schools, etc. Another portion will go towards my local church in order to impact the local community through things like youth projects. I speak on many occasions to many different groups about the Gospel, about not giving up, overcoming problems, developing leadership and how to do evangelism.

It doesn't really matter if the Gospel is for you – that is your decision – but you do only have One Shot at life, One Shot at making a difference, One Shot at how you spend eternity. As a sniper it was One Shot – one kill. Now it is One Shot – one life for all of eternity with the Gospel.

If you want to email me, my email address is

neilobbard@greatcommissionsociety.com

Connect with me on Facebook:
my page is One Shot One Kill One Mission

Acknowledgements

I would like to thank my lovely wife Tina and my sons Ben and Jon, who never gave up on me even when I was at my lowest point. I love them all so much.

I would like to thank my parents for everything they have done for me.

I would like to thank the Great Commission Society for being there for me, for encouraging and mentoring me in order to help me develop into an effective evangelist.

I would like to thank The Mothers' Union (in particular Winchester Diocese and the late Dave Elms) who gave me the Gospel whilst away on the Away From It All Holiday. Also for having enough faith in me to make me at present the male team leader on the same holiday that literally saved my life. I also want to thank Ernie, my predecessor, for some great laughs.

I would like to thank all of the people whom I have had the privilege to help on the Mothers' Union Away From It All holiday as they have all shown me something and helped me on my own journey.

I would like to thank everyone whom I have had the pleasure to serve with in the British Armed Forces. I have seen many acts of courage and leadership, not only on operations but also in everyday life. Like many of the Armed Forces, emergency services and in ordinary everyday life, there are many unsung heroes whom I would just like to thank for their everyday service.

Neil Obbard